T0203305

Digital Organizations Manufacturing

**Intellectual Technologies Set**

coordinated by
Jean-Max Noyer and Maryse Carmès

Volume 5

# Digital Organizations Manufacturing

*Scripts, Performativity and Semiopolitics*

Maryse Carmès

WILEY

First published 2018 in Great Britain and the United States by ISTE Ltd and John Wiley & Sons, Inc.

ISTE Ltd
27-37 St George's Road
London SW19 4EU
UK

www.iste.co.uk

John Wiley & Sons, Inc.
111 River Street
Hoboken, NJ 07030
USA

www.wiley.com

Library of Congress Control Number: 2018937246

British Library Cataloguing-in-Publication Data
A CIP record for this book is available from the British Library
ISBN 978-1-84821-907-6

# Contents

# Introduction

*"In a violently poetic text, Lawrence describes what produces poetry: people are constantly putting up an umbrella that shelters them on the underside of which they draw a firmament and write their conventions and opinions. But poets, artists, make a slit in the umbrella, they tear open the firmament itself, to let in a bit of free and windy chaos and to frame in a sudden light a vision that appears through the rent – Wordsworth's spring or Cézanne's apple, the silhouettes of Macbeth or Ahab. Then come the crowd of imitators who repair the umbrella with something resembling the vision, and the crowd of commentators who patch over the rent with opinions: communication. Other artists are always needed to make other slits, to carry out necessary and perhaps ever-greater destructions, thereby restoring to their predecessors the incommunicable novelty that we could no longer see. This is to say that artists struggle less against chaos (that, in a certain manner, all their wishes summon forth) than against the "clichés" of opinion. The painter does not paint on an empty canvas, and neither does the writer write on a blank page; but the page or canvas is already so covered with preexisting, preestablished clichés that it is first necessary to erase, to clean, to flatten, even to shred, so as to let in a breath of air from the chaos that brings us the vision."[1]* [DEL 91]

---

1 The text by D.H. Lawrence that Deleuze and Guattari are referring to is the introduction he wrote for Harry Crosby's *Chariot of the Sun*, first published in 1928. It is available online and

The purpose of this book is to describe how organizational digital policies are achieving the development of strategic models and socio-technical dispositifs, and both the changes and the supervision of the practices of employees, as part of the production of organizations.

The phenomena discussed here are a testament, not only to the transformations taking place (or claimed as such) since the decade of 2000–2010, and affecting the Modes of existence within the workplace and the frame of reference for managerial actions, but they also resonate more broadly with a general trend toward the digitization of our companies.

The organizational factories studied here are coupled with digital machines, collective enunciation assemblages that serve as a milieu for strategic model-selection dispositifs, as libidinal economies attached to the complication of the techno-politics of organizations, as local adjustments from local pragmatic approaches, and pragmatic approaches carried out by the proliferation of interfaces.

On the basis of several ethnographic analyses, we propose both a description of the processes for the formulation of these policies, a *"manufacture"*, *as it is made, experienced and stated*, as well as a general reflection on the methods and research that allows us to examine these processes.

Thus, this same movement is linked with the concept of *"assemblage"* by G. Deleuze and F. Guattari [DEL 80] and to the approaches of the *actor-network theory* by Bruno Latour and Michel Callon [AKR 06]. In this way, an analytical framework is created to adapt this ethnographic work to organizations. Our exploration stretches from the offices of project leaders to symposiums and other events dedicated to the self-glorification of the best practices of organizations in the era of all things "digital", through workshops where employees meet, and extends to the observation of social-digital practices.

Starting from the examination of the battles that are waged in the context of the design of an information system, of the strength relationships and of the tests that are made there, but also by contextualizing it in front of an entire set of performation processes and with the installation of how it is laid

---

is really worth reading. Gaston Bachelard wrote something strikingly similar in his book on *The Formation of the Scientific Mind*: https://aphelis.net/poetry-philosophy-communication/.

out in its techno-political dimensions. One of the purposes of this book is also to show the extent to which digitization requires us to put the question of politics at the heart of our analysis of interfaces and the "molecular revolution" that characterizes it [GUA 77, NOY 13, NOY 16]. Therefore, we attempt to explore, with great attention, the status and functions of interfaces, by relying on several cases regarding the interlacing of the political economies of the semio-policies that these interfaces demonstrate.

Based on approaches to pragmatic sociology and socio-technical approaches, the issue of politics lies at the heart of the comprehension of organizational production processes and the production of digital milieu, which we focus on in this work.

Organizational production processes are described through the lens of several phenomena and dynamics of formatting: the implementation of socio-technical scripts taken in conflicts and the relationships of various forces, the creation of a generalized "narratique" framework [FAY 72] nourishing desire for permanent innovation, moving towards "a data-centric imperium".

*Chapter 1* presents an ethnographic survey carried out over several years, referred to as the Moeva case: it concerns the creation and changes to digital policy and an associated dispositif in a large organization.

This survey examined an assemblage in the process of transforming and describing the manufacture of organizational techno-politics. The scripts were shown to be very dynamic "actants", including in their agonistic and confrontational dimensions. They are at the heart of performative processes and the source of disputes: they are framework entities, activity patterns, design routines and professional models anchored in practice, constraints, and perceptions given to project managers and to users, but also to the programs of practice enrolled in the interfaces themselves. On this basis, digital innovation in the organizational environment and its manufacture thus presents itself as a combination of scripts: with each script, we encounter a mixture of narratives, drawings, experiences, desires, and semiotics: an assemblage of all these things.

The scripts are immanent to the organization, its project, its practices, its frames of reference for dominant actions, and the technologies that are put to use. We show that producing the organization is the equivalent of creating a script.

It then becomes a question of seeing how they are designed and how the cooperation that occurs in them is put into place: their form of mobilization (how one script mobilizes another script), their reinforcement, or their conflict (the imposition of another activity model or another techno-political approach). By being attentive to "what they do and what they require to be done," we show a part of the chain of events, of formatting, given that they are processes of performativity.

And when a trial-event is found, there are at least two scripts that clash, and with them all the forces they carry. And we show that examining the production of a digital organization factory is akin to these conditions, to produce an "ethology of the forces" similar to the Deleuzian school of thought as expressed by its heir, B. Latour [SAS 03]. The question of defining the empirical or the observable elements provides access to a kind of "concrete ethology of the forces". This issue is far from being resolved.

In this work, we essentially insist on scripts, as an organized set of utterances (not exclusively linguistic), having the ability to affect and to bring about the world they designate. Innovation can be seen as a struggle between scripts, for the conquest of the superior position or the control of its environment, such as the resolution of strength relationships between the performative processes in which the scripts are included and of which they are carriers.

*Chapter 2* expands on the phenomena of performation already described in the case of Moeva to describe, in support of other areas, what we designate as a *general "narratique"* [FAY 72] *of digital organizational policies*: we envisage it through the story that the actors give themselves, from the self-referential processes, of dynamics that are also hetero-poetic, but also by examining the "innovative reasoning" thus brought into play. Here again, it is power relationships within the assemblages and between utterances that are discussed in particular. The assemblage, in an indissoluble way, is "the machine assemblage of desire and the collective assemblage of enunciation"[2]. The assemblage is a way of thinking about the

---

2 As such, these phenomena are regulated through various modes (not exclusively linguistically), the production and distribution of the statements, "what is said and

relationship, the connection, and the composition of relationships "that hold these heterogeneous elements together". The assemblage is defined in particular by the "alliances", "alloys", "attraction and repulsion", "sympathy and antipathy", "alteration", etc., which it facilitates or censors and thus, also by means of the potential for transformation, it allows. It is no longer a question of posing the problem in terms of the spread of technologies, practices, orthodox discourses, cognitive equipment, etc., based on the assumption of a clearly defined center, but to consider the dynamics, the connections that are aggregated, the relationships between a plurality of actors and localities. These features of the layout prove to be close to phenomena described by the *actor-network theory*, which can be considered to have been inherited in some respects from the Deleuzian philosophy. For testimony of this proximity, M. Callon redefined performation on this basis. We envisage processes of performation, based on theoretical orthodoxy and experimentation (for example, when the managerial world develops a theory from its own practices), of performation opened up on the outside (via the formatting of organizational environments from the realm of the internet or other information systems designed for other organizations), of technical performation, etc., all these phenomena being considered in a process in which performation is desired. The organization is immanent in the pragmatisim of the scripts, the processes of alteration/creation that they bring, as well as to the energies, impulses, and libidinal economies that are affiliated with them and/or that are their byproducts. Again, under the same framework of interpretation, we are led to examine pragmatic communications from the consequences that we have already evoked from the rise of the performativity through "speech acts", celebratory practices, the clutch-like functions of these watchwords. For these watchwords, just stating them is sufficient in order to be able to see the entire organizational and managerial script that goes with it, because again, it is the collective assemblage of enunciation that comes first, and the watchwords are merely both the expression and the expressed idea of the assemblage that gives them strength and efficiency. In doing so, we present a summary of the evolution of narratives from a "network-centric" perspective to a "data-centric" perspective. This shift and the diversity of the performation processes are illustrated by the case of the creation of an open data policy within a project group in the public sector.

---

exchanged": "the utterance is the product of an assemblage, always done collectively, which puts into play, both within us and outside of us, populations, multiplicities, territories, fates, affections, and events" [DEL 96].

Thus, we explore different performative configurations, and do so in order to especially elaborate on the description and understanding of how the populations of technical beings and human beings are woven together with their grammar and combinatory elements with the complexes that pass through them or that produce them. In doing so, we follow the considerably long networks of the powers that act at the heart of this manufacturing, whilst examining their transformation and their morphogenesis.

Finally, in *Chapter 3*, we insist that what has been presented so far is a *political economy of the interfaces*, or *semio-politics*. By this, we mean the entire set of rules, constraints, and arbitrations taking shape in digital interfaces or that are delegated to them. This delegation is partly carried out in the dark, because it sometimes instantiates itself out of any mastery and rational choice, of decision-makers and of users, thus under programs conceived elsewhere.

By making use, in particular, of the "signifying / a-signifying" theorems of F. Guattari, we highlight the way in which semio-politics affect the potentialities of digital practices, their extent and their richness. They play out and distinguish themselves according to several archetypal regimes: *a regime of signs* that becomes a regime of "capturing" and intensive encoding of relational processes; backed by the first, *a connectivity regime* that defines the rules of association/dissociation and therefore access, as well as a *reflexivity regime* from which the fields of visibility and the mastery of scales are defined. The analysis of a corporate social-network platform serves to illustrate the design and the concrete action of these regimes.

Semio-politics insist on the action of non-linguistic semiotics, on the exponential growth of digital data traces and the automated processing of these, on the movement of semiotics as the major players in the performation of practices and of an organizational political economy. Thus, we consider that the negotiation and evolution of *these new means of semiotic management,* under the current socio-technical conditions [GUA 83] are essential today, and we sustain that making history, building the memory of the interfaces, determining their power to open new futures within the organization and understanding the manner in which this affects the metastability of these collectives, is a major political task.

Finally, we turn our attention to the variations that affect organizational semio-politics and we show the complex relationships (with their related problems) that are interconnected with digital methods and analytics. We thus indicate the ways to analyze new empirical elements and to emphasize the rise of algorithms within this general process of transformation and the manufacturing of digital organizations. By placing ourselves at the heart of the creation of new socio-cognitive and techno-political ecologies (from the example of platforms for "online socialization" used by employees), we suggest the development and the enrichment of methods and ethno-digital approaches, requiring these elements to be located as close as possible to the assemblages, amid their complexity.

# 1

# Manufacturing the Organization, Manufacturing Scripts

## 1.1. Pragmatic sociology and the pragmatism of scripts

### 1.1.1. *A few requirements*

The transformation of organizational environments arising from the deployment and complexity of digital apparatus has already been widely studied for several years and across all continents. As we may recall, after the first waves of computerization, the "webification" of work processes (especially those involving the use of intranets) was marked by the same desires for the disruption and reconfiguration of practices – a rather banal process. The companies' ICT level of equipment was also present as an indicator of economic development. This profound shift is analyzed, or perhaps thought about, starting from the basis of efficiency problems (the optimal economics of the equipment/productivity ratio, for example), working conditions (the psycho/sociological analysis of stress and surveillance situations, compounded by their digital component) or also with regard to the evolution of collective work (after the work done by the CSCW in the 1980s[1], cognitive sciences and engineering sciences continue to be common objectives for the design of ever more intelligent interfaces and applications). What we are facing are multi-faceted, complex objects and

1 CSCW: *Conference on Computer-supported Cooperative Work* – a term used in 1984 to designate an interdisciplinary conference that has been held for several years since (the 20th conference was held in 2017 in association with the CMA), which brings together research related to the contributions of digital technology to collective work practices.

processes that bring several disciplines into play. For a long time, research work has been (and often continues to be) categorized not only according to the disciplines they are connected with, but also according to the "time" and "level of scale" with which they were involved. Are you an economist? Well then, look at the macro sets and productivity statistics in the deployment phase of technological solutions in these business sectors, or look at the "mid-level", that is, the scale of the company, by linking the investments made by trendy applications with the efficiency of an industrialization of administrative processes (and while they're at it, making projections on the possible reduction of staff). Are you a semio-cognitive scientist? Then go see how other players, such as paid beta-testers equipped with eye-tracking devices, react to a new search engine company to formulate the best possible recommendations to the publisher or developers, in the hope of improving functionality and making them more affordable. If all the disciplines of the Humanities and Social Sciences are entered by digital means into organization, we also know which obstacles they face when the levels of scale and temporal events are found to be fragmented in this way, the actors and the processes are broken down to their bare essentials. Here, as in other areas (since digital practices outside of working hours are also involved), the quantitative studies of the spread of a technology, or the studies of "user-centric" uses, have told us little if anything about what is being placed within the framework of a technical continuum. How can we explain the failure or the success of the implementation (its description in these terms) of this kind of application, or digital system? What is it that is being configured and recomposed in the context of the design and the implementation of the use of digital apparatuses? What does an ICT project of an organization in the process of redefining itself tell us?

When put to use here, pragmatic sociology may help us to provide some elements in response. Several principles describe this approach (perhaps presented as a vast nebula)[2]. In the case of France, the currents that emerged

---

2 For an analysis that brings together the various related works, see the article by [BAR 13], in which the main theoretical and methodological markers of this current are established. They are the heirs of pragmatist philosophy, whose biggest proponents include Pierce, James, and Dewey. Among the French authors associated with this movement are: B. Latour, M. Callon, I. Stengers, P. Lascoumes, L. Boltanski, L. Thévenot, E. Chiapello, N. Dodier, A. Desrosières, D. Cefaï, J.-L. Chateauraynaud, P. Corcuff, Y. Barthe, D. Linhardt, C. Lemieux, etc. (some of these researchers were able to collaborate at times, and have separated themselves scientifically from the others). Concerning organizational and collective

here in the 1980s and that may be attributed to that have the notable common characteristic that they have all broken away from the critical posture of Bourdieu. For F. Chateauraynaud [CHA 15], there are three of these currents: actor-network theory, or "sociology of translation", brought about by the Center of Innovation Sociology of the Ecole des Mines (Callon, Latour, Akrich), the sociology of action regimes (cities and justifications) (Boltanski, Thevenot) and situated action (Quere, Theureau) [CHA 15]. Others like J. Noyer [NOY 16] or C. Liccope [LIC 08] by extending, at right, the perimeter to English and European research, bring together within what is presented as "the approaches to activity", the current of distributed cognition [HUT 95], The psychological theory of the activity [THE 04][3], the ethnographic approaches of the situated action [SUC 87][4] and the theory of the actor-network. Antoine Hennion also highlights all the influences the American work has had in the development of the approaches of the Center of Sociology of Innovation [HEN 13]. For J.-M Noyer, the objective of precisely located and distributed approaches is to "understand the conditions in which cognition unfolds in networks, the modes of circulation of information, the norms in usage and the intellectual technologies involved. These approaches branch into many varied strands [...] we only need to mention that one should think of the co-determination of thinking entities and tools, of cognitive processes and intellectual technologies as situated in the *milieu* of collective assemblages of enunciation, in the milieu of collective equipment of subjectivation, of complex and hybrid actor–networks" [NOY 16].

In this context, specific branches are formed, such as "the cognitive anthropology of modern situations" [THE 96, THE 04][5] all the while passing

---

analysis approaches, the references that can be mobilized relate to works called activities, situated action or distributed cognition. In Information and Communication Sciences (a specific academic discipline in France), links can be identified with the Ecole de Montréal in Quebec, Canada (with J.R Taylor and F. Coreen being representatives).

3 Participatory approach to research (case studies and action research) is part of these work-situation analysis movements (workplace studies). Y. Engeström gives a summary of the psychology of Vygotsky and the study of the "superior psychological functions" by putting the focus on the mediation provided by the tools, signs, and culture.

4 Suchman proposes what Theureau describes as an "empirical science of human action in relation with technical devices".

5 Theureau describes cognitive anthropology as a branch of cultural anthropology from the 1980s, indicating that it can be traced back to Malinowsky, by way of Lévi-Strauss and his "savage thought".

through a painful separation of the problems on the basis of their disciplinary fields through the subjection of classic anthropology (its heritage) to a dialogue with philosophy, the cognitive sciences, and sociology. The central project of these surveys on contemporary and concrete situations would be [LAV 88]:

– "The empirical and theoretical characterization of situationally specific cognitive activities";

– "To arrive at a theory of active social players, localized in time and space, acting reflexively and recursively on the world in which they live, and at the same time, that they transform";

– "Take the localized nature of the activity (including cognition) as a given, and begin to explore its dimensions".

These empirical approaches to the activity (which, as a result, involve anthropologists, sociologists, historians, and researchers in information, communication and cognitive sciences, etc.) bringing together an entire collection of surveys led on the fields of organization, research, art, on controversies, law, public action, digital practices, etc.; a vast array of landscapes and subjects, understood through the prism of analyses of ethnomethodological inspiration to describe concrete situations (at the present or in a "genealogical" fashion), the actions conducted within them, and the mechanisms that come to govern and contort them. Though some branches differ in their scientific applications, *at a minimum*, they share this "astonishment with the terrain", as well as a large part of their methodology. From within this continuity, we present four essential prerequisites for our own work.

First, we consider the question of the inter-definition of organizations and the digital realm, as an object that demands a "pluridisciplinary pragmatism". Not only because this object may be seized on by the various obediences of the Humanities and Social Sciences, but because it is there that extremely varied acts and processes can be found. At certain times, we must play the role of a legal scholar to understand the co-construction of the law and the policies of cyber-surveillance; at other times, we will put on the glasses of an organizational theorist, to attempt to live through the transformations of work; in still other situations, we will need to live in the world of mathematics, statistics, and digital technology, to incorporate the actions of algorithms used for digital information processing. "Playing the role of…" does not mean that the researcher is improvising from time to time as a data scientist and management specialist, but that he is located in a complex interwoven environment of problems and actors of very different natures, and that he has to live in this environment: this means giving himself the capacity to make use of multiple propensities that are presented to him, including "human/non-human things"[6] and phenomena. Objects, like other entities, as well as individuals, assume the stature of actors[7]. They act: a notion imported from semiotics [GRE 86], the "actor" is "any element that presents a difference within a course of action and that modifies the outcome of a test" [BAR 07].

In this continuity, by placing the researcher in the situation and without interpretative presuppositions, J. Denis insists on the need for a change of perspective and angle of observation during the same survey. This is one of the points where sociology breaks from the dominant parallel uses in France in the 1970s through the 1990s [PRO 15, DEN 09]. It no longer involves considering "isolated uses in a possibly artificial face-to-face exchange between a user (or group of users) and a certain type of technology, but the emergence and the consolidation in essentially stable socio technical chains in space and time" [DEN 09][8]. This transformation requires the researcher to shift from the role of the spectator observing the uses of techniques, to a

---

6 From the works of the CSI, from the 1980s and 1990s, to the recent works of B. Latour on the climate [LAT 15], we have begun the shift toward a refusal of the "big share" between human and non-human elements, between all things natural and all things artificial [LAT 91].

7 This symmetry, proposed by B. Latour and M. Callon between human and non-human actors, nature and society, attachment and detachment, has been seen as an empirical continuity of the *strong program*, or "relativist", by D. Bloor. Starting in the 1960s and 1970s, Bloor and his colleagues in the Edinburgh school began to consider that the *study sciences* should respect four axiomatic principles: the principles of causality, impartiality, reflexivity, and symmetry. These principles apply both to sciences as well as to beliefs (whether true or false), in that they do not constrain a rational cause within the confines of a social cause of the second. This does not imply that therefore there would be "equal validity" between provisions. By consequence, "the concept of truth" only exists within the state of conventional particular knowledge, historically contingent and relating to social and cultural factors interacting with our sensory experiences. Regarding the evolution of the *strong program,* see [BRI 08].

8 "This posture consists of varying the points of view as much as possible, and thus the targets of attention. The second targets the creation of stories, which involve surrounding an observable situation in a limited unit of time" [DEN 09, p. 13].

decoder of meanings and classifier of appropriations (a term still used often, and quite poorly when referring to statistical tables of users) to a person in motion and curious about all situations.

Secondly, our perspective is related to sociotechnical approaches, and more broadly, to the anthropology of techniques, which has largely shown (but nevertheless must constantly recall) the drama of the great separation between "technical" and "human" elements. In the organizational analysis, the same difficulty was expressed logically: the example of the "contingent" or "systemic" readings of technology shows how it can still be studied as a simple "ingredient" or as an independent variable (one that is independent from politics in particular). Conversely, other works insisted on the analysis of the co-determination relationships which remain current, of which B. Latour cites some major works of the 1990s [LAT 94, 88, 06a]:

> "The works by Leigh Star on computerized work sites [STA 10], of Ed Hutchins on cognition anthropology, of Lucy Suchman and Charles Goodwin on coordination into work sites, of Laurent Thévenot [THÉ 06] on familiar courses of action, in addition to the studies by social historians of science, and sociologists of science turned to organization like John Law point to a complete redefinition of the divide between the two worlds. In the following sentence 'information science and artificial intelligence in human organizations' only the two copules 'and' and 'in' have remained unscathed! Each of the six other words have been reformated beyond recognition"[9].

The third principle that we retain is that of the association of the levels of scale: "Globalize the local" and "Locate the global", these being a condition of renewal of the sociology for B. Latour [LAT 06a]. Connecting, associating, following the trajectories, which have been artificially described as micro, meso, or macro-levels and then, just as artificially, relying on them. The engaging presentation made by a group of researchers [BAR 13] of the theoretical and methodological positions commonly found in pragmatists leads us to repeat this obvious fact: the localized approaches of the organization and work collectives do not erase the situation, the action of law, social norms, or of any other institution which, instead of being rejected in the past, "far away" or "high above", cross through the "here and now" of

9 http://www.bruno-latour.fr/sites/default/files/61-COMPUTERS-GB.pdf.

collective interactions. Among the many ways these entities can become apparent are as strategic resources (interests, justifications, denunciations) but also as cognitive resources (decision support, representation, information filtering, etc.). When Edwin Hutchins observes the decision-making process on a military boat, he sees the role played by maritime charts and the compass that have this specific nature of being a means of transport, in this place, the Ministry of Maritime Affairs, the Defense, cartographic services, their practices and legacies in the long run... Thus, in a large amount of these works, the "micro" level is not conceived in opposition to the "macro" level but, conversely, as the plane where, from situation to situation, the "macro" level itself is accomplished, realized, and objectified through practices, devices and institutions, without which it could certainly be deemed to exist but, however, would no longer be able to be made visible and describable... This posture is valid for sociological reasoning itself, which, in this respect, cannot claim any kind of privilege: the social sciences deserve to be understood and analyzed as contributing to the processes societies use to reflect on themselves and take control [BAR 13]. Moreover, Latour considers that removing ourselves from levels of scale becomes a requirement for getting rid of the *a priori* nature of the hierarchy of essential characteristics, when one wants to study translation and transformation as major communication processes: as ANT holds, there is no equivalence, there are only translations.[10] Thus, for example, we would be more interested in the processes of performation, as opposed to concepts such as "Culture" or "Structure" (these concepts – if we still want to rely on their existence – must be shown precisely in their processes of designation, transformation, and formatting by digital practices, and not taken as an explanatory variable, etc.) [BAR 13][11].

Finally, the last point on which we want to insist concerns the analysis of the phenomenon of politics. Contrary to what some authors claim, the question of politics – far from being removed from pragmatic approaches and socio-technical approaches (something that was presented as the expression of a break with the critical theories of Foucault, Bourdieu, etc.) –

---

10 Technologies contain a variety of political, social and economic elements as well as science, engineering, and the particular histories of these practices. Translation, as developed by the French philosopher Michel Serres, is a term that attempts to overcome the arbitrary divisions between these related aspects. See Darryl Cressman http://faculty.georgetown.edu/irvinem/theory/Cressman-ABriefOverviewofANT.pdf.

11 Actor-network theory, also known by its other name: the sociology of translation.

is at the heart of the apprehension of organizational manufacturing and the manufacturing of the digital environments that interest us here. The fact that the Marxist reading of technologies has been abandoned does not mean that the phenomena of power have been erased from the analysis; but it must be understood that this concept is used without an *a priori* critical (or worse, ideological) view beforehand, that it refers to a political economy of relations and to an analysis of the assembly of forces in presence (something that should be understood as "power relationships", and thus irreducible to a mere conflict of forces). The focus is not on the processes of domination and class struggles, but class struggles are reconfigured considering the hardships, power relationships and associations between forces, particularly with ANT, which has enriched the description tremendously. B. Latour formulates one of the limits of the Marxist critique of technology in this sense, mainly seen in an antagonistic relationship (capitalism/workers) for which he induces and reduces the passage to the number of the phenomena and dimensions in play[12]:

> "Whenever the introduction of a machine does not attack the workers, many Marxists are left speechless and start talking about technical factors and other determinisms. When a machine does deskill textile workers they know what to say; when companies create new highly skilled workers they see this as a puzzling exception, or even, in MacKenzie's terms as an "obverse trend" [LAT 88, 06] [13].

---

12 This does not mean they have disappeared. And an entire series of engaging works make it possible to place the question of work within the framework of an extension of what has been described as "cognitive capitalism", and the formation of a new class known as the "cognitariat". In this regard, see the work of Yann Moulier Boutang (Moulier Boutang, 2007).

13 B. Latour grants that Marx "saw that a machine may lead to a new job position" in his text "The prince machines and machinations", reducing the analysis to merely an "antagonistic positioning" of the Marxists, according to the terminology of [MAC 84]. He goes on to say: "[… ] Thus, when it is clear that a new technology cannot be explained by class struggle, they must then either fabricate an excuse, and in so doing, claim it has escaped everyone but them, or – worse still – admit that some aspects of technology may be "neutral" or "positive" after all" [LAT 88, LAT 06].

### 1.1.2. *A few trials*

In our view, the problem or tension that proves this is the controlling condition materiality has on the situation (which serves as a trace) and by which proof is provided for the understanding of power relationships. It is a requirement of empirical analysis and has been one since it began: the second proposal of irreductions is "there are only trials of strength, of weakness. Or more simply, there are only trials. This is my point of departure: a verb, "to try"" [LAT 93].

The descendant of pragmatic philosophy, also known as empirical philosophy, French pragmatic sociology presents itself as a "sociology of ordeal" [LEM 07, BAR 13, MAR 15], but according to these authors it deviates from the proposal – which we believe is central – of irreduction. In the situations considered here, we are not interested in a social order or a socio-historical complex that would be processed as an inseparable whole, but a combination of elements taken from the same position as the place of the organization. [LAM 00] take the discussion of the term *épreuve*, which translates to "ordeal" or as Latour describes it a "trial of strength", in English further by stating: "In the Francophone world, however, the term has a more complex meaning, referring also to 'trial', 'ordeal', and 'proof'. This approach has been developed in terms of an international comparison. Assuming that individual members of different national groups are, in principle, equipped with the same competences and have equal access to the *cites* permits us not only to pay attention to similarities that are commonly overlooked, but also to shed light on actual differences without having to reify them as 'natural', 'self-evident', or 'culturally determined'" [LAM 00, LEM 04, NAC 98].

Moreover, it does not apply exclusively to the long term and the macro-level, for which we have already pointed out the limits for the analysis of socio-technical couplings. Rather, a radical empiricism of technical and organizational policies would require us to consider a discontinuous chain of adjustments that will need to follow the uncertain paths. When examined between intervals of time, the organization is merely the result of bifurcations, and from among these oscillations, sometimes the smallest. To this end, we will show in this work how the digital forces require us to put the question of the politics of interfaces, and the "molecular revolution" that characterizes it, at the heart of our analysis [GUA 12, NOY 13, 16, MAR 15].

With regard to trials, the pragmatic approach adopts both an epistemological position and a methodological position, since this phenomenon is that each of us must think and make the situation able to be grasped and described. As Dewey points out, quoted by Martuccelli, for "any judgment resulting from a problematic situation, the important thing is to determine what problem or problems are posed by a problematic situation in the investigation" [DEW 93]. Among the various currents in the sociology of conventions [BOL 91], currently in an uncertain situation, a trial of strength represents a problem of the construction of judgments, a construct conceived on the basis of the placement of opinions into confrontation (or into equivalence): junctures, couplings, and assemblies between different "orders of magnitude" (commercial, religious, etc.) are thus the basis of disputes and then arrangements (agreements), either local or more extensive arguments analyzed as common higher principles, more generally, conventions (institutions) and therefore, a set of social relations, described here based on how individuals set out to justify (make right) their behavior and decisions (without presuming interest or rational calculations) [BOL 91][14]:

> "Thus, beyond the success or failure of an action, it is important to understand how actors base their beliefs about sanctioning proof considered as fair. Ordeals are at work in case of litigation (within the same city) or in disputes (between various cities), they are also the source of arrangements or compromise, in fact, they come into play every time there is a question of resolving a controversy in court through a trial" [MAR 15][15].

---

14 In the approach to the theory of conventions, the "common higher principles" or "orders of magnitude" feature sets known as "cities". In [BOL 91], there are six of them: inspired city, domestic city, city of opinion, civic city, merchant city, industrial city, and then completed with one more: the city by projects, in [BOL 99]. For the authors, this last type of city merges for authors with the dominant connectionnist perspective, in which the metaphorical figure of the network dominates (in which the connectionist world precedes the formation of a city). Each city brings with it its universe of explanations, its justification criteria mobilized by individuals. One of the major points of disagreement between Boltanski and Latour remains the persistence of a structuralist sociology, claimed by the former and denied by the latter.

15 Martuccelli describes two main uses of the concept of ordeal in the Humanities and Social Sciences: the "trial-sanction" mainly mobilized, in his opinion, by the theory of conventions and by the ANT; and the "trial-challenge", associated with work related to existential

If the trial is relevant here (but only partly) regarding a question of power relationships (between registers and delegated authorities) and their transformation [BOL 99], we cannot agree in our approach with either the logic of "these large sets" that would comprise shared higher principles that are dominant (at least in the use that was made by then), the issue of the method of construction and empirical selection, of which they are the product (which we find to be of interest in the first place), nor the domination of the verbal enunciation of the theory of conventions, which, incidentally and at the risk of a "psychologizing" reading that the project by Boltanski and Thevenot has nonetheless sought to avoid, may slip into the reduction *a priori* of the action of objects, or even the time and space, into a "context" – even if they have been included in his remarks. For us, the forces acting within the structures of enunciation come first, and the contents of the words come second[16,17].

For science studies, a trial of strength comes to describe the formation process of scientific controversies, or when they are exhausted, their processes of closure [CAL 91, LAT 84]: we are dealing with multiple trial-sanctions in scientific research, for example, in proof-stabilization in the controversy for the ANT, but also in trials of strength that are relaunched, opening new opportunities and confrontations. Thus, we find that these collective disputes arise, as a way of putting to the test not only relationships (hybrids, since they are not only inter-personae) but more broadly, the assemblage itself, within which these relationships are built (the term "assemblage" is now preferred by Callon and Latour to the somewhat

---

problems and self-training. For the author, "regarding the proof-sanction, much of it depends on the strength, the evidence and the legitimacy of the sanction, whether the objectivity of the world, the success or failure as criteria of truth and of the verification of the action, or also, a possible role of closure and escape from controversies through relationships of power and justice". We advocate another approach.

16 We don't feel it would be useless to "decide", as desired by Martuccelli, between a trial of strength presented as either a punishment "directly controlled by the objective reality itself, [or] conversely, as a sanction [...] dependent on elements external to the inherent objectivity of the world" [MAR 15]. We stressed the incompatibility of the dichotomy of "internal/external" with the project of the analysis of socio-technical elements and fixtures.

17 However, in 2004, Latour stressed the possible convergence between Luc Boltanski, Laurent Thevenot, and his work, the need to abandon the covering of "reason". "We relate certain evidence to situations, and we don't add a test of reason to the tests," he said, in [LEM 15].

confusing "actor-network"). Our perspective on "trials" or "events" thus relates fundamentally to a political dynamic, formed within the frameworks of Gilles Deleuze and Felix Guattari, following the thinking of assemblages. To describe the organization-digital connections, we cannot limit trials to situations of dissent. Describing and understanding the transformation of assemblages implies that we now consider the trials as "events": when the individual, the rules or the object resist, when the desires compete, including technology "that no longer wants to work", at the time when new alliances are created between laws and computer standards, when an algorithm for recommendations on the Internet and the recommended clicks it performs, etc., each time we experience a trial-event. What are the trials that characterize the establishment of a socio-technical process? What are the events experienced in the digital manufacturing of organization? What are the driving forces in the experience that are related in these tests, to ensure the performation (the result of these tests)? And we will still need to see how the test is participating in a shift – even one that is infinitesimally small – of the assemblages, in the two-way movement of "deterritorialization" (from which it takes its capacity to transfer) and "reterritorialization" (that it selects and makes use of as a given medium until a new deterritorialization) [DEL 80, LAT 06b] [18].

### 1.1.3. *Following the scripts in action*

On the occasion of these trials, the actors demonstrate their ability to affect and be affected. Multiple mediations take place, taken from what we describe as socio-technical scripts. The movement of the organizational assemblage is tested in terms of the power of scripts and the propensity for deterritorialization / reterritorialization they authorize.

One of the first objectives of this ethnographic study is to observe the process of development and mediation borrowed from these scripts. Putting the phenomena of performation and trials at the heart of these processes involves seeing what they do or "cause" and following the tensions that aggregate around these particular actors. Again, we form part of the continuity of the works of sociology of innovation (1980s–1990s), but this

---

18 Procedures, testing protocols, evaluation, various instruments of scientific research, funding, etc., can all be an opportunity for multiple tests. See also [LAT 79].

survey will allow us to discuss certain contributions and pursue our reflection on the regimes of enunciation. To claim that this interplay of scripts has been instilled in our research on organizations is an understatement. As we will try to show, we see it spread throughout all parts of the work because it has to do with their microtranscendances and their macro/meso colleagues. Because it concerns the establishment of particular livelihoods organized together, as well as between organizations and beyond them, as regards our relationship with the state of digital affairs. In short, it refers to those elements comprising the framing beings who act: how they happen, what do they do and how to spot them? We try to offer some answers by including the digital manufacturing of the organization within our study, that is to say, the establishment of the way that organizations and their components exist, the codetermination of ICTs and organizational practices (from workshops for employees to management offices). Since these technological agents are routinely put to use in order to meet the demands of change and continuous innovation, this socio-technical perspective and co-evolution will be one of our connecting threads[19].

The approach places processes of inter-definitions of social and technical elements, and the varied nature of their connections, at the heart of the analysis. It highlights the components of pragmatism, or as Guattari writes, "a generative pragmatism corresponding to the mechanisms of the linguistization of semiotics and a transformational pragmatism that is not transformational, not meaningful". To take it even further: it bears on semiotic pluralism in its very heterogeneity and hybridizations.

Rather than ask the question of the "social significance of technology", it is preferable to find one that aims to examine the technical construction of all things social, the performation of practices and subjectivities, the weaving together of populations of technical beings with populations of legal, moral, or managerial entities. This leads to conceiving innovation as a process that gives rise to an invention, the ability or lack thereof to meet the

---

19 On the concept of creation with Souriau and its differentiation from construction (of constructionism), see Latour B., "Take the fold of the techniques" *Networks*, No. 163, available at: http: // www. cairn.info/revue-reseaux-2010-5-page-11.htm. "The artist, as Souriau tells us, is never the creator, but remains the founder of a work that comes to him but, without him, would never come into existence".

conditions of happiness that will allow it to incarnate, to update and produce, with a singular purpose, a world of meanings.[20]

The antithesis of a "shot sequence" in film, a plan to file without interruption or editing, innovation in the organizational field is overly coded practically everywhere: it is applied to times, places, situations, objects, diagrams and it is connected by slogans, legitimization, rationalities, and strategic models, often afterward. The socio-technical, techno-political couplings of the digital organization operate as redistributive slices, constraints, and desires. The scripts are one of the actors. To clarify our direction, let us elaborate a bit further on the film metaphor. Established on the basis of a plot, a film script is a document, providing various pieces of information: reproductions, behaviors of the actors, the technical data required in the shooting (lighting, sound, etc.), staging elements (sets, spatial configuration) and camera movements (tracking shot, close-ups, etc.). In production, the script makes reference to the person in charge of ensuring the continuity of the movie, that person will work on the connections between plans, scenes, and sequences, connections that will allow for continuity, compliance with the plot (for editing) and that, by making continuous adjustments to the script, will "document" it (registration). In reclaiming the project and its purpose (a work to be "projected", as it were), by embodying and bringing it to the screen, this initial document serves three purposes: descriptive operator, connector and modeler. It is also the mission assigned to the "Project Leader" in businesses[21,22].

Thus, as with designing a cinematic apparatus, here the project organization, approach and associates are all placed together, varied elements in businesses, which are objectives and management requirements, distributions in space-time, situations and singular contingencies, objects and material constraints, programs and interfaces, individuals and their roles

---

20 Commenting on the work of Latour, Fischer says, "We need not celebrate "humanity as technological detour", but focus on the "peopling of technologies"" [FIS 14].

21 The concept of the script has enriched much research in the human and social sciences: social anthropology (sexual scripts, criminal scripts, etc.), cognitive sciences, the sociology of science and technology, and the sociology of uses. It has been adapted in favor of these movements. The many uses cognitive sciences have made of the world of film have been discussed by [PER 01].

22 In the world of film professionals, the distinction between "scenario" and "script" can sometimes seem unstable. In the cognitive sciences, the difference is slight.

(principal, MOA/MOE designers, developers, experts, spokespersons, users, etc.), text (annotations, data, images, diagrams, explanations, language elements, etc.), routines and professional standards. This forms the first type of script: the script draft. However, unlike the cinematographic elements, the technical-organizational scripts are, firstly, immanent, practices and the organization itself (can you imagine a film without the start of a script and only designed from improvisation?). From the initial idea to the handoff to the users, the scenario of a digital apparatus in an organization can always be replayed differently, and change the assignment of duties and roles of the various "human and nonhuman" entities that it composes, becoming secondary or at least asynchronous from this perspective. The characteristic itself of the projects is the uncertainty and instability of the actors, who are impossible to list in their entirety at the beginning of the design and thus to define their attributes and behaviors *a priori*. This is the paradox of "project-risk management" in the design of information systems where inductive approaches have to face the innovation process itself, namely the existence of blind and uncertain areas.

The script presents itself as both the process by which links are created (between different entities), and as the program that reassembles courses of action [THÉ 06]. As such, the sequences, the narrated segments, can be edited independently (as in the context of an organizational "narrative" in film); we then proceed to make "connections", associations between different themes/planes, doing so in order to ensure a level of overall consistency and to serve the rational nature or the goals of the project (participants may have only partial knowledge). Thus, in a project intended to design a new digital apparatus we adjust our actions in response to the events that occur over the course of the project and the order of the presentation of the arguments. They are enriched and modified by other narrative sequences.

In the same sense as "actor-network", "problematization", "controversy", "stakeholding", etc., the script is one of the key concepts of the sociology of translation. More recently, Latour has devised one more of the major means of analysis, the "modes of existence" and the two ways in which they tend to work (difficult to hold in place), metaphysically and pragmatically. What does it mean to him to read our social groups through their scripts? In particular, we need to contact the "beings of passionate interest" (economic interests, for example) and "attachment beings" (which will be connected): in this context, "that which we refer to as "Society" is not, from the viewpoint of this mode, the effect of scripts stacked on top of each other, the exact nature and type of the stacking has been lost from sight, and to those, a giant dispatcher was surreptitiously added, by way of confusion with politics; this meta-distributor, this providence that would allocate seats, roles, functions, without our being able to know in which offices it would exercise its wisdom, nor by which mechanisms it would transmit its orders, its formats, its standards" [LAT 12]. To unfold and deconstruct scripts requires us to discard any temptation to reach transcendence, without giving in to the excesses of constructivism and relativism. The concept of mediation will help us in this[23].

The anthropology of Modernity proposed by Latour is vast, and to the extent that it focuses on organizations, we must consider this mode to be in different areas of application: business, government, religion, the market, etc. Thus, regardless of the field, "the organization" does not emerge as an outcome, but as a process, an institution whose dynamics we must analyze, in addition to as a mode of existence in itself. Yet, several issues remain common (how are entities within a script connected? What is their performative force and where is it drawn from? What is it that ensures the effects that frame this? What mediations does it employ[24]? How can it be transformed in time and what is it that transforms it?), phenomena to which the connected scripts may vary, depending on the point of view from which we examine it and what we look at: a set of organizations (in our case, for

---

23 In the chapter entitled "Correcting a Slight Defect in Construction" [LAT 12] Latour responds to the double critique (he claims to be neither relativist nor constructivist), emphasizing the need to equip us with new tools. Among these, he includes mediation. In his view, to mention science or an organization they are built from, for example, would mean saying three things at the same time. The first: we are facing mediations that "cause us to act". Second: the author of the construct becomes a mystery. The situation we have here, by contrast, is one of oscillation, varying alternatively between the construct and the constructor, and the hand of the puppeteer to the puppet. Third point: "to remove oneself from this oscillation", he adds an ingredient. "Saying that something has been built implies the introduction of a value judgment, not only on the origin of the action [...] but on the quality of construction". Therefore, this commits us to take seriously the act of construction in itself, in order to study it. This is something that constructivism, according to Latour, can no longer do, since he has cast doubt on all the "artifacts" and their veracity. Given the heavy connotation of the term today, he agrees to substitute the concept of design for that of construction, which he borrows from Souriau.

24 For the 12 ones proposed in [LAT 12a], see the following address: http://www.bruno-latour.fr/ sites/default/files/110-ORGANIZATION-PASSOTH.pdf.

example, a company and the army of partners and stakeholders that are related to it), a specific company, and the various internal processes that characterize a particular situation of working in a team, or the work done by an employee on his computer. Perhaps, we may already sense that these different levels of scale can be considered discontinuously. In this first part of the work, the scripts indiscriminately take us from the office of an employee to the CEO of the company, at times passing through professional rules and others, through the settings put in place by a digital developer. We show that manufacturing an organization is the equivalent of producing scripts (and not exclusively linguistic scripts) and that they are no longer a matter of "floors in the building that is the company's headquarters", but the creating of relationships, as well as power relationships. In our view, following the scripts and their heterogeneous grammar (their production and action) amounts to performing a crossing of arrangements. They are constructed and from them, distributed themselve in others.

We therefore agree with the ambitious vision of Latour and the fundamental position he gives to scripts in his analysis of organizational phenomena. However, we will try to clarify the elements that attach and tie together within these scripts, to extend the length of the networks that feed into them and stem from them (especially in the study of the process of performation, discussed later). Finally, our work here involves describing what is presented as a study of the conflict between scripts (the conflicts or the reinforcements between them) while placing the issue of digital semiotics at the heart of organizational performation process. Where did each of these scripts get their names from? And what is the role of their creators (which is difficult), their materials, their spokespersons/representatives, their intensity, and the place from which they express themselves? Besides the common phenomena that we have already indicated, what is it that will distinguish them from each other? This will be revealed over the course of the investigation and the trials that we highlight here.

If we are interested in the construction of theories on managerial actions (ranging from academic theories to orthodoxies on digital strategies), the scripts, "stories" produced in this way, travel and move from company to company, and repeat themselves until they become idea archetypes (an established framework, or frame) [MIN 75]. Thus, some of these encounter fortuitous conditions that allow them to dominate. In this sense, they may be able to have a relatively automatic nature, and approach the script of cognitive science or IT, which emphasizes the automation of sequencing and behavior. For us, the figure in this case relates to "stabilized" decision-making models (within a short-term period for the company), to frequently repeated inferences: the responses given by managerial, conceptual and normative scripts (we will see further the role that celebratory practice have here). But when, on the basis of the landscape and its contingent weak points (scripts of localized activity), we come to understand that the script is susceptible to the arrival of a new actor (who plays the role of a "Hitchcock", taking pleasure in punching holes in the logical construction of the filmmaker, who offers to collaborate on a film that has already been scripted), who requires that changes be made, new programs of action be devised, new holes be made in the scripts. Creation and innovation are at play in the introduction of this difference itself [MIN 75][25,26].

Drawing from Latour and his anthropology of modes of existence, the act of organization (or "organizing") in the sense that we understand it, and its maintenance and stability, are conditioned by "a connection, an accumulation, a formidable layering of successive disorganization: people come and go, they carry all kinds of documents, they complain, assemble, separate, grumble, protest, assemble again, they organize once again, they disperse, catch up, all in constant disorder, without ever being able to define the boundaries of these entities that continuously expand or shrink like an accordion" [LAT 12].

According to this philosopher, the script is basically immanent in the organization, an organization that manufactures them, disputes them, and tests them, but a script that, almost simultaneously, it acts out and sets in motion:

> "Scripts are not presented as a tautology (we produce the same
> society that has produced us; at the same time, we are bound
> externally by the standards to which we nonetheless aspire) that
> if we forget the slight delay in time, by which it is never exactly

---

25 "A script is a structure that describes appropriate sequences of events in a particular context" [SCH 77].

26 For example, see the computer scripting languages that are used to initiate and coordinate the implementation of programs. AppleScript for Mac OS is a scripting interface designed to operate in parallel with the graphic environment. The principle of this script is to automate tasks, reducing the time required to complete these tasks and reducing the possibility of human error.

the same moment and never with exactly the same capabilities that we find ourselves "above" or "below" the same scenario. This sinuous nature, so unique to scripts, is unfortunately not to be found in the concept of tautology And even if it could follow this expansion mode, this does not always make it capable of serving as a template for politics, religion, law and the psyche – not to mention one's first or second nature" [LAT 12].

Another figure who in this case leads us specifically to technical materiality, described in detail by M. Akrich, deals specifically with interfaces, with the proposal made by the designer of a technical object to the potential users of this object. Again, this is a scenario of a predetermination of situations of practice. This proposal (which, to varying degrees, can be binding or relevant from the point of view of the user) is accompanied by several movements [AKR 87, AKR 91]:

– indications (as found, for example, in operating instructions);

– descriptions (the formation of a customary meaning, decoding of the scenarios, the singular adaptation of this).

In this chapter, we will have the opportunity to analyze these two movements, and we propose to view them in their continuous state of flux, a major feature of digital apparatuses in organization. The investigation of scripts thus also involves following the trajectories, in addition to numerous iterations and updates made to the socio-technical configuration.

From our perspective, we therefore give the concept of "script" an extensive meaning: scripts are immanent to the organization (in fact, they themselves are organization, through and through) and giving their mobile nature, are based on a semiotic pluralism.

The investigation will not only include this particular level of scale that includes the linkage "localized" between an object and a user (a practice of confrontation between an individual, a situation, and perceptions, and a script framed by a digital program), but also extend to other places and processes that constitute the assemblage within which organizational action programs are produced. In this specific case, the design of digital apparatuses in business, what are the locations and entities that become involved as a result?

The designers and suppliers of ICT solutions, a project group whose members come from a single company or from other companies (project managers, managers of different services, consultants, IT companies, etc.), the employees of this company have do their jobs from multiple applications, and may also include Internet users, trade unions, journalists echoing the achievements of companies, professional associations, and some clubs, which organize meetings and other events, etc. A large collection of objects and inscriptions are utilized in the design processes: specifications, schedules, PowerPoint presentations, reports, email exchanges, financial indicators, computers, software programs, URLs, access codes, cookies, viruses, network and bandwidth infrastructure (which, in some cases, was subject to being devoured by rats[27]), "quality" standards, the company's internal regulations, legislation work and ICT law, some of the best known websites and online tools (Google, Facebook, etc.). In a way, each of these actors crosses through "worlds", in which they is linked, and each one "speaks" at their own level but leaves a mark on the group as a whole; everyone participates with varying levels of intensity in the production of scripts, working together with or against the other actors.

To summarize up to this point, we have found at least three precautions to take to prepare for the investigation.

We will be looking at an aggregate script, at hybrids, and then our task will be to "seek to bring to the foreground the materiality of the apparatuses they use to stack up and merge together" [LAT 12]. The attention given to trials and the equipment of these trials will assist us in this task.

On the basis of the regimes of enunciation, whose scripts are both the expression and material that is expressed (as they are immanent to the organization) and the mediations that they borrow, the materials (registration) that are preferred vary in quality and intensity: linguistic materials (speeches, reports), non-linguistic semiotics (interfaces, programs, digital codes), corporeal elements (behavioral postures, physical movement, or activity routines), architectural materials, etc.

---

27 This fact was reported to us by the RATP: the appetites of rodents work to undermine the maintenance of networks that run the lengths of the lines that connect transportation sites by digital linkages. And the tastes of these animals are the same in other countries as well; in 2005, field mice were responsible for cutting telephone lines for the entire region of central Sweden for 20 hours, after chewing through the area's fiber optic cables.

Finally, several scripts can take action simultaneously: digital innovation in the organizational environment appears as a combination of scripts and power between performative processes in which they are included, and which they carry.

## 1.2. Setting the stage

### 1.2.1. *Two gray suits at the Belmont bar*

It's the end of a late autumn day, at the bar in the Hotel Belmont. The bar, with its *Belle Epoque* ambience, is nestled within the heart of the sixteenth arrondissement of Paris. Here, two men have made plans to meet. One is the manager of a communications agency, paid for his hours of consulting with major corporations. His claim to fame is his ability to detect "technological innovations" in the HR field (he was the one responsible for importing the American corporate communications model on the Internet to France). The second is a human resources manager at a multinational company. He has been described as a "strong advocate of social dialogue" and is preparing to carry out missions on a larger scale. The company has just joined with several business branches within a single group (which involves delegated activities of the management of public services: water management, waste management, public transportation, and heating systems). In the coming days, a certain Jean-Marie Messier – with whom, outside of his HR ties, his relationship is not very warm – will be named the CEO. Both of these professionals address each other with a cordial tone, befitting of the aristocratic demeanor of Parisian businessmen, while showing some signs of connivance maintained by their closeness within the same networks. If we were to follow his connections, we would find other CEOs and managers, politicians, key figures on television and in other media, former military officials, technicians, writers who were formerly communications representatives, or vice versa... leading him to "a group to be built". Because of this, and even though he has no knowledge of digital technology, he feels, he guesses, he knows that there is a fundamental link that will be established between ICT, his organization, and achieving its objectives. He senses the potential of an HR information system to serve his strategy and transform the company (even in spite of the company itself):

> "This system, you see, could help to break up the local power brokers, a legacy of the autonomy of the subsidiaries. If the new group could be made known through the system, together

within a single space of communication, and ensure that everyone works in the same way, it would be very effective".

Under "the system", the HR director would thus be its ally, working toward the purpose of federating multiple entities within the territory, to gain independence from local authorities in order to carry out an "alignment" (of the processes and organizational strategy). The contract is concluded quickly. The consultant is given the mission to create a single digital communication system dedicated to the management of recruitment and the mobility of employees in the future group.

What will his frame be during this meeting? What forces give credibility to the forces acting between these two? What are the various accounts which operate (and the protagonists who give them)? How are these narratives intertwined and linked to other semiotics and non-linguistic elements?

The description provided here, and the analysis that follows, are intended to identify an initial set of phenomena. Other descriptions follow in the text, which will complete the process at work in the production of digital apparatuses in organizations.

A few preliminary remarks: firstly, we may question the level of permanence among managers, the organizational models of action attached to computerization. This conversation at the Belmont took place in 1999, yet it could just as easily have been 1975 or 2015[28]. Secondly, this scene shows us we must remain attentive to the stories of a project (those within the ethnographic event, and those that we give, or which are fed to us by professionals). The production of organizational projects requires us to consider the status of stories that will be given alongside these projects, the motives that support them, and whose initial rational backings, as expressed here may not correspond to those which are written "after the fact". Finally – and this is no small task – we must address this astonishing phenomenon that grants these technological objects (even decades after the wave of determinism swept through the management sciences) an ability to affect the

---

28 Beginning in the 1970s, led by IBM, Honeywell and Bull, digitized management began to be implemented in various company departments (staff administration, accounting, inventory management, etc.) and the organizational changes related to it have already been the subject of several studies. The link between HRIS, management control, and the decision-making approach – forming, at a minimum, a dashboard for HR processes – is also a target put in place during the 1970s–1980s; see [ROD 10].

organization, subjectivities and the processes at work, to express and be a political power in action.

The research builds on an investigation inspired by ethnomethodology lasting seven years (2000–2007). This choice of methodology prompted us to choose this action as a preferred temporal space for observation The monitoring of the daily actions of various actors and the written record of their interactions, the developed interfaces and applications, the documents produced, the exchanges of electronic messages, interviews, etc., are the materials used in the "Moeva case". This project involves the implementation of a digital apparatus made up, firstly, of two "front office" extranet jobs/mobilities dedicated to employees of the group, and a website for external recruitment and, secondly, a "back office" made up of an intra-extranet, available to HR teams (roughly 400 people at the end of the project) who are required to manage thousands of applications and other documents incorporated into HR processes in this way. This is similar to a groupware system, in this case centered on automated business processes (workflows) and the sharing of information resources (supported by defining user profiles)[29].

To conduct this investigation, we will move from office to office, listen in on official and intimate discussions (outside the project, located in the halls of head offices, or on the phone), allows us to bring users together with the bugs in the functionality, read hundreds of pages of reports, data, and specifications, and thus observe the theater of operations from as close as possible (including the staging of meetings and version releases). We are on a level that is neither beyond nor below these messages (meetings, symposia, professional press): through participatory observation, we attempt to navigate between different plans, around which, for example, a newspaper article may be brought up, because it is circulated by the project manager: this is not so much about describing its "content" in detail than to be attentive to how this article is involved in the process.

The digital production of organizations invites us to navigate within the various narrative orders (first and foremost, the order of objects) and take

---

29 The study of ethnomethods, that is to say, the rules of conduct, all that constitutes and everything that people use naturally and implicitly in everyday life, can be said to be "the study of current practices of the members, experienced in everyday life, through the analysis of the rationalizations given for their actions and their words as reflecting their interpretations".

advantage of traces of varying natures. This survey is the description and analysis of how locations, strengths and actors, are progressively woven together. By dispensing with any *a priori* definition of "social clusters" and the forces that are in play, by not sacrificing field studies for analytical instruments, by following the associations as given by the actors themselves[30] in producing this ethnotechnology, our purpose is, in taking after the sociology of translation, to produce as rich a description as possible, even if this framing may still only be unfinished, incomplete, with a few holes still left[31].

The history of these forces, of their stability and instability (with "meta-stability" being a condition for the perpetuation of the organization), convergences and divergences, a story that therefore does not begin and end "around a cafe", is presented below by following a path from one stage to the other, stopping to examine tests, approaching the project as a continuous and chaotic evolution.

### 1.2.2. *A parade of participants*

The Moeva case brings a multitude of entities into play (actors from group projects, writings, speeches, information systems, internal regulations, etc.) that we understand as many individual actors, that is to say, as entities having the capability to affect or be affected. This perspective of the actors (beings and objects)[32], allows us to embrace the complexity of organizational situations, guarding against the temptations to analyze only written language and action (the analysis of speech "on" or "in the action"). In a digital project in the process of organization, what are the forces that are expressed, evaluated, that collide with each other, and how does their composition transform itself? To answer this, we must start by following these actors

---

30 On these points, see the methodological breakages that were proposed by this current of the anthropology of science and technology, and in particular the work of Michel Callon and Bruno Latour.

31 The incompleteness of the description refers both to the complexity of arrangements (networks of actors in which the actors form linkages and act) as well as the inability of the researcher to transcribe everything in a book while continuously monitoring individuals and objects.

32 This is a notion that Callon and Latour have borrowed from semiotics (Greimas) to enrich the context of the work of the sociology of science and technology.

involved in the situation, in a design activity[33], or to put it another way, an activity done in various locations and processes of an assemblage. Thus understanding the relationship between these particular entities, and the levels of intensity that circulate, thus leads us to consider the construction of a digital apparatus such as an ecology of relations between actors.

Let's now take a look at one of these ordinary situations: the proceedings of a Moeva meeting in a large office area of La Defense in Paris. Here, we meet:

– the main players in this mission from 2000–2001; the implementation is based on three traditional categories of "project actors" in charge of creating the system. There is the "project management" category: DG of Moeva (which we will thus call the enterprise involved with this research), the management of human resources (the project leader) and a selection of functional managers (from various entities) form some of the targeted users. Then, the "project management assistance" category: internal advising (communications management and the management of Moeva's information systems); the consulting firm specializing in human resources communications, "HRConsult". The "project management" category: IT solutions for publishers and other external technical service providers. In seven years, there will be changes in different responsibilities or in the people involved, but the profile of actors and the roles remain the same;

– statements produced over the course of the actions taken (verbal interactions, PowerPoint presentations, e-mail exchanges, etc.);

– numerous material registrations (interfaces, databases, repositories of schools/professions, specifications, minutes of meetings, notebooks of functional indications, communication plans, training, user guides, etc.);

---

33 Ethnomethodology, the anthropology of science and technology, the approaches of situated cognition, activity theory, in addition to other concepts, have compelled researchers to leave behind the paradigm of "sociological uses" from the 1980s, overly focused on the solely technical objective and its interaction with a user, or on long representationist patterns (values, cultures, etc.) to follow closely what the actors and objects caught in the same situation make. This still requires researchers to take an "unpartitioned and non-exclusive look", because it must embrace situations with many possible viewpoints: sometimes following designers, sometimes computer programs, sometimes the targeted users, sometimes the legal requirements, sometimes documentary analysis of a project and its history, etc. [DEN 09, LIC 08, PRO 15].

– CVs: this is indeed an element that will gain strength. By changing their material nature (they have become digital), candidates will be transformed into data flows, which will have to be recorded, processed collectively and more "industrially". They will be quantified, indexed, and taken progressively as the indicator-descriptor of the activity of a recruiter. CVs: in Latourian language, they become a "little thing", which will permanently put the "big thing" (the company) to the test.

Thus, from the Belmont to the meeting room, the layout is inhabited by a multitude of individuals, objects, places and designs. And it was true that "there were already a lot of people[34]" since the beginning of history and thus, we are really looking at more than two men in a cafe, except when we consider that they are only the expression of these forces, being the black box of these forces."

Added to them, this list of entities will provide the project with slogans, screens, codes, files, other individuals. The Belmont or the project manager's office is simply not able to contain the actant networks. Over time, whether deliberately or by chance, the incessant calls to form new entities "cause the network to flee", scattering in all directions:

– other targeted users that are employees and applicants seeking employment (who apply on the website). We will often speak in their name, the name of their desires, and the digital practices they assume;

– prescribers and other spokespersons, such as associations and the trade press, whose slogans sometimes become arguments from authority for the project managers;

– a multitude of companies whose policies of interfaces, strategies, IT developments and arguments are displaced within the apparatus through cases of benchmarking (competitors or companies thought to be role models) and offers of thanks to publishers;

– a prime minister, government policies for employment and economic data (at a specific time, the group will need to respond to a recruitment effort explicitly requested by the highest entities of the State); institutional partners

---

34 Deleuze and Guattari their book *A Thousand Plateaus* with their famous formula: "We have written *Anti-Oedipus* as two people. As each of us was actually several people, there were already plenty of people involved" [DEL 80].

(such as local authorities sought through recruitment operations from their establishment in cities);

– internal standards (recruitment management rules, mobility, etc.), legislation (the Labor Code), the CNIL, then other legal constraints that will be indicated again as part of the deployment of the device internationally;

– and, in addition, a whole collection of other "things" that they are still connected to! "How many actors are there? We will have no way of knowing this before measuring others" [LAT 84].

Depending on the constraints and variable modes of expressions, all these bodies operate in the same design process involved in the production of networks that are generally extensive, being codetermined by subjective considerations. By allowing ourselves to be guided by the successive connections at play, taking to heart the principle of symmetry between objects and individuals, we are given the opportunity to free ourselves of the heavy burden of "invisible elements" (especially those acting to conceal the collective unconscious, imaginations, representations, and theoretical models, of all social elements), their over-interpretive classification and givenness as "natural" (a pre-established decryption that, incidentally, frees acting individuals on a mass scale)[35]:

> "What is a force? Who is it? What can it do? Is it a subject, text, object, energy or something else? How many forces are there? Which ones are strong and which are weak? What is at stake in this force and this measurement? Is it a battle? Is it a game? Is it a market? All these questions will only be defined and deformed by other events" [LAT 84].

Thus, we follow the forces involved, we create a map of these heterogeneous actors from the trials that arise, we identify and update them,

---

35 One of the areas of interest to the sociology of translation is to have made individuals exercise their power to act and to avoid any explanatory detours through "social magma". These are "the actors who make everything, even their explanatory frameworks, their own theories, their own contexts, their own metaphysics and even their own ontologies" [LAT 06c].

and redistribute the powers around them, according to the specific collective arrangements of the project. This means that the story is woven together by events, and sequences-events that push them toward other events.

## 1.3. Moeva "Beta": building a theatre of operations

### 1.3.1. *The English temptation and the IBM test*

In the spring of 2000, the firm HRConsult began its mission with the goal of identifying technology providers that could offer innovative and efficient solutions in terms of Internet application management system (external candidates) and intranet (a system for the mobility of internal employees). At that time, the Moeva group had not yet officially been established, and the project only concerned the branch dedicated to public transport and waste management.

In a book he published in 1997, the manager presented the Internet as a "revolution" for communications for recruitment and "the marketing of human resources". In particular, the proposal was based on the recommendations and experiences of US-based agencies specializing in the field. Whether idealized or real, once the legitimacy of the Anglo-Americans had been obtained, the first editor selected was English (with a list of multinational corporations added to his assets). "Personic" indicates: "In 1998 around 1.3% of the entire US workforce was placed in employment using Personic software". Thanks to the mediation of HRConsult, meetings are organized within the company. Designated by the HR Department, the Project group is then constituted by the manager of recruitment and mobility, and the manager of internet/intranet communications. But a few weeks later, the Information Systems Department is asked for an "opinion", and adds three representatives to the device. Soon, several constraints emerge: the publisher must provide a solution that offers compatibility with ERP HR Access (an ERP Enterprise Resources Planning), marketed by IBM (each system is installed on different databases including both Oracle and Microsoft SQL Server). Led by the DSI, the project involves the modules for training and payment, but also the range of features for recruitment-mobility. The balance of power is then in favor of the DSI-IBM pairing, and against the alliance of HRD-HRConsult. The location of Personic's development teams, outside of France, and their technical and financial constraints (their budget approached a current equivalent of 500,000 euros) are the foundation for expressed rationality[36].

Note that the Moeva-1 project was intended exclusively for the short term, the territory of France (that is, the external candidates and ten thousand employees with access to an internet-enabled computer), a historical space from which the future group would put in place a new identity (thus excluding from the scope the many entities already present all over the world who were, in turn, already equipped with their own HR management system). International expansion will only truly be considered after several years. Seven years later, after which period (representing a significant portion of the career of a project manager!), yet another version of the system will allow for the possibility of integration with another country (England). In fact, the international presence of the company faces constant difficulties in being reflected in the apparatus.

After three months of discussions, aborted quotes and conference calls made between the two sides of the English Channel, another technology provider was presented by HRConsult. This company, without any references abroad (at that time, pragmatism would prevail, prompting it to forget about the world for a certain time), had designed an online recruitment management solution for its own activities. Essentially, this is a small team, competent in the area of digital developments, and enthusiastic about creating a number of extensions to its "DevX" system.

Simultaneously, the HR Access constraint from IBM weakened: at the time, PGI suffered from insufficient "web compatibility" (large ERP systems had not fully carried out their shifts to digital technology, particularly in terms of user interfaces) and recruitment modules were not sufficiently developed to respond to increasingly precise expressions of needs (formalized in a document and quickly adapted into a specifications file). It also involved a head-on opposition to the digital "culture" computer between the DSI, connected with mainframes, and project managers boasting of an innovative and much more "agile" vision, offered by the online world The DSI-IBM/HR Dept.-HRConsult confrontation ended with the argument of the expected completion times: the transition to the new version of HR Access would take two years. The first of these two called for a long-term

---

36 See http://www.sourcewire.com/news/4372/personic-pioneers-e-recruitment-technology, accessed October 5, 1999.

vision, while the second wished for it to be brought online in early 2001. At the company's headquarters, no amount of "coffee breaks" soothed the manager's impatience. In early fall, DevX was selected under the last condition established by the DSI, that of repairing databases for future HR Access. The HRConsult/DRH/DevX coalition readily accepted it: they never asked for the data for the ERP.

This was the operational theatre, or at least one of its updates.

### 1.3.2. *"We want to think for ourselves!"*

What reflexive actions can be developed by a collective action on the things that move it and run through it?

How can this group take control of the script that is at work on its performance? Luhmann or J.-M. Noyer might ask, what are the instances and processes that are self-simplifying (by the script) that allow it to be used as instances of its own operations?

We will look at the status and role of the interfaces later on. To continue with the action, under the constraints of a rationalized decision-making process to be completed, the arguments meet, collide, reinforce themselves, cancel, or dissolve. The forces that are present are revealed and put to the test. In presenting, first of all, its prestigious list of references, and second, the economic valuation of the return on investment of their solution (that DevX would never risk) Personic seemed to have the balance of power in its favor. Certainly, the obligatory transfer by DSI, unfavorable to a project that was beyond its scope of legitimate action, was an insurmountable obstacle to the sale. But the gradual shift towards an ad hoc approach (partially proposed by DevX), also reflects another perspective opened up by the project manager, Moeva, who said one day in July 2000: "We do not want standardized solutions, we want to think for ourselves!" On this basis, there is no need for benchmarks, "business-cases", references to extensions, and functional modules ready to use (the "good project engineering manuals would eat these pages"), which corresponds to the approach of Personic (a strategy that is already lost) and also to the HR Access approach.

What does this claim mean to the project manager? The argument made by this manager contradicts the process in progress, but this statement allows for the allocation to be made of a place, a position at each camp, to define its opponent, and as Machiavelli suggests, it allows it to take a hold of time. Incidentally, there is an affirmation of an ability to be autonomous, a desire to express it. Even if we know that "ideas never escape the networks that make them" [LAT 84], the demand for autonomy is an indicator of an organizational world continuously inhabited by a desire to create itself (here, we have the opportunity to recall this, to be used in other areas). The project leader is defeated in his attempt to transfer the DSi connections with the project, and weakens the technical constraints. Invention is pitted against replication, specific programs against rigid systems marketed by the heavyweights of the digital market: this is the word of the day. With a reasonable budget and time limits in the schedule, the project can proceed.

The question of the spread of organizational models of action is part of a tensioning of the distributed, nomadic performation processes. The project manager, despite his statements, responds effectively to internal tactical redistribution of forces, but only has a mastery of the design of the apparatus. HRConsult and DRH design specifications that describe and update models of experiences and relatively heterogeneous practices (methods for the management of recruitment and mobility adopted by hundreds of different managers); interfaces proposed to candidates-users as well as staff-Intranet users, features that were nevertheless studied (separately, by actors) on other business websites; computer programs and features already developed by DevX and used by its clients. True, it is expected that other features will be created, but from the beginning, the design is incapable of being sealed off from "an outsider" or "a forward". So, here we have it: a new trial and a new way to carry it out.

This sealed-off nature, claimed and brought "to value", is placed explicitly under the phenomenon of organizational standardization done by information systems. Indeed, the programs and their interfaces (PGIs and other software packages) are an aggregation of contingencies (environments with special characteristics), practices, managerial processes of other organizations, in which the editor draws a temporarily established compromise, corresponding to the most common situations, and assuring optimum commercial potential. This compromise allows for the establishment of a standard offer, which after successive iterations, must meet the configurations and demands frequently made by future customers. Thus, by appropriating the work of many groups and projects, and by selecting "the activity scripts" of other places, a normalization of the processes of information management and organizational action by direct action programs: a technical performation moving companies in business is operated[37].

The publisher often offers functional enhancements and also introduces specific developments that other customers have been able to achieve. The process of innovation is thus the result of the cross-fertilization of the systems between each other. This practice also represents a particularly advantageous economic model for the service since, as we have directly confirmed, it involves achieving a return on investment on developments sold to specific customers by later offering them as "standard" in the product. Thus, the project manager also positions himself against this phenomenon, with the key word becoming the "personalization" of the system, its adaptation to the particular context of Moeva. However, the acceptance of such a strategy – this personalization – cannot be carried out without a debate: some called for the rejection of formatting, and the reactionary nature of the company in the area of the "context" ("it is unique in its field"), others counter-arguing by emphasizing the costs of development and the risk of not being aligned with solutions (and thus to organizational models) already tried elsewhere. Is this a specific case within business innovation strategies? The story about the pairing of "peculiarism/standardization" is actually quite commonly found in the world of management, where everyone puts forward large amounts of demonstrations of their efforts to testify that, when confronted with "technology", it is the organization that is always right. The enemy has been identified: technological reformatting. It then becomes a battle between different actants for a transformation of the organization, and once this transformation occurs, it will often be recalled that technology is "an ingredient, nothing more". But at the same time, the normative imitation[38] and isomorphism in which companies and their advisors are actively involved are widely considered to be a virtue[39]! This is the case for companies, as it is for "all entities (who) seek not to appropriate external

---

37 Drawing on Callon and Muniesa, we defined this as a process of innovation, bringing into conflict the forces acting based on various types of performation, with technical performation being a special case. See Chapter 2 of this book.

38 Here they are considered as a replication of the same.

39 We will come back to this and the case of imitation in Chapter 2.

entities, but for them to be appropriated by them", and each monad "aspires to the highest degree of possession" [TAR 93, TAR 99].

What the project team progressively begins to perceive is that, by financing the developments of the DevX application, it will directly allow the publisher to capitalize on the new features that will be created for Moeva, and that the contingency and the power of the "Invention" that it is related to will be put into circulation and available to other companies, which in turn will be able to reconfigure them... or take them back as-is. It does not object (contractually, it is not allowed to do so) and even finds a way to be proud of its actions: its management script takes the form of a possible model.

### 1.3.3. *Writing the management script: its manufactured-manufacturing making*

Based on a framework document presenting the expected main features of Moeva, DevX carries out what is known as an "adaptation study". The purpose of the evaluation is to evaluate the difference between the existing "standard" in their solution and "the expression of needs", thus identifying the field of the developments to be achieved, and ultimately defining the corresponding financial investment.

At the level of the back-office (the HR user interface), the processes for recruitment or internal mobility proposed as a standard by the publisher are made up of the following functional building blocks:

– offer management: creation of an offer from an input mask, sending of a possible offer to a superior or an operator, publication on the website, search engine for offers following 10 standard criteria;

– applications: a table listing the electronic applications received in relation to an offer, multiple selections of candidates (for sending a group message), a candidate's record and a candidate's qualification (unprocessed, negative, called in);

– recording of an application (received by conventional mail or by e-mail);

– a multi-criteria search engine for the use of the shared pool of candidates (10 standard criteria);

– a search engine for events (meeting, notes from the recruiter, level of urgency, confidentiality, etc.);

– a collection of email templates (replies addressed to external candidates);

– an administration of users: coordinates and rights according to two possible profiles (recruiter, manager).

These different "building blocks" make up the script for a professional practice: programs, settings, and application data offer a specific outline of the processes used for work and processing (based partly on automated tasks) of information. Using an interface, this script assembles and models courses of action and operates at the center of the performation of procedures. Some sociological works vividly describe the formalism and standardization of systems of human resources management and selection, a process presented as a "professionalization", which is summed up in framing judgments and "extending the jurisdiction (HR services) within the company" [FON 14]. Each time, and as Edwin Hutchins pointed out, the distribution of models is developed through mediations: through interactions between agents, and also through artifacts [HUT 00, CON 04][40].

Various requests for specifications of this functional base are expected by the project manager and the HR manager. In particular, developments must take into account the practices that continue to be carried out within the company: initially, a desire to reproduce the organizational processes is therefore strongly asserted. This "expression of needs" is given together with a detailed presentation of the internal processes, as they are perceived by the central hierarchies and by the 10 colleagues who will be the first users of Moeva. This expression takes the form of a management script, with a specific form of modeling: it specifies a "life cycle" of a job offer, of a document (the internal or external CV), as well as the various actions that can be performed at each step following the responsibilities of each person in the process.

---

40 [CON 04] indicates that for Hutchins, the distribution of cognition is often presented as involving two sides: an ecological side, where cognitive processes are distributed between an agent (or several agents) and artifacts (utensils, equipment, texts, symbols, computers, etc.); and a social side, where cognitive processes are distributed among several agents coordinating within the same site [HUT 00].

Translated into the application, the script advocates a template for:

– the creation and validation of an offer before publication;

– the processes of acquiring a job application, in two possible ways: the "sourcing" is carried out by the website (the registration of the CV by the candidate) or by using conventional mail, through the post office, which requires a registration of the job application with the HR user in the database;

– then, the next step is the selection, involving the viewing/analysis of the folder and the "qualification" step to indicate which status is assigned to the candidate;

– finally, there is the follow-up after the meeting, and the results of the interviews, and the process is completed with the assignment of a position to the chosen candidacy.

On the basis of this process, there should only be minor adjustments made to DevX. Nevertheless, the temptation of the HR manager to "reverse" the established extended application process that allows for the management of applicants quickly leads to a problem: would this then lead to an increase in development costs? After another iteration (a series of exchanges between DevX and project managers), will the requested features be "useless"?

Thus, a few elements in particular are discussed but not retained:

– the enrichment made to the file of the candidate recruited for the job (managed in another existing system: different applications are used interchangeably in the management of the employees);

– the ability to publish offers, not only on the HR site of the company but also on job boards[41]: This proves to be too complex to carry out and requires an approach to these particular sites;

– the addition of a new stage for online applications selected by recruiters. This stage involves asking candidates to send a document via mail called a "standardized CV": This return to printed messages, which had the advantage of creating files built and enriched according to internal "standards", was also abandoned, in favor of enriching the electronic application form.

---

41 Job boards are websites specialized in spreading job offers.

On the other hand, new features will be designed, again at the request of the project managers, allowing them to move towards a digital "office" of recruiters (with the possibility to record the time of the interview and reports from that interview), dealing with the particular case of spontaneous applications, of re-injecting "paper" applications into the system (via a form and digitization process – the latter of which will always be judged as imperfect, as the users believe the ideal procedure in this case would not require any action done by humans), to communicate to the directors and to each recruiter indicators of the flow and tasks (the number of replies to an offer, the number of CVs to be processed, negative applications selected, etc.). A "personalized" space will also be offered on the candidate interface: this will include a history of the positions sought, an update of their CVs, the option to indicate that they are no longer looking for a job, a password management system, and later, it will be integrated with a function for alerts on new offers).

Finally, the forms and the many "list areas" offered on the interfaces are enriched and backed with a production of various "repositories", operating as an indexing of documents (CV and Post Offers) and events. The specifications are enriched with several pages, with toolkits that are generally rather extensive. They concern:

– the job offers: the status of the position to be filled (to be validated, publicized, suspended, filled) – the expected candidate profile (beginner, experienced) – localization (list of departments, regions, countries, continents) – level of training expected – the list of domains, professions at Moeva, etc.;

– the applications: education level – type of training – location – languages and language levels, etc.;

– management: list of HR users, subsidiaries, companies – list of tasks and events (convened, maintenance Tel, etc.) – List of typical e-mails to be used and data form for the preparation of selected mails, etc.

Essentially, at this stage, the work on the instrumentation of the employee's practices would appear to reach its peak.

With regard to mobility, certain specifications are also expressed, though in a more marginal way: the same functional schools of thought are applied to external employees and candidates and they are applying at the time from the same website. On the other hand, the back-office of the recruiter will distinguish between the two types of applications (the candidate is asked to specify whether he is an employee of the company). Ultimately, they opt for the strategy to attempt to apply a de-partitioning of mobility, through Moeva "Beta", by bringing together and by sending out notifications directly to employees for the job offerings, without passing through a hierarchical validation. This is part of the policy direction of the management. However, this point will constantly be debated.

At the beginning of the second semester of 2001, Moeva "Beta" began making its first "receipts"[42] of deliveries (including the final validation of the features by the project management): We have already been delayed by a quarter compared to the deadline projected one year earlier.

### 1.3.4. *What happens in a recruiter's office?*

The design of the apparatus is based significantly on the perceptions and desires, the normative (and labile) worlds, of two HR professionals who form part of the project team, and take part in mediating it. They essentially become the spokesmen for their few other colleagues who will be the first to use Moeva. This produces a device that has yet to be optimized to reach its full potential, but is intended to be suitable for the most commonly-encountered situations.

Nevertheless, if someone were to go to the office of a Moeva worker to observe him work and to have a discussion with him, this tangled web of action programs described above would weaken, become more complex, coexisting with other scripts. "I'm used to doing it this way", "Well, it depends", "There are special cases", "The processing of responses is done by two service employees, who have their own methods", etc., this person would tell us. On his table, we see stacks of files with a written title designating the type of applications they contain. This classification differs somewhat from the "statutes" provided for in the application: there are "urgent" files, files "selected to invite", "waiting for the opinions" of other colleagues, "applications recommended" by a third party (a senior manager, organizations or, by an acquaintance), etc. The latter in this case is "a

---

42 The term "receipt" refers to a developmental phase where the conformity of the product with the expected specifications is verified. This phase is also called the acceptance test.

delicate issue in terms of adding into the future system, because it should not necessarily be known by all the users". Against the walls are stacked piles of archived boxes with applications from the last year or more, and "there are also some in the corridor". Furthermore, for those sent by mail: "I print them all out!" "That makes it easier to review them". Indeed, we can see him doing this, quickly ranking all the applications (which are still quite different from the paper files) in his messages, and which – as you can see – does not allow for the attachments to be searched. "So, I print out the message and staple it to the CV, in order to know who it was that sent it to me and the message they sent". Finally, there are the files with sensitive information, from employees who have responded to a mobility offer: "We need to ensure that their direct supervisor has given the employee authorization to change positions".

In another office (on a much higher floor), a 50-year-old HRD describes his organization and practice, which reintroduces certain specifications in relation to the first one. For the time being, his biggest concern is to reassure himself about his future ability to use the Moeva system. We put ourselves in front of the screen, then we pick out a page at random: "When we get the hand that appears here on a text that is highlighted in blue, is this where we click?" We agreed, at his request, that this conversation would remain confidential, regarding the other participants in the project ...

These observations are a reminder that a digital script and an organizational script are merely limited models of practices, and if the adjustments made by each of these practices can pose various problems (delays in processing, a lack of coordination (among stakeholders, etc.), these are also conditions of the development of the uses and the efficiency of collectives. Taken as a constraint imposed on recruiters, the Moeva device has given itself the objective of working on the homogenization and standardization of work routines: this will only be the case for certain processes (the management of bids, the use of standardized answers), but it is likely that new workarounds would need to be used. Does an information system have the ability to capture all local and widely varying practices? The performative power of semiopolitics is always prone to washing up on the shores of subjective particularities[43]. It must contend with micropolitics and

---

43 We should stress that the use of massive data, or "data mining" and the enormous potential of operations allowed by "big data" tend to make this relative failure uncertain, by reinforcing the power to capture and format specific data points.

diverging desires, while combining with the specific grammar of the interfaces and scripts that form its ordering (up to the risk of creating disorder). *Organizational micropolitics and "libinal economies" in the managerial world lie at the heart of the question of contemporary "Collective Equipment of Subjectivation"* [GUA 89][44]: debates, conflicts, celebrations, tests, sanctions, alliances, etc., spring up from the processes of subjectivization within organizations, within digital apparatuses, processes that are facilitated or censored to varying degrees.

## 1.4. Extension and celebration

### 1.4.1. *Going forward, even blindly*

In September 2000, our team was hard at work, with the goal of creating an apparatus for two companies whose HR management processes were almost identical. But this led to the various different activities of the group, and the IPO of the group, which now expands to include four companies, being carried out during the summer. The director, who we met in 1999, became the Deputy General Director. The CEO of the group remained the same but a new president of Moeva was appointed. In its internal newspaper, this new organization was legitimized. "Moeva needed to offer a better readability of its activities. The strategy of refocusing over several years has clearly led to the emergence of two concentrations of skill sets, both of them being particularly dynamic: the environment and communication. In the sector of the environment, to strengthen our global leadership, we must now give our professions more coherence, autonomy and the means to develop"[45]. Moeva became the first global group in its activity area (public services delegated in the field of the environment). In this process, some

---

44 This "collective equipment for subjectivization" may be of a religious, political, technical, artistic, or organizational nature, etc. While F. Guattari holds that subjectivity is currently devalued because of the control exercised by mechanisms of power, these also hold the possibilities for change. "Subjectivity is now controlled on a mass scale by devices of power and knowledge that put technical, scientific and artistic innovations to work toward the most backward aspects of social life. However, other mechanisms of subjective production – procedural and individualized mechanisms – are conceivable. These alternative forms of existential reappropriation and valuation can soon become the foundational principles of human communities and individuals who refuse to leave themselves at the mercy of the deadly entropy, characteristic of the period we are going through" [GUA 89].
45 Internal Magazine of the group, July 2000, annex 9.

point to a gradual movement towards disengagement that was initiated on the part of Jean-Marie Messier in relation to these activities (more discreet than on film or television). The CEO is reassuring: "Moeva's stock prices are not a sign that its principal shareholder is losing interest". Nevertheless, at the end of 2002, the Vivendi group sold off the entire environment branch.

Our project team navigated in sight and, it must be said, in the foggy areas within strategy, maintained by the leaders. The design that continued for several months remained focused on the initial perimeter. It was assumed that the basis for the needs and features would not be very different in a configuration that potentially widened the perimeter to two additional companies.

It was not until spring 2001 that HRConsult was asked to take an interest in the specifics of water and energy activities in order to create a new specification. The first developments made by DevX therefore had to be modified by taking into account new informational content, new repositories, and potential new expectations. At the same time, the last tests of a delivery carried out by DevX were completed by the project team. For the pilot of this project, it was a matter of valuing the developments already made with the new teams, of integrating them into the process, and to do this, he felt it was essential not "to arrive with a blank page".

### 1.4.2. *Making newcomers into allies*

At that point, we'd come across a lot of spokesmen. And they expressed themselves here and there by sketching an initial figure of application users that are HR managers, employees and people looking for jobs. With the extension of the perimeter and a "participatory" approach extended to other HR managers, we heard new voices (those of HR officials from other companies) who made their constraints "talk", and this mixture informed the employees and candidates to a certain extent. By enlisting the requests of the place, we then exited the project manager's office, to then occupy the open halls of other directions; we added seats around design tables "as large as a board of directors". We entered into an environment of solemnity.

The landscape was prepared: the main leaders of the new activities were previously contacted, or met face to face with the project manager and HRConsult. In reality, the process required using a certain art of diplomacy to manage the apparatus, anticipating the frustrations that may arise (everyone could already own a management system or envision leading such a project), and reassuring and convincing them that the issues were relevant.

With the inter-intranet manager now positioning himself as the project manager for the entire group, the objective was to unite the four activities – referred to, rather paradoxically, as "divisions" – into a collective design process. Here, it was important to consider another dimension, one that was very political, associated with this methodology: the Moeva project is one of the first HRM devices commonly used within the newly created group. For its senior executives, this was an opportunity to meet the HRDs from the various subsidiaries, and a perfect opportunity to "bring the other directors in line".

Three project meetings took place between June 2001 and March 2002: at these project meetings, officials from all the activity areas and various subsidiaries were present, about twenty people in total, who at this time represented about one hundred of the users of HR functions. HRConsult played a special role in project engineering: it was both the guarantor and rapporteur of development with the assistant director of the group, co-editor of specifications and tester like other members of the project team. This mediation was a characteristic dimension of the missions intended to assist the project managers: the challenge in this case to facilitate dialogue between a digital technology provider and the company. This was a two-way process: from IT engineers to HR managers, from HR to DevX (explanation of user needs and managerial issues that computer scientists cannot understand):

> ""An actant can only gain strength by associating with others". So he speaks on their behalf. Why don't they speak with their own voice? Because they don't have one; because they are made to be silent; because, by making too much noise, their voices cannot be heard when they all talk together. Someone interprets for them and speaks in their place. But then, who is it that is speaking? Them, or it? Translation is treason. If an actant is challenged on his faithfulness, he shows that he does not say anything other than what was meant by the others. The demands of the forces, without any other purpose than that provisional one, that an alliance built on weaknesses may impose" [LAT 84].

By reinforcing the role of some spokespersons by the number of actors involved, by operating by selecting/filtering, extending the perimeter of the entities and actions targeted, we had another aspect of the geopolitics of the actants and the foundation of scripts that was expressed.

### 1.4.3. *The first debates*

"Why do it?" What is the purpose of engaging individually and collectively in such a project? A "manufacturing of consent"[46] initially took place here, beginning from frequent reminders (by the project leader or by members of the group themselves) of "higher interests": if "engaging" had meaning for an individual whose mission was to recruit and support the motivation of employees, this HR manager could hardly oppose a project with the issue of "human resources development" and the enhancement of the "intercultural wealth" of the company. As a result, the first questions related to two other dimensions. The first was organizational and managerial: "Before it thinks about the technology", the company must take advantage of it to rethink the problems related to the valuation of its professions (wage policies), the assistance with the mobility of the employees and the internal rules that govern it. In the "off-the-record" conversations (in the hallway), some of them indicated that they didn't "recognize" themselves in the formation of a new identity group, driven by a holding with no connections, of the terrain, the "big bosses up there somewhere" who thought for the "workers on the ground", who are too far away from these bosses and their concrete concerns to know and understand their daily problems in a relevant way.

Faced with this confusion, there were some that confronted it with optimism – but not all participants shared this judgement. These introductions (which, since these "meta" constraints are necessary, imposed on everyone, are sterile) must be terminated, and progress made to the second axis of discussion developed by the new members the team: with regard to the constraints imposed by the Moeva device, what were the gains that each actor was able to obtain from it?

---

46 See this issue of the "manufacture of consent" in the work of N. Chomsky, M. Foucault and F. Lordship.

At this point, we entered into a sequence that would be repeated many times over: the presentation of the features, their justification, and the collection of the requirements. There was always some kind of project meeting coming up, bringing into play material recording, managed according to a meeting agenda that was generally respected. The key actants here were the specifications, the description of the databases (repositories), the "demo" (the state of the developments made by DevX and the Web pages with editorial content), and retro-planning.

The features described in the specifications were commented on according to their state of development. The strategic and organizational issues, as well as the basis on which the features are put in place, were not negotiable, but given a degree of leeway, and were open to the participants. In this sense, the process of interest [AKR 88][47] was based on the presentation of a sufficiently wide space of evolutions and enrichments, such that everyone could express their desires. However, by accepting the other constraint of a collective agreement, they were therefore obliged to negotiate and to reach a consensus.

The different rules and standards used, programmed within the device and directly related to their professional practices, applied to the data: what information should be collected on the candidate (i.e. the design of the electronic "CV" form), on the status of his file (in process, unselected, reply addressed, convening, hiring, etc.)? What automated information processes should be provided for (the multiple *workflows* used to update the recruiter's dashboard, the candidate's information, the hierarchies in the case of an employee who is a candidate for mobility, etc.)? What toolkits should be established, and what data should be used in the search engine?

It was, therefore, a question of designing a common grammar within the profession of HR, and codifying the various processes involved: the sequences of the process and the various data associated with it are an activity script. Moeva made these scripts part of its interfaces and programs, it put their practices into its contract. This "contract" was embodied in the principle of sharing information, a unique specification file, but also, later, by the training devices and other user manuals that would be produced. The strategic aim of standardization of the various management processes

---

47 The incentive model was proposed against the dual model of the diffusion of innovation (an actor who designs, a passive user) in [AKR 88].

between disparate entities was gradually carried out, and in the process, given the reflexive exercise required (on its recruitment, mobility management), Moeva offered a potential for transformation of scripts and business routines that had previously been prevalent. Nevertheless, it became clear that this was more complex, and that the "technique", despite its performative power, would often break down when faced with the local practices that each HR actor deployed.

Given the magnitude of the work to be done and the necessary mobilization of HRs to the supervising intermediaries on the sensitive subject of the mobility of employees, the fact was that the effort must be made in the short term on the website, and therefore on the external communication.

In the long run, where was the interest for future users of Moeva? This was recalled in the specifications and illustrated by the outcomes of the developments that have already been made. There are three areas that would seem to be the main cause of membership.

From an economic point of view: the extension of a direct communication without passing through recruiting firms, paying portals for job offers or the press; the possibility of lightening the administrative load of CVs on paper, a "task without added value" and that requires significant time resources for the people who have the responsibility. However, the argument from management is based only on relatively uncertain assumptions: "We will always need the big firms to advise us", "We need to keep getting press coverage". At the level of skills management: the potential of a "pool" of candidates to be used by the various activities; a release for the hierarchical mediations for a better distribution of internal offers to collaborators (although conflicts related to this rule are explicitly provided for). Finally, the external attractiveness of the group, by demonstrating innovation in digital issues, demonstrating its ability to be a provider of jobs essential to the French economy, by deploying a common "HR offer" (in this case, it is the editorial content of the site that takes this role) positioning it at the same level of companies judged to be the most ambitious in the matter (whether competing or not).

The prospect of these gains would appear to replace the many constraints that would affect users: it acted at the very heart of the acceptability test. The collective agreement seemed to hold, but remained fragile. Indeed, these project meetings were characterized by many debates, and over the years, the same ones that were believed to be closed tended to re-emerge (in particular, as the uses of Moeva developed, and during version changes).

### 1.4.4. *Self-glorification: setting the stage for September 2001*

In September, version 1 of Moeva was no longer accessible by the candidates, but training for HR users had already taken place (this would be another occasion for other recommendations to be suggested). The project team sought to achieve a goal of being adopted by eighty HR managers within four to five months, and in the process, spreading to a wider level of deployment: nearly a thousand were possibly affected. These formations allowed them to initiate the process of job offering postings, a condition *sine qua none* for the launch: the volume of these offers therefore needed to be sufficient, because this would make it a Moeva in which one could find only a few dozen positions for a group that, as we recall, employs a hundred thousand people in France.

We left the center of Paris to head for the city's suburbs, but the buildings all shone with the glow of success, new, massive, and gleaming in an immaculate white. The room was imposing: The announcement of the launch of Moeva 1 was well worth its event hall, and three hundred managers had come not only from everywhere in France, but also from other countries where the company was located. The event was called "The Annual HR Convention". The event was important, given that it presented the structuring policies and strategies developed by the general management for the entire company, unified under one identity. The digital apparatus entered into the program between the announcement of the launch of the business savings plan and the new European governance of social dialogue! It was given twenty minutes. The general manager of the group (and of the coffee shop two years earlier) gave the presentation. Here are some extracts:

> "An expression of the synergies existing within Moeva, the group's human resources website would be accessible as of November 2001".

> "The Internet and intranet sites are one of the first concrete demonstrations of our synergies. They were made in

collaboration with you, the HR managers from our different professions".

"Intended for external candidates, its goal is to present our ambitions in terms of human resources policy as well as the positions to be filled within the group".

"Recruiting involves an initial presentation. By designing a joint communication for all recruitment audiences, Moeva offers a coherent and attractive image of the employer that will reinforce its reputation and success with the candidates".

"This project demonstrates the effectiveness of collaborations and the intercultural richness of Moeva".

The order words are characteristic of organizational enunciation arrangements. They are well-known and clearly defined performativity processes. This type of utterance is only based on its pragmatic implications[48] and we can consider at least three of them: the on-the-spot introduction of individual participation in a new organization that has just "taken shape"; the simultaneous execution of the word of order and the intensity of the desire (in this case, one of narcissism) which is then acted on; the promise of a professional efficiency that brings into play the abilities of the leaders, the project managers, but also that of the users themselves (since the design mechanism is collective, each of them can have a share of the responsibility that may arise from any possible successes or failures).

The future developments concerned this time were announced, and firstly, the applications dedicated to the employees of the group in France: this V2 was also presented as their first commonly shared information system. The choice of the narrative and staging was no longer considered classic in business practices, and offered a new example of the way these elements could be considered. However, the successive versions of the device benefited from a much more "confidential" communication of its launch. At this point, the players in our scene at the Belmont believed that

---

48 For the order words, see the set: "Postulats de la linguistique", Part 1, in [DEL 80] and the reference to Jean-Pierre Faye on totalitarian languages. We go back to these points in the analysis of the performation processes.

their strategy was a success, and that the follow up would be more than following up on to tactical variances.

Thus, the end of this period involved the presentation of a celebratory narrative within the same performative device, with the collective and reflexive message taken over the course of activity (the experience of the project device) and a semiopolitics of interfaces. This phase showed the interlacing of performativity processes in the production of the digital devices in organization, given that these having presented themselves as tests where networks of extremely diverse actants were brought together. The disturbances continued, intensifying and stretching as they went.

## 1.5. Years of continuous developments and testing

We now return to a long phase characterized by many debates, a multitude of adjustments, constituting of just as many new events for Moeva.

New actors came into play: seven "administrators" were appointed at the beginning of 2002. Led by the project manager (assigned to the headquarters), these administrators, who were also daily users of the application, represented the four activities of the group and the major affiliates of the group. They were given the task of creating the list of users of their companies in the application, assigning them rights (management of applications according to their area, the creation-modification of form letters, etc.), advising them throughout their practice and also ensuring the proper application of the rules of the processing (in particular, the practice of the "compulsory qualification" of all applications).

### 1.5.1. *The intranet mobility takes over the transformation of the modes of cooperation*

The specific category of actors who are external candidates was not integrated through studies, but presented an ideal as a "projected" entity of the process, typified and embodied in the form of an application, transformed into a stream of data. Starting in January 2002, the regular points consulted on the website were made by the HR manager in charge of changes to the functionality (5,901 candidate files were available by March 2002). This objective of the "candidate" category supported the legitimacy of the project and increased the visibility of the map of the external audiences defined in this way by the company.

The second "target" category consisted of employees: version 2 of the device referred to the design of an intranet intended to energize professional mobility within the group.

This version was the concrete application of the project of intranet mobility that had been formulated in the first year, but as it was more complex to achieve on a political and managerial level, its implementation was only carried out after the first version for external candidates was made. On the technical level, the intranet site dedicated to the employees of the group offers "dynamic" features (based on databases) identical to the external site: searches for offers, application submissions, the ability to subscribe to offers (based on job criteria chosen by the candidate, with automatic receipt via a workflow of an email with an offer corresponding to the candidate's choice), with an update of that applicant's candidacy. In addition, this time, the category of "internal candidates" was mobilized within the design process: collaborators from the group were interviewed on their perceptions of the mobility process and on their experiences in the field, with this phase responding more to a communications objective than to a study of the experiences of employees. Thus, the testimonials were distributed on the site as successful mobility models. The proposed features were the product of a scheme that interconnects the logic of the collaborators and the logic of the human resources managers, in which the following were conceived: a specific form for this target and a workflow designed to perform the process of the processing of a mobility request. New rules are communicated through a "mobility map"[49], among other methods, which formalizes the internal standard of a mobility process and commitments between three groups (employee, starting entity, and host entity). Indeed, the technical apparatus upset the usual procedures; it was necessary to define the new mechanisms resulting from the "de-compartmentalization" of the information and the collaborations now required between the HR teams of the different divisions: Job offers were accessible without the employee having recourse to his supervisor, HR managers received applications from employees belonging to entities with which they had previously little exchange, etc. As the development of mobility gradually began to assert itself as a strong policy enacted by the HRD group, the term Moeva quickly

49 Mobility Map of the Vivendi Environnement group.

became the "umbrella brand" of the entire digital device dedicated to human resources in the group. The digital device then took charge of the transformation of local practices, which nevertheless continued an endless cycle of adjustments, and questioning of the politico-technical scripts imposed.

## 1.5.2. *Third identity and access policies*

In 2003, in a break from what had been announced by the CEO during the formation of the new firm and its strategy of aggregating all its subsidiaries, Vivendi disengaged from its "environment activities". With a new leader, the group then strived to build a distinctive identity of its own around the delegated public services (including a change of its logo and name: the company became "Veolia Environnement"). The three web sites constituting the Moeva apparatus underwent their third evolutionary shift since the project had been initially devised. The management of digital developments and coordination returned to the HR project manager, recruited at the end of 2001. The public relations agency HRConsult then played a strategic advisory role and involved itself more in editorial production and less in the dimensions of testing and functionality. As applications for developments were enriched throughout the year 2002, Moeva ultimately did not want to be put online until the first quarter of 2003: this involved the design of an internal communication plan targeted at the HR network and at the collaborators. As with the external recruitment site, regular consultation points were created. An intense negotiating session had also taken place in order to define the access policy for Moeva: was it be necessary to make the site available through the group's intranet, or to design an extranet (a site secured through personal codes) allowing all employees to access Moeva from their home? The first option was contradictory to the project's ambition, as only 20% of the group's employees actually had access to the intranet within the company. The HRD then requested the firm HRConsult to carry out a short survey on the practices of organizations in this field (consisting of a comparison with other groups, and reviews of the press conducted on enterprises & careers)[50]. The extranet solution had the arbitration in its favor, considering the problem of internal connection, but also because it was a completely new strategic opportunity. In fact in 2001,

---

50 A weekly publication in the French press geared toward professionals in human resources management.

Vivendi CEO Jean-Marie Messier launched a plan to equip all the company's employees with access to digital technology. Computers were provided almost free of charge. The only constraint was the start-up screen: the Vizzavi portal, marketed by Vivendi Universal, and presenting "home" commercial offers (at the time, Vivendi's workforce totaled to more than 300,000 people, the same number of users as these online services). Within the continuity of an approach promoting accessibility to information technologies, Moeva was thus launched on the Internet, since the company had seen an increase in the number of personal devices possessed by its employees.

As for the HR teams, they were given access to a "recruiting application" that was also made available through an extranet to solve the problem of access to the unevenly deployed intranet of the group. Training for users and HR was organized on a regular basis, not only to "update" the knowledge of the older employees, but also to echo a strategy for integrating new HR managers from newly-owned subsidiaries affiliated with the group used by the human resources department at the headquarters.

### 1.5.3. *In search of external recognition*

The functional changes continued endlessly, and resulted in the launch of a version 3 in 2005; their creation arose from trained administrators and users. In order to further understand the relevance of these requests, a study of the practices was called for in 2004, but this was not carried out before 2006. Also noting a fairly large number of messages sent by the employees using Moeva to the attention of the webmaster (the HR project manager), a usage guide for the site was written and sent to them. In 2004, the cross-intranet manager would implement various "publicization" actions of the Moeva case on external media. Based on an interview with the manager, an article from the website "Le Journal du Net" ran in March 2004, with the title "Veolia Environnement recruits on the net". In this way, it was echoed by the structural specificities of Veolia ("a very decentralized organization") and the disparate practices developed in the subsidiaries in the field of recruitment tools: "the problem is that each subsidiary develops and uses its own management tools". The issue expressed here was one of homogenization and the image given to the candidates: "to give the candidates a feeling that they have truly become integrated into a large group and not just in a regional entity". The manager justified the technological choice made in 2000 based on the budget and, "above all, because it is a solution created for and by recruiters". Secondly, the Veolia representative referred to the methodology of the project (working groups, the solicitation of a consultancy agency) and the launching of Moeva on the Internet (the representative refers to the Messier plan for the equipment of the collaborators). Finally, the weakness of the evaluation and the monitoring of the processes (the statistical module was not created until 2006) were highlighted by the journalist. But, in response, the Veolia representative stated that "during the demonstration, the recruiters understood the tool right away". The difficulties of the project and the many debates that flared up within the day-to-day activities of Moeva for several years were completely erased. But somehow, magically, it all worked.

At the same time, the company entered Moeva to the "Intranet Award" contest organized by the magazine *Entreprises & Carrières* (Enterprise & Careers). This "price" practice in the professional world was characteristic of another performativity process based in this case on self-reference [LUH 90, 11][51] and which we will go further to describe as a process of "experiential performation".

### 1.5.4. "Villepin's 100 days"

In 2006, an extensive operation was launched, with the goal of recruiting three thousand people in France for positions involving so-called "industry" professions (bus drivers, technicians, etc.)[52]. These recruitments were carried out either externally or internally (through a mobility process). This was

---

51 Following after N. Luhmann, this leads us to observe how the systems produce their own models of action [LUH 90, 11].

52 It is rather astonishing to see that some major groups in France, both public and private, perpetuate this choice of vocabulary to describe the different categories of employees. The terms designating the first levels in a hierarchy (which in fact include the majority of employees) such as "exploitation" or "execution" (terms used respectively in the RATP – the Paris transportation authority – and the SNCF – the public operator of rail transport in France) are very far from the idea of a "non-hierarchical" organization whose "collaborators" would all be managers, actors, pro-active members, a perspective that has run through the messages of management since the 1990s, the construction of which was described extensively by [BOL 99].

echoed by the press in many articles[53]. This path forward was the result of a thinly veiled request from the prime minister, made to the largest companies in France: to set the wheels in motion to create employment in less than three months, and to make sure everybody knew about it. This was referred to as "Villepin's 100 days". And here is how the issue was presented in the nightly news:

> "David Pujadas: 'Let's return to the details of it a little bit.' There's just one point to make: you have not made any commitment in quantifiable terms. Last week, we heard you talk about 100 days, 100 days to change the economic climate. Is that a goal you've now abandoned?

> Dominique de Villepin: 'I did say that. No, not at all. 100 days to recreate the conditions of trust, that is to say, to set in motion all the apparatuses that will enable us, day after day, week after week, to do a better job. That's what I said, I'm a pragmatist. I want to create a situation where hiring clicks into place, I want to recreate trust, and I am convinced that from there, we will recreate jobs in our country'"[54].

At the plenary meetings (with nearly 25 participants), everyone was aware that the 3,000 recruitments would correspond largely to internal mobility or jobs that had already planned to be created before the Prime minister's announcement. "The 100 Days" stirred up additional tensions within the project group: how could they respond to this political directive within a short period, persuading the teams that this was not a forced coordination between the agenda of the company and the agenda of the government, and convincing them that this was a rational action by Moeva, focusing on recruiting using apprenticeships (branded as "Moeva Compétences", or "Moeva Skills") and not an act of political maneuvering

---

53 "Veolia Environnement has placed its bets on training, recruiting three thousand young people using apprenticeships or professionalization contracts. This decision came following a change of course in the group's strategy, with Veolia wishing to target the large industrial market, while up to that point the company had been focused on municipal contracts. These agreements allowed it to negotiate on several HR areas. These included training at Veolia Environnement; support for external mobility at Tokheim, Air France, or SFR; employment for senior Citizens at Areva and Alstom", *Entreprises & Carrières*, no. 827, October 10, 2005.
54 Excerpt from a dialogue between David Pujadas, host of the evening newscast of the channel France 2 and former French Prime Minister Dominique de Villepin (in office from May 2005 to May 2007), accessed December 15, 2015, available at: http://discours.vie-publique.fr/notices/ 053001900.html.

by the government? Indeed, how could they interpret the presence at these long-running meetings of an observer, a specialist in political communications and a communications adviser, very highly regarded by the French political (and economic) elite[55]?

In the company, the apparatus was based on investing heavily on freshly appointed regional HR delegates, dispatched throughout France and representing each of the four areas of activity (now known as Veolia Eau, Veolia Énergie, Veolia Transport, Veolia Propreté). A great deal of operations for communications "events" were organized in dozens of cities in France: buses were equipped with computer stations to welcome job applicants; a logistical system for connections was designed (including a satellite connection, at a time when urban WiFi did not yet exist); the press and local elected officials were invited (who, as we recall, would themselves be the first customers of the company Moeva). During this period (the 100 days), the president of the Republic himself (Jacques Chirac) – a close friend of the CEO – honored them with a visit to one of the group's training centers [LES 15].

This operation required adaptations to the application and the creation of features and a new site in advance, formalized by the drafting of a specification, which was therefore committed to, and already shows indications of what would later become version 4 (an opening projected for 2007).

This phase was characterized by a confrontation between two coalitions. On one side were the ICT representatives (now affiliated with the Information Systems Department) and the digital editors, who called for, at a minimum, modifications to the application and its functional relevance with regard to the requirements of the Movea Compétences operation. On the other side were the leaders of the operation and the project managers, who defended the need for new developments in the applications, bringing in the end users of that application as their allies: "The tool was made for them"; "I'm working on behalf of my users". Taking into account several requests for changes that were still "overdue", including those both related and unrelated to Movea Compétences, it defended the transition to a fourth version. Moreover, since 2004, the relations between it and the publisher have deteriorated considerably, as evidenced by delivery delays and frequent

---

55 A few years later, she had taken another position as a communications advisor for DSK.

technical problems (these problems are not recognized by the other opposing camp). Arbitration (between these two sides) was done through a director of human resources, the consulting firm, and the policy officer of the operation: they proposed carrying out a study on user practices. The study and the conclusions to be made would therefore be the deciding factors on the extent of the developments to be achieved and the legitimacy of a new version. The methodology chosen was based on observations of practices and interviews: some 30 situations of usage were analyzed. The conclusions of the study highlight requests for changes and technical dysfunctions, but also reveal significant organizational issues. The areas that are actually brought up relate to the challenges of work practices, the acquisition of user skills (a lack of training and information), the constraints associated with the device and, finally, the meaning given to the large-scale deployment of the Moeva system (an overview of the criticisms is presented in section 1.6.2).

### 1.5.5. *Conflicts and paths of rationalities*

Looking back to the very beginning, back at the cafe at the Belmont, the structural changes of the organization put its political legitimacy toward the digital project: it was an issue of aligning the objective of integrating the identities of the multinational firm and the objective of standardizing human resources practices in the field of recruitment and mobility management. The upper management, by contrast, was seeking a mechanism that would allow it both to respond to this demand for incarnation through a process of semiopolitics, and to issues of efficiency. But, as it turned out, *the desires of management would gradually shift toward the second plan.* The group's leaders were not interested in the potential gains associated with the automation of certain tasks (such as managing flows and transferring CV recordings in the database of the candidates themselves), sharing the information between HR teams at different companies (which may explain the relative lack of interest in the practices and the feedback of the experiences at other organizations). The argument by management was only made to better serve the political argument, and while the first of these proved to be weak, the commonly-shared greater interest was thought to be powerful enough to be called upon.

In all the exchanges, including in the interactions between management, the consulting firm and the head of communications the political element remains: the leader needed to remove the structure in autonomous subdivisions, which had been prevalent until then, to set up a network structure which implied, first of all, a de-compartmentalization and coordination between the business units, and secondly, a level of control reinforced by the integration of decentralized sites with a single digital system:

> ""The Human resources Intranet forms part of a strategic commitment to foster internal mobility". It must promote internal behaviors in line with the objectives of the Human Resources Department. Currently, the mobility approach depends mainly on the direct hierarchy (compulsory validation) and is carried out in a very informal and ad-hoc manner (between regions). The incentive device and the material accompaniment seem to have improved. The behaviour of the remaining team seems to be marked by a very strong autonomy of actions"[56].

The design of a "generic" and integrated commercial offer of all the activities of the group[57] implied, in particular, that the management of human resources must be carried out in this new frame of reference.

On the other hand, communications to field users was based on functional legitimation and on a principle of accountability (a respect for commitments, objectives). The contents of the communication were based on the solicitations of a professional agreement and the excellence of HR practices: "HR officials are responsible for providing the needs in terms of the skills of the entities they are responsible for"[58]. This was the rationale for the Moeva apparatus. In 2000, the human resources intranet enabled "the development of geographical and functional mobility by promoting the transparency of the internal market through the spreading of job opportunities"; raising awareness of the benefits of mobility; responding to a strategic recruitment need; publicizing the training offers that are a pre-requisite for the possibilities for change; offering a dynamic work tool; creating a medium for information, exchanges and the sharing of values between the different

---

56 Minutes of the Project Meeting, Human Resources Intranet, July 2000.
57 The availability of Moeva worldwide was built starting in 2002 but initiated as early as 2001: it involves, for example, providing services to an industrialist, waste treatment services, water, cleaning, energy equipment, etc.
58 Intranet mobility specifications, July 2000.

subsidiaries of the group"[59]. These multiple challenges were functionally retranslated into the specifications of the information system, which must allow for the following:

> "– to provide vacancies for the employees of their entities and of the group as a whole;

> – actively identify employees with a profile corresponding to their needs, and likely to be candidates. This identification can be done from the pool of candidates established by the application management software;

> – to have access to a collection of practical information and a space of exchange with all the professionals playing an HR role"[60].

An echo was also made in terms of the employees of the group, for whom the technical apparatus must be able to "satisfy their desire for individual advancement"; express these wishes; inform them of the opportunities that exist in their company and in the group as a whole; provide access to practical information that is part of a logic of forming close ties with the HRD of the group"[61].

The permanent availability of the Moeva Intranet at all times and in all places (and thus of the job offers) became, after certain fears that non-employees would enter into the system reached a tipping point, a decision with a large amount of political content and the mobilization of "markers", slogans of what was at the time associated with the "e-organization", became explicit: in particular the concepts of "transparency", of equality, of "hierarchization" (the process of mobility without one's hierarchical superior becoming aware), of extended access, of informational efficiency. Once again, the vocabulary used exemplified the order words associated with the digital production of the organization.

The Moeva project may constitute an exemplary case of the manipulation of the technical object for purposes that are not merely functional or

---

59 Minutes of the Project Meeting, Human Resources Intranet, July 2000.
60 *Ibid.*
61 Specifications file, July 2000.

managerial, but above all, political. But we can see how these two levels are inextricably blended together. Moreover, it is also a question of not demonstrating the ignorance of these ends by the internal teams: the HR managers of the various companies are sufficiently lucid about the underlying organizational issues of the project and it is not uncommon that in the project meetings, greater demands would be made on managerial policies and the means to optimize mobility flows than on the technical specificities of the intranet[62]. This argument may also be an expression of a questioning of the purpose and relevance of the de-compartmentalization sought by management. With regard to the effort required to transform their practices and routines, what interest does each HR actor have in integrating the system? And, on a more radical level, can the intranet be the single answer to the management problems faced? These are questions that come up at working sessions, and not criticisms expressed in the plenary, because they are perceived as risky (that is, they would be likely to rouse suspicion from higher-ups about the commitment of anyone who would have the audacity to express these questions).

The exploitation of this theme made by some opponents of the project allows for doubts to remain and makes use of a known problem in digital projects: the current inclination of leadership for the formulation of an expression of needs in terms of technical solutions. In our case, the "maneuver" is the result of a clear desire of the management: for the intranet to be one of the solutions to the organizational problem. The project and its overall functional characteristics are therefore not negotiable, but the adaptation of areas of application inconceivable and left to the discretion of the HR network to be agreed upon. The posture of the management is no longer classical in its strategy: it is a question of giving its subordinates the possibility to decide the modus operandi, while maintaining the illusion of having control over the entire apparatus. This brings to mind the notion of a "strategic coup", as described by T.C. Schelling:

> "A strategic move is one that influences the other person's choice, in a manner favorable to one's self, by affecting the other person's expectations on how one's self will behave. One constrains the partner's choice by constraining one's own behavior. The object is to set up for one's self and communicate

---

62 In this way, the wage policies, the accompanying modalities and the political rules governing the mobility within the group are convened in the debate.

persuasively to the other player a mode of behavior (including conditional responses to the other's behavior) that leaves the other a simple maximization problem whose solution for him is the optimum for one's self, and to destroy the other's ability to do the same" [SCH 60].

We completed this survey at the end of the year 2007. The director, who had been at the Belmont a few years earlier, left the group to raise cattle in La Creuse (the last CEO of the group became EDF's CEO). The next trial will be for the project manager: the new director of Human Resources asks him for a "PowerPoint" presentation with three slides to understand the Moeva digital apparatus, its purpose, and its uses (no need to give an extensive history of the past eight years).

## 1.6. The designation and description of the scripts

### 1.6.1. *Scripts put to the test of professional criticism*

"Characters in the script dispatch roles, appointments, performances in a space and time trajectory which is also going to produce novelty but not of the same kind as that of the story" [LAT 95].

First, the criticism of the political and strategic model of Moeva fed on a regular questioning of the initial aims of the device, namely the economic integration of the various subsidiaries, translated by a semiotic and technical integration. The message regarding the efficiency and the sharing of an "intercultural" wealth is opposed by a forced inclusion in the system (and thus, in the new organization) and the loss of autonomy.

At the same time, as the decentralization of the management of information (the reversion of tasks on the premise), also puts in place a system of direct control or delegation of the practices (via application administrators designated by subsidiaries) and the tacit evaluation of users (headquarters seizes the opportunity for traceability offered by the tool). The so-called *reporting* features (the user dashboard) are seen by some as having initially been intended as monitoring tools. At the same time, some of the HR managers regret the loss of control over the processes of mobility: the access that favored the job opportunities "without screening" by higher ups (deciding on the employees concerned, communicating the offers selected by these employees) opens a loophole in bureaucratic power. For others, on the contrary, the ambitions of management and the resulting application do not mark a fundamental break with the prevailing business routines: maintaining, in the process of processing the mobility of automating workflows, the information of the supervising manager when an employee positions himself for an offer, for an example.

The confrontation could be summed up as an opposition between the neo-managerial model, valuing the role played by an employee who is a manager of his skills, and his career, and a rational/legal model of mobility within a company.

Political criticism is rarely openly expressed. Instead of the actions of flare-ups, the network of users prefers a soft consensus and functional criticism to the disputes over the strategy. Thus, several arguments weaken the managerial script tending to equate the rationalization of processes and the creation of values (time, resources, relevance) with business practices. The operational gains announced would not act as a trial of strength and, instead of offering greater efficiency, the application now assimilates to a time-consuming process, not compensated by any qualitative leap forward.

Below is the interface for entering recruitment and reporting: it is a question of declaring, through a specific interface, the movements resulting from external recruitments and internal mobility, integrating periods of training. The process involves: the recording of a job offer (34 criteria or text information fields); the possible manual registration of the candidate file (if the applicant has not applied via the sites); the registration of 23 criteria qualifying recruitment and referring to so-called "strategic" reporting data.

A target of these critiques, some interface actants present themselves as victims in a privileged position: the repositories presented in the form of a Web "list area" (Figure 1.1), the lists of files to be analyzed and incessantly enriched with a continuous flow of new files, the indications of "to be processed" on the files, the reporting forms on recruitment actions (Figure 1.2) ... all this translates (being described and re-described) as a permanent need for tedious tasks to be carried out, and as a reduction of the autonomy of the professions, as a lack of knowledge of the "realities on the ground" (a critique that could be quite political, and current, at one of the company's sites and of its executives). The critique of technology is always a critique of the script within which it is included. But, while some seize on technology to denounce this "industrialization of HR processes" without too much "practical" meaning, others, on the contrary, demand that it be intensified: they formulate the proposal of another script that would be characterized by "more automation" of treatments (automatic replies to candidates, integrated matching as soon as an offer is made, the removal of the steps of "human" analysis).

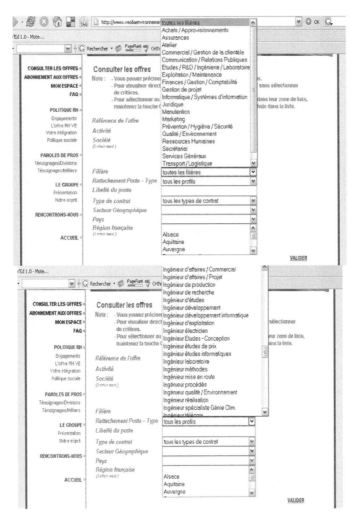

**Figure 1.1.** *The frameworks and standard positions of the Moeva case*

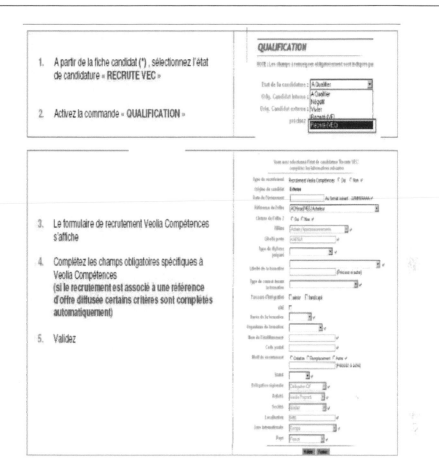

**Figure 1.2.** *The reporting interface of recruitment actions*

Finally, the socio-cognitive dimension that complements the tangled web of criticism is essentially traced back to the tension that constitutes the sharing of information. A new standard, defined in version 1 and which will continue until version 3, establishes the information regarding what is known as the pool of applications as a "common good". However, this can only be relevant if each recruiter considers that he must process all the CVs received in response to an offer (in electronic or paper form), since these may potentially be of interest to other users of the "base" (in reference to the candidate database). This rule implies, for example, that a recruiter for bus drivers would be required to process the application of an engineer (for example, to qualify the candidate as a "pooled" resource[63]. This also induces (until version 3) that all spontaneous applications received by mail must be recorded in the database. As a last resort, the requirement for pooling will be imposed by the functional constraints of the tool. The logical consequence we can find of this is an overload of work. The change in recruiter practice that takes place is accompanied by a relative perplexity as to the gains that could be derived from this pooling of resources. With the goal of clearing up these doubts, the communications media (including the training guide from which the following quotation was issued), highlighted the strengths of the recruiting intranet:

> "The recruiter application is intended to optimize the search for applications, to facilitate the management of recruitment and the distribution of offers. With a shared database, you will be able to search for candidates from within the pool of applications of the entire group. This database will be decentralized: each recruiter in the group will be able to manage their own applications and administer them. This application offers you many features designed to develop relationships with potential candidates"[64].

But two years after it was put in place, the pool appeared to be under-utilized, and the spontaneous applications received by mail would only be recorded in a systematic manner. This requirement disappears from the policy of the deputy head from 2003. Similarly, the constraint imposed by the tool used to qualify all spontaneous electronic applications upstream would be removed: this type of flow will be managed automatically and integrated into the pool without any special treatment (i.e. a reading of the CV and a response from the HRD) being required.

In addition, a specific feature has been put in place: the "booking" of candidates. In contradiction with the objective of capitalization of knowledge that had previously been acquired, it was this area in which a recruiter could regain some control over the resources he wished to share, or not to share, in terms of what the application will make visible or not. Lacking in the standard configuration of the editor, this feature was created in an ad hoc manner. As a sign of a continuing restlessness and the

---

63 A qualified candidate (classified within a pool) is usable by all users.
64 Training Guide version 1, December 2001.

instability of the scripts, two years later, this restriction of the consultation and operation of the files would be abolished and replaced by a "notification". Here, the change was justified by the adverse effect of "reservations": recruiters would keep files "on reserve" (or they would "forget" to disable this function) for several months, which made it impossible to share them with other users, or to process a mobility request end to end, and to do a precise analysis of the flow[65]. The principle of notification overrides the simple delivery of information to a workflow of processes, leading to an overly bureaucratic logic. It was deemed preferable to value virtuous behaviors (which some users demand).

More broadly, these different debates express the challenges of reflexivity, an issue at the heart of the policy of interfaces. This is an issue of positioning oneself in relation to the practices of colleagues, placing information and local data within a larger set while maintaining the ability to control what can be shared, in terms of what I myself see about others and on what others see about me. The isomorphism between the areas of visibility and the organizational structure, the hierarchy, and the distribution of powers, having become very political, is subject to various discussions as illustrated by a multitude of user reflections. On the indexation of a job offer and the publication rights: "Should we partition it up to the company level?" or should we "default the activity logo and, using a checkbox, allow the possibility to activate the display of the company logo?" On the management of users: "We propose to offer the possibility to create a user solely within the scope of the activity of the administrator" and "the only events to be seen should be the ones that I created for the candidate, the events of colleagues

---

65 This is reminiscent of what [STA 10] observed in terms of collaborative practices and maintaining informal areas as conditions of use. "[...] groupware and other technologies of the same type were built as technical infrastructures for assistance to the members of an organization by linking the physical, temporal, and functional domains. The experience with groupware suggests that highly structured collaborative applications will not be able to integrate with local work practices [RUH 96]. On the contrary, long-term experimentation has led to the emergence of a complex web of applications and inventories, combined with pockets of knowledge and locally-available skill sets. These systems begin to become more and more common to formal infrastructures and create a unique, ever-evolving hybrid. This development is facilitated by that which, in its formal structure, helps to redefine roles at the local level and the emergence of communities of practice at the intersection of particular technologies and types of problems. These observations call for research on the evolution infrastructure over time and how a planned, "formal" structure merges (or doesn't merge) with an "informal" structure arising at the local level".

do not interest me". In relation to the recruiting office, the training manual states "after the identification, the application displays a home screen, allowing the user to obtain a personalized analysis of the management of applications and offers". On the objectivity of the flows and work activities by the traces made available digitally in this manner: "Someone can transfer an application to me and I can see the comments made by other recruiters. Anyone can see the comments made by other recruiters, and some things have shocked me; we all must have professional ethics! Only those who are involved in the applications should be able to access the comments. There are some things that are not to be shared, even between HR members"[66].

As we will see for other cases presented in this book, the setting of the areas of opacity and transparency is a key characteristic of the techno-politics of the digital aspect of organization. It is not only a condition for the modes of cooperation, but of the operation of the organization itself, namely its metastability. The scripts, as a whole, operate on the systems in metastable equilibrium[67]. The tensions that run through the design, the friction between its clashing scripts, and the local adjustments that characterize it, offer the organization a capacity to continue its movements of adaptation, reinvention, and even innovation (even the hardest conflicts can reflect this metastable nature, with the exception, in some cases, of the closure of the company, and thus a new state of stability).

## 1.6.2. *Naming and distinguishing scripts*

At the beginning of this chapter (see section 3.1 as well), we asked a number of questions about the designation of scripts, how to qualify them,

---

66 Interview, survey 2006.

67 Metastability: a system is in "metastable" equilibrium when certain variations can cause a breakage, a transformation of the equilibrium. Death is a stable state (no longer open to any possible transformation). A collective (for example, a company) is in a metastable state: various variations and tensions (even minute ones) run through it, which are the condition by which it is perpetuated, the condition of its change into other systems that are themselves meta-stable. According to G. Simondon, "In all domains, the most stable state is a state of death; a degraded state from which no transformation is possible without the intervention of energy from outside degraded system" [SIM 89]. And the comments by D. Dekiss: "A stable state is a state that is not susceptible to change, except through an external impulse" [DEK 04].

and we suggested different possibilities: through the subject of mediation (computer codes, speeches, etc.) that they borrow, through their spokesperson or principal delegate, by the intensity of the force it carries, by what they do... in the end, these events are encountered in situations that have given us the salient elements to begin to distinguish them from each other. Among these events, we find processes described by Akrich, though the analysis grid of these processes forms only one side of the possible analysis.

The sociology of innovation has stressed the need to take into account the object in the action and the foreshadowing of a user immediately involved, associated with the design of the techniques. On the one hand, according to Akrich, presuppositions are part of the technical object, and are translated into the interfaces (the first movement of the script), and in the developments which the designer postulates that they will agree on, that they are the most suitable for general conditions of future use and certain conventional *subscriptions*[68] (the necessary use of electric current by an electronic device, for example). Different developments, strategic models and other tips can be aggregated into several scripts designed by the publisher of a software solution, all of which join with other professional statements (the second movement of the script). On the other hand, the designer continues to repeat this action incessantly, going back and forth between it, the technical object, the user, the object in the situation and drawing, in the end, the form of the interaction – the coupling that could operate. M. Akrich, in the sense he intends, proposes "a script, a scenario which is intended to be a predetermination of the stagings that users are called upon to imagine from the technical device and the prescriptions (notices, contracts, advice, etc.) that accompany it" [AKR 87]. The managerial script often comes in the form of a legitimizing narrative, with a performative vocation. The rationale for the project that the organization gives itself can be the following:

> "The recruiter application is intended to optimize the search for applications, to facilitate the management of recruitment and

---

68 According to Madeleine Akrich, an innovator may consider that the destination environment of the technical object already bears the markings that define its relationship with its future environment; these prerequisites, it goes without saying, are subscriptions. "By adhering to the scenario proposed by the apparatus, the user, in a broad sense, subscribes to a number of prerequisites which emerge from his sole responsibility" [AKR 91].

the distribution of offers. With a shared database, you will be able to search for candidates from within the pool of applications of the entire group. This database will be decentralized: each recruiter in the group will be able to manage their own applications and administer them. This application offers you many features designed to develop relationships with potential candidates"[69].

However, users may not know this presentation and these prescriptions beforehand. It is, therefore, once faced with the interfaces that the user operates the different possible descriptions in the sense of Akrich. This movement of *de-scription* corresponds to a phase of interactions in action, in which the meanings of the use (the third movement of the scripts) are updated. During this movement, some possibilities other than those provided for by the initial script will be explored. On the basis of the usage it carries out and its critical analysis, our employee, when obliged to interact with Moeva, creates a description, moves and updates the "generic" or managerial script that has been proposed (designed by the project group and the publisher of the application) but also its activity script put in place, that lives alongside a business script. The use of the concept of "profession" refers to two phenomena: the willingness of project managers to take on the practices and expertise that each employee may claim (with an ongoing struggle to determine who is the rightful holder of "business knowledge").

Regarding the Moeva digital device, de-scription (which is done by both the project group and the target user network) is quite easy to learn, and this is learned from anxieties and criticisms expressed during design and after the production of various volumes[70]. The arguments arise both as what fuels the creation of a script and as traces of the updating/activating of the scripts in which the individuals confront each other. In our case, negotiations and criticism focus on three main dimensions: the business model and the standardization of processes, the socio-cognitive dimensions and the modes of cooperation, the politico-managerial and strategic model.

---

69 Training Guide version 1, December 2001.

70 This approach, used by the tests of the processes of the de-scription must be completed by the analysis in situation of the practices, or also of the different traces of practices and data related to it.

| | Managerial Scripts | Interface Scripts ⇐⇒ | Business and Activity Scripts (users) |
|---|---|---|---|
| Politico-strategic dimensions | Efficiency of strategy and communication (scale gains), operational efficiency and economic gains by the federation of entities. | – Information system commonly shared with all recruiters<br>– Reporting and tracking tools for practices<br>– Extranet, meaning less hierarchical filtering for employees<br>– Management of opacity/transparency by setting the data status | – Forced Inclusion of entities<br>– Loss of autonomy<br>– Loss of control over the hierarchical chain of internal mobility (extranet for employees) or, on the contrary, critical of too much of a response on the information-mastering routines that were previously prevalent |
| Procedural Dimensions | Optimization of information flows (time and density) through the streamlining and standardization of processes | – Automated management of flows and alerts for workflows<br>– Shared and obligatory data repositories | – Claims of singularities<br>– Work overload<br>– Request for more automation<br>– Maintenance of pre-existing practices (paper return)<br>– Request for an emphasis on the delegation of tasks within the tool by mass-scale treatment |
| Socio-cognitives dimensions | Creating value for decisions through resource sharing, storage shared on a mass level, and access to new information resources (knowledge) | – Meta-model of practices<br>– Structured databases<br>– Automated and manual features of flows and data indexing | – The need for control over its local resources (conditions of visibility and indexing shared)<br>– Weakness of the means of exploration in the data<br>– Instead of cooperation, the placement into coopetition |

**Table 1.1.** *Scripts and criticisms of the Moeva apparatus (simplified model)*

Table 1.1 shows these three arguments or dimensions described in the case of Moeva, from the confrontation between the managerial scripts (involving the main logical assumptions and causalities that characterize them) with the criticism of the users who present themselves as both business scripts and activities. Managerial scripts are not overhanging "mega-scripts". Managerial scripts (associated with the project group) and business scripts (associated with the activities of users and their perception of "their profession") coexist. The scripts of interfaces appear as their preferred mode of movement. The tensions that express themselves are the trace and the updating of the scripts.

So now we have a list of the scripts that we have provided here from the words of order outlined by the project management for managerial scripts, major digital processing for interface scripts and the main criticisms by users of the business/activity scripts. It goes without saying that we can determine a direct duality in the activity script as seen by the project management on the one hand, and by the users on the other hand. In summary, we thus observe at least three areas of the test that act between them and in which they can also be confrontations or alliances.

A script is always incomplete in relation to the situation it is seeking to format, since carrying it out implies an active participation of the user and other entities, conditions, with which it is connected and which its designer cannot fully foresee [AKR 98] or know. This incompleteness results in a tension between a world inscribed by the designers in the object and a world described by its displacement:

> "It is in this context that we have to agree on the meaning of the description that we propose, such as the identification and analysis of the mechanisms that allow this connection between a form and a meaning that (and who) is the technical object" [AKR 87].

For example, an information system for a business (as is the case with a car, a telephone, etc.) is based on a proposed script for use made to an employee from a prefiguration by the designers of a process of work and associated tasks, assumptions about the aspirations and motivations of uses, inserting them into an enlarged framework that will take into account, in an essentially piecemeal manner, the characteristics unique to the situation of usage (temporal elements, places of consultation, postures etc.), individual capacities (instrumental and cognitive skills), technical constraints (server power, program interoperability, etc.), and managerial and economic constraints (expressed by one or several companies), normative or regulatory imperatives (which format organizational processes), etc. This incompleteness also determines, in the first instance, the existence of creative areas and adaptive workarounds.

The technical object thus presents itself as a mediation and a system of connections between heterogeneous actants, following more or less long networks, and it is in this unified relationship between the situations and the material constraints, between the worlds of designers and users, that the differentiation of socio-technical couplings occurs.

It is the network between the different scripts, as well as the forces that are associated with them, that will describe the configuration we are dealing with more precisely.

The list of scripts can be filled in as follows:

> – *interface scripts* affiliated with applications, their semiotics, programs, algorithms, information architecture;
>
> – *scripts of situated activities* associated with routines, courses of action, unique practices of a technical object, and modes of interaction between employees;
>
> – *profession scripts* associated with the institutional and professional standards of each trade or that the particular collective is given;
>
> – *editor scripts* associated with the proposal, not only commercial but also to the functional and technical proposal of the IT developer;
>
> – *managerial scripts* associated with the organizational and practice model defended by the departments and project managers;
>
> – *projects scripts* associated with the engineering project: methods, distribution of roles and tasks, timetable, steps, deliverables, determination and updating of the results, etc.;
>
> – *theoretical and theoretico-doxical scripts* associated with academic knowledge (which can be found in the training of decision-makers) and the worlds of professional narratives, external prescribers, consultants, associations, trainers ... and opinions;
>
> – *regulatory scripts* associated with laws, business or collective, national or international regulations, applicable to companies and their digital apparatuses.

**Box 1.1.** *Different families of socio-technical scripts*

Each category of scripts brings with them special forces and mediations, specific vehicles they make use of to move around. For us, the interfaces take a separate place in these configurations, since they have the ability to link the different scripts, to ensure the passage between scripts. They are conditioned by the cooperation of the categories and allow the updating of the materials that are distributed, spread out within other scripts.

## 1.7. Models

### 1.7.1. *Cycles and dynamics*

The problem with a table (see Table 1.1) is that it presents materials in an essentialistic manner; it freezes positions and oppositions. Those things we do not yet see with full accuracy are precisely the phenomena described by the empirical approach, and among them, the reciprocal passages (passes) between managerial scripts and the business scripts, but also the passages between dimensions and their transformations. Indeed, and to complete the perspective of M. Akrich, we consider that the movement of scripting (scripts) is inseparable from the movement of descriptions: the work of the project group (the managerial script) carries out a decoding (de-scription) of a business practice that it will then overwrite (in-script) with an action model, and whose interfaces will mediate, with the target users then decoding this second element, and bringing it into a relationship (at the time of a reflexive moment) with the singular script of their own practice, which in turn disrupts the collective script proposed by the management or the project group in charge of the design.

In addition, the perspective of Akrich reverts to a narrative version of the script, which is defined in part, certainly by its effects, but which is no longer immanent to the organization and which acts in a separate way, following a classical dualism: subject/object, human/non-human. These are the "relationships", influences with one another that should be thought through more extensively beforehand.

This leads us not only to abandon the linear modeling of design processes for information systems (including the now-standard V-model) but to also offset ourselves in relation to other proposals that have integrated the logical processes of updating – confrontation in a short circuit (in agile methods, the integration of the user from the outset of the process), but also to offer another view of the "Vortex model" of the sociology of innovation[71].

This metaphor that we propose here, based on a sine wave, has several interesting points.

It allows for us to consider the combinations of different forces on the same design cycle and to think about the question of asynchronicities in the different movements that characterize the manufacturing of a digital apparatus. The variables selected in this way are:

– the magnitude of pressure exerted by a force;

– the time and pace, the moments of interventions of such an individual actant or of such a phenomenon, as well as the cutoffs and restarts of a cycle.

It commits us to thinking about the successive movements of scripting and descriptions (their recordings) according to their reports on speed and slowness, a temporal shift, a movement of scripts (which one could imagine moving like vibrations on a rope).

The lines of force are lines of scripts, and they intersect, respond, and oscillate at the pace of the discussions, technical developments, and practices.

In the following figure (Figure 1.3), the bubbles on the left side are the names of possible script lines:

– the scripts provided by the project group (interaction between the scenario of strategic action posed by management, standardized activity patterns, and the rules defined by the project management cooperating with the few members representing user networks);

– the scripts proposed by the editor and the various technical constraints;

– the unique scripts attached to situations and professions (user perspectives).

---

71 In [AKR 88], innovation is described as a process following iterative loops, integrating all actors from the outset, a search for compromise and interest. Each ring corresponds to a "pass" and socio-technical transformations.

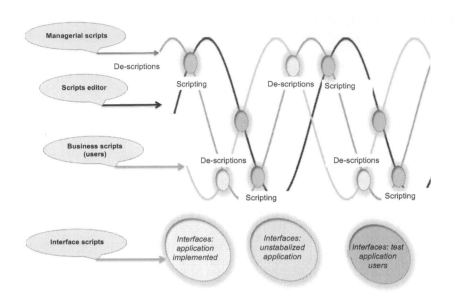

**Figure 1.3.** *Sine wave model of the dynamics of in-scription/de-scription of Moeva*

Each crossing gives rise to a new state of the interface: at each of these nodes, the scripts of the interface give us a form, and the semiotics redistribute and relaunch other scripts.

Each node can correspond to a particular moment of a technical confrontation: the application is in the process of design or significant change (first node iA), therefore in the phase of translation/programming of scripts (in-scription in the features and semiotics), for example, carried out by the collaborative work between the publisher and the project group; the application enters the test phase (node iB), a phase characterized in particular by the interactions of the user/publisher/project group that then negotiate the description of the activity model (which is more or less appropriate); the application is put into production (IC node), which means that it is accessible by all recipient users. The interface carries out a mediation before a possible new phase of negotiations and in-scription/de-scription is resumed.

In this example, the lines of forces have the same amplitude (symmetry with respect to the x-axis), but it goes without saying that one could vary the degree of intensity as time progresses, or add new strengths, new groups (of actants) (with scripts fed mainly by legal constraints, for example).

In the sine wave model, the question of asynchronicity, and more generally, that of the differentiation of time, of paces and rhythms, that is of diachronization, is essential. As B. Stiegler points out for organizations and institutions, we see each of these social systems "formed by specific tendencies that instantiate the dynamics of synchronization and diachronization. [...] Each new stage of instilling introduces new synchronization processes, that is new meta-stabilization regimes" [STI 10a][72]. We also touch on one of the fundamental aspects of the semiopolitics of interfaces.

We still need to go through one more step. According to B. Latour [LAT 12], to report on the course of action means to describe the movement "by which passionate interests and scripts are linked"; the description is then nothing more "than simply the bending of the scripts".

This implies specifying which of the actants allow these "passes" and the mediations that take place: the local "prescriptions" of a higher-level manager or a colleague; a meeting; a specification or even, for example, as seen in the case of Moeva, a prime minister (with the tour de force here being to create a relationship, within the same script, between the pace of CV processing by a recruiter in Rennes with a discussion in Paris on the settings for automatic alerts and the success of "Villepin's 100 days").

The description of the Moeva years allowed us to account for a course of action specific to business practices and to situations of the design of a digital apparatus, but also to unfold these scripts that are immanent to the organization.

In support of information and observations on the ground, a second modeling of the relationship between the entities of a script can be presented as follows (Figure 1.4). This script is presented here in the form of semiotic-semantic relations, that is, each actor conceives, in its argument and

---

72 At the social level, which is the level of the organizations and institutions of the collective individualization, the meta-stabilizing tendencies for the synchronization, a condition of the unity of the social level as a whole, work both for and against the tendencies toward diachronization, which constantly jostle with these meta-stabilized structures through collective individualization [...]" [STI 10a, STI 10b].

its actions, a system of relationships between narratives and words of order, the routines of professional actions and a catalogue of functionalities, technical information (the catalogue shown in the central bubble "Moeva Interfaces").

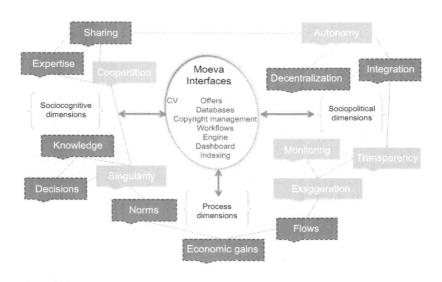

**Figure 1.4.** *Example of relationships within an assembly of scripts*

The labels in blue (e.g. "Norms") refer more to the managerial script-linking features (which can be put to use in the argument to support or criticize the apparatus), the reasons for the application to exist (such as gains) and the execution conditions (such as the changes to internal standards). The labels in green correspond to the semantic register of the criticism: this script can be the emanation of the course of action of a user during which he is in a situation to treat the daily alerts presented on his dashboard (Workflows indicating the delays in its processing). He thus considers that he is in a situation of a work overload (he is suffering from the flow of CV data) and monitoring his practices without compensating them in terms of access to more qualitative resources (he no longer has the time to study and identify the relevant files, thus making the idea of the capitalization of knowledge and better decision-making tangible). The name of his business script is no longer "recruiter", but "CV indexer".

The power of a critical script like this one seems to be very weak in the face of the overpowering nature of the introduction of the internet and digital solutions within organizations. In the case of Moeva, this resulted in a gradual distancing of the CV actant, which became very disruptive (it has outsourced its treatment and introduced more automation in the operating mode), in order to realign the tasks of a recruiter with a profession for "Creating Value".

## 1.7.2. *Other dynamics*

This survey examined an arrangement in the process of transforming and describing the manufacture of an organizational techno-politics. The scripts have proven to be a very dynamic and high-performativity process and as a source of disputes. Indeed, during a trial event (in the process of in-scripting and de-scripting) meeting there are at least two scripts that clash, and with them all the forces they are carrying. Studying the production of digital organization is akin to these conditions, to an "ethology of forces" similar to the Deleuzian school of thought as expressed by its heir, B. Latour [SAS 03][73].

The case of Moeva also described a set of phenomena that characterize the processes of establishing an organization on the basis of its digital projects:

– the construction of narratives at different levels of scale, their confrontation, their instability, and the differentiation between their status: managerial decrees, narratives, celebratory practices (from the first launch to the micro-celebrations that came with each new version), the prescriptions of the editor, questions from users, etc.;

– the need to link the "messages in the design process" with the many different modes of formalization of narratives, and among these modes, the "documentary" recordings and mediations (with specifications files and User Guides essentially being the consensual culminations of many disputes);

– scripts that travel from organization to organization: scripts are nomadic, and one of the vehicles they use is the application itself. This can be considered as a strength (since the models already selected by others are

---

73 Any singularity calls for an "ethology of the forces", a consideration of the environment that formed it, that made it appear as a "consequence", an "effect" for the "system" [SAU 03].

returned to themselves, and these "others" can be considered exemplary) or sometimes (as in the posture held in some cases by our project leader), as an admission of a low level of capability to determine themselves. Therefore, what is needed is a hybridization of scripts: specific developments are added to a replication of the features and interfaces chosen by others, in other places;

– unstable forces and forcible reversals, that is, a transformation of the networks linked to each of the members (transformations of the links that leave from them and that connect back to them) and the internal relations within the scripts;

– "capture/modeling" operations on the courses of action, and thus the placement into scripts of a local practice, always done on a partial level: the scripts' incompleteness is the basis for both their weakness and their strength, as well as their unique intensity;

– a design process characterized by asynchronous wavering between moments of in-scriptions (for example, scripts at project meetings, in the workbooks and in the application programs) and moments of de-scriptions that bring together the actants (project group or users) in the presence of each other, and the latest versions of the interfaces;

– fluctuating rationalities, antagonists, and models of economic efficiency are not always conclusive. Since we see the project being continually revived, we consider that the very condition for the meta-stability of the organization may be the act of moving forward, and doing so blindly to a certain extent.

As B. Latour says:

> "To organize is not, cannot be, the opposite of disorganizing.
> To organize is to pick up, along the way and on the fly, scripts
> with staggered outcomes that are going to disorganize others.
> This disorganization is necessary, since the same beings must
> constantly attempt to juggle attributions that are, if not always
> contradictory, then at least distinct. Instead of anisotropy, it is
> heterotopy that wins out" [LAT 12].

Formatting systems are always in a state of tension brought on by the possibilities of closings and openings: creation and innovation can no doubt be carried out only against these constraints even by phenomena of "resistances" (so decried by management), by the expression of relationships of forces that they will engender. We have shown how the scripts clashed, as did the different figures and rationales that were linked to it – and each time a script enters into play, we are dealing with a combined set of narratives, diagrams, or activity routines (with a specific location), desires and semiotics, with an *assemblage* of all these things[74].

Each combination or fitting can lead to forces and coalitions of forces of nature and different scales (these are in fact different places, connected with each other). Sometimes, the power relationships seem to be on the side of the management/editors, sometimes on the side of the network of the business users and their representatives, and still other times on the side of the computer code and the functional constraints. In its arguments and actions, everyone designs a system of relationships between narratives and words of order, professional action routines and a catalog of technical features.

The various adaptations that the digital apparatus has seen are the result of the obligation to reach a compromise, the strength of certain arrangements, and the collective or individual strategies related thereto, the investment in the project by uniquely differentiated desires: the confrontation between the requirements of the tool (and of its interfaces) with the scripts for the activities of the professions, to the perceptions-subscriptions of the users, to the particular interpretations, make up the iterative formation of a new technical coupling, of the transductive relationship [SIM 89][75] that is established here. If presenting this interaction, a director of information systems would likely want to remove the "user test". In 2007, while the technical solution was actually going to be replaced by another one (as evidence of how thankless a task the creation of computer applications is; after barely completing a seven-year development cycle, they

---

74 "The minimum real unit is not the word, the idea, the concept or the signifier but the *assemblage*. It is always an assemblage which produces utterances. Utterances do not have as their cause a subject which could act as subjects of enunciation, any more than they are related to subjects as subjects of utterance. The utterance is the product of an assemblage – which is always collective, which brings into play within us and outside us populations, multiplicities, territories, becomings, affects, events" [DEL 96].

75 Transduction is the operation by which a *one-by-one* action is "exercised" between elements that have already been structured and new elements. It is the "most primitive and most fundamental model of amplification." "By transduction, we mean a physical, biological, mental, or social operation, by which an activity spreads from one agent to the next, within a domain" [SIM 89]. For a brief overview of the key concepts of Simondon G., see [DEB 04].

are promptly pushed aside for a new one), this manager indicated that the user was "a waste of time". The functional standards, and thus, the semiotic scripts (imported from other client organizations in the interfaces and programs), had to become established, facing an overcrowded and heterogeneous collection of desires. According to this posture, the performance device of the business world would have already completed its work of "selection", the identification of what is deemed appropriate, and thus had no need to go out and investigate on the ground. Thus, the most direct powers of performance may attempt to annihilate subjective spaces, but remain blind to all the "heterogeneity" that they will seize (despite this) in the scripts imported from other companies, and thus refreshed.

The forces that are performing constantly call for innovation, but the question is whether they open up socio-technical and professional outcomes.

The question of how multiplicities are written into "organizationally situated" scripts ultimately leads us to difficulties associated with this investigation, to difficulties which are in some respects the ones that may have been highlighted in some of the works of B. Latour on the ethnography of law and organization [LAT 12].

One of the first limits of the approach lies in the requirement in its methodology for the monitoring of actants and events which are able to be seen, without adding any events or any other information that would not have been revealed when these events occur. This has two important consequences: the focus on disputes and the absence of an exterior level. The analysis of the composition and the actions of the scripts have actually been strongly based on observations of salient events, such as the criticisms and battles between the members of the project, on the model of what could be described as "situated controversies" [LEM 07][76]. Since the scripts become known primarily when they fail or when they are "dissonant" [STA 10][77] or also when the forces they associate with are few in number, what happens

---

76 The classic characterization of controversies, for example by C. Lemieux (which is not exclusively scientific or technical) could be compared to the specificities of organizational conflicts [LEM 07].
77 "An infrastructure that is invisible when it works, becomes visible when it fails: a server crashes, a bridge collapses, the electricity is cut off. Even when there are emergency mechanisms or procedures, their existence only highlights the infrastructure that has become visible" [STA 10].

with the others? The ones that don't make themselves understood who would appear to have met all the necessary conditions of happiness, and would have no need to be made to be understood. However, would it be necessary for us to remove them from the survey, and how do we come upon them? Some scripts can sometimes run through our routines or have enough consensus to "shut us up", while others may still require the researcher to live with the actants outside of the situation set out for the inquiry!

In describing the organization that is being done, we therefore seem to require more than the recording of the tests during "passes": there is no passage here, of the movement of a folder, such as in the Council of State studied by B. Latour, although the specifications of Moeva and its different versions may have common traits (with even a "fetishism"[78] at certain times in the Moeva process, but the contractually binding document was quickly neglected). We must follow in the footsteps of a multitude of people who stretch the network of observable things far beyond the corridors of Veolia Environnement and its partners. Admittedly, the orthodoxy of pragmatic sociology[79] might raise an objection against us here, asserting that this would be the responsibility of the invisible or "weak" entities, for they are seldom summoned in the course of experience by the actants, and therefore have no scientific interest: this is the landscape on which the "sifting" of the facts is carried out, which gives rise to observable differences. However, would we be able to exclude groups such as the councils and the professional associations from the organizational arrangement, which some members of the project group belong to, and which they hardly ever mention in this experience? Should we even go so far as to find out what they read and look up their background in training?

More generally, investigating other places and long networks does not appear to be unnecessary.

---

78 In "The Manufacturing of the Law", Latour describes a veritable fetishizing of the files (papers) that are manipulated, traced, indexed, taken from a continuum, marked with stamps, and each action is performed internally ("They are watched like milk on a stove top", p. 93), until they are published in the Lebon. All these manipulations are the passages that this sociologist describes as the subject of the law. "The judges do not reason, they hassle with *legal files that act on them*, that pressure them, that exert a force on them, which make them take one action or another". Nothing remains that would give the impression of any resistance, of anything, of any cause. "Nothing more material, more real" [LAT 04].

79 B. Latour prefers the notion of "empirical philosophy".

Another question relates to this particular regime of enunciation which makes up the organization, which, like the twelve regimes he describes in his *Anthropologie des modernes*, is according to the author, irreducible to others. Presented by Latour as the preferred language and grammar of this scheme, is the script so fundamentally original? Could the potential performing nature of the script, its ability to assign roles and aggregate heterogeneous forces, its ability to launch trajectories, etc., be able to be assigned to another enunciation regime such as the law[80], science or religion, for example? Moreover, didn't he write in 2004, that the texts of the law "[...] allocate roles and functions, assign abilities, distribute authorities, create all parts of different entities, provide redress procedures, and so on, covering as many scripts as the myriad human interactions – which are still, somehow, below these scripts that give them their action plan, their road map? [LAT 04].

In addition, instead of a principle of the autonomy of the regimes in relation to the others, and as L. De Sutter and S. Gutwirth rightly note in their critique of the ethnography of the Council of State, we would then be in a situation in which the regimes interlace, and not merely in a situation of coexistence of these regimes.

> We believe, on the contrary, that what this story demonstrates is that it is the nature of the law to belong to other enunciation regimes than its own – or at least to participate in them. [...] The law is has always responded to the shifts in modern demands: science, art, politics have always governed the way in which the law is said, they have always distorted the determinations of the game of accusations that had been its own" [DES 04].

---

80 The production of the law is based on legal deeds, discussions, tests, instruments, and a regime of declarations. "Law engenders human beings, without it itself being made by them". It belongs to the category of fetishes. "This regime of enunciation does what no other one does: it keeps track of all the disengagements, by tirelessly reattaching statements to the persons making them, through the perilous path of signatures, archives, texts, and files". In fact, more than any other action, the signature reveals this very particular form taken by the law [LAT 04].

# Performation: Out of Bounds (and Beyond Language)

## 2.1. The question of performativity, at the heart of the production of digital organizations

### 2.1.1. *Inheritance and openings*

The Mocva case has shown us how an entire array of scripts could be created, and how their co-functionality could be implemented: their form of mobilization (how one script mobilizes another script), their reinforcement, or their conflict (the imposition of another activity model or another techno-political approach). By being attentive to "what they do and have done" we have made explicit a part of the chain of proofs, formatting as they are performative processes.

It should be recalled that the scripts are presented as an organized set of utterances (not exclusively linguistically) with the capacity to affect and to bring about the world they indicate. Innovation can be seen as a struggle between scripts, for the ability to gain the upper hand and to impose their models of action.

We are going to make use of other cases as well, in order to examine different performation configurations, to deepen, in particular, the weaving together of the populations of technical and human beings with their grammars and combinations with the many interconnected passions that run through them. But this will also serve to deepen the new offshoots that these textures support in their assemblages (both in the private and/or public sector, and in the area of government policies). Thus, they follow the generally long-reaching networks of the powers that act[1], their transformations, and what gives them their morphogenesis.

Firstly, we want to emphasize the need to break away from the linguistic model of performativity. A brief review is in order.

The question of performativity has indeed been developed in the field of linguistics, including the seminal work of J.L. Austin: *How to Do Things with Words* [AUS 62]. At this point, it might be necessary to recall some of the essential concepts of linguistic actions in Austin's work.

Two concepts are proposed: that of the denotative or constative utterances that describe the world, and that of performative[2] utterances that perform an action. These two concepts will be complemented by others. Austin then describes[3] "illocutionary acts", which create an obligation at the same time as enunciation and the perlocutionary act, which expresses an enunciation in which the intention of the speaker is invoked (with an effect on those who receive the enunciation). He therefore proposes a general theory of "speech acts", which distinguishes the case where the speaking of a sentence in itself transforms the relationship between the speakers and performs an action (the illocutionary act), and the case in which the speech has an effect on the speaker or perlocutionary consequences, whether voluntarily or inadvertently (the perlocutionary act).

What matters the most to us here are the things we will list in what follows. This consideration of the performative dimension has important implications for the linguistics that Gilles Deleuze and Félix Guattari have

---

1 In some respects, in the works on organizations, French works have often maintained a dissociation of "endogenous/exogenous", in/out, when, as F. Cooren points out, it would be better to consider the *ways organizations have of existing and of the ways they are organized, by reassembling the local and the global levels* [LAT 06], in order to be able to address these issues from *both a constitutive and a performative point of view* [COO 10].

2 According to Austin, performative utterance is related to the question of performance, or even to that of "performativity" (of an organization, of procedures, of a system, etc.) and in this sense, to the evaluation of an efficiency, to the measure of an effect, of an *input/output* ratio. Another meaning will be given to us through the concept of "performation".

3 Additionally, a "locutionary act" defines the thing involved in a statement (irrespective of the meaning).

summarized in their series *"Les postulats de la linguistique"* from the Mille Plateaux, namely:

> "It has made it impossible to conceive of language as a code, since a code is the condition of possibility for all explanation. It has also made it impossible to conceive of speech as the communication of information: to order, question, promise or affirm is not to inform someone about a command, doubt, engagement or assertion but to effectuate these specific, immanent and necessarily implicit acts" [DEL 87b].

Another consequence, for our purpose, is that "it has made it impossible to define semantics, syntactics, or even phonematics as scientific zones of language independent of pragmatics. Pragmatics ceases to be a 'trash heap', pragmatic determinations cease to be subject to the alternative: fall outside language, or answer to explicit conditions that syntacticize and semanticize pragmatic determinations. Instead, pragmatics becomes the presupposition behind all of the other dimensions and insinuates itself into everything" [DEL 87b].

In short, to obtain the essential elements of what concerns us:

> "Language is neither informational not communicational. It is not the communication of information but something quite different: the transmission of order-words, either from one statement to another or within each statement, insofar as each statement accomplishes an act and the act is accomplished in the statement" [DEL 87b].

### 2.1.1.1. *When saying is doing, and when doing is saying (Austin/ Lyotard/Ingold)*

Our concept of scripts is partly rooted in this design, and grows increasingly deeper still as the scripts begin to operate in a heterogeneous field, in what we might be able to call the social field of the organization. The scripts, in the sense that we understand them, are "social" in their enunciation because all of their enunciations, according to the concept put forward by Deleuze and Guattari, solely refer to "collective assemblages".

And the pragmatics that we have already called for previously, is a policy of scripts (as it is a language policy in linguistics) where statements and actions mix together, are revived, manufactured, and altered, etc.

From a certain point of view, which we will attempt to explain, the extended scripts "involve" the organization and the "doing" comes to the forefront within the scripts, but always with "everything against them", over the course of the practices, the work of installation[4] that bears the alteration-creation, innovation and dysfunction at the same time[5]. Our analyses would appear to demonstrate that while the organization may well be immanent in its scripts and in the performative pragmatics, there is nevertheless a permanent openness to future outcomes, an alteration and creation present within the psychic and collective individualization of the organization. When we mention "the weaving together between populations of technical and human entities with their grammar and combinatorial arrangements", we understand this performative knitting together as intricate interlacing, made from transformations and translations between linguistics and semiotic regimes, between grammars and syntaxes through the process of linguisticization-semioticization of grammars, syntaxes, and semantics, including artifacts, as well as computer codes (non-meaningful semiotics) so important[6] at the core of the scripts[7].

When we refer to this weaving action and these fabrics, we understand these as being unable to be reduced to languages and speeches within the organization and about the organization, nor able to be reduced to the scripts embedded within the organization... but to the opening of a wider experience, of a greater otherness. Here, we draw on the concepts of J. Derrida, for whom text and texture "implies (or imply) all 'real', 'economic', 'historical', and 'socio-institutional' structures; in short, all possible references" [DER 71].

---

4 In the sense of Souriau.

5 In this area, we rely on both G. Simondon, G. Deleuze and T. Ingolg.

6 It is widely recognized that a level of importance should be given to non-meaningful semiotics and the roles it plays in "Integrated Global Capitalism" (Guattari). We will return to this in Chapter 3.

7 F. Guattari and J.-M. Noyer.

This is because there is an internal pragmatic–performative scripting of the scripts (in their pluri-semiotism itself), that there is a possible interconnection and translation towards an external pragmatic-performative (in its dimensions, this may still not exclusively involve language). This shows us the way forward to develop a political approach to the "outcomes", the processes of alteration-creation within the organization.

To give to the scripts, in our approach, the powers of the collective assemblages of enunciation and the mechanical assemblages, of which they are both the expression and the expressed, therefore implies that we abandon once and for all the exorbitant privilege that we have given to language:

> "For a long time we believed it to be transparent and only a product of all actants involved; it had no thickness, nor any violence. Then we began to doubt its transparency, and we sought to restore it by cleaning language, as one might do with a glass. So much did we prefer language to anything else, that we have made critiquing it the sole task of the generations of Kant and Wittgenstein. Finally, in the 1950s, we realized that the language was opaque, thick, and weighty. Instead of ending its privileges and giving it back to the other forces that translate it and that it itself translates, we wanted to instead reduce all other forces to the material of the signifier. We then made text into 'the' thing. This was during the glorious sixties. We have exaggerated a lot. 'Everything they say about the signifier is fair, but it must also be said of every last pipe dream. There's nothing special about language that would make it possible to distinguish it from everything else long-term [LAT 84]."

This has led us to consider, as we will see a bit further on, a kind of general narrative, and one that is not exclusively linguistic at the heart of organizational performation. The organization is therefore inherent to the practical elements of the scripts, the processes of alteration/creation that they bring, as well as to the energies, impulses, and libidinal economies that are affiliated with them and/or that are their byproducts. Also, within the same framework of interpretation, we are led to examine the communicational practicalities on the basis of the consequences we have already referenced on the assemblage of performatives through *speech acts*.

In *La Condition postmoderne*, Jean-François Lyotard reiterates Austin's major categories of enunciation and the acts they produce (the acts of language), to examine the tangled interconnections between themselves and open themselves to the question of the power relationships between the statements themselves.

> "Lacking what he calls the "simplicity" of scientific pragmatics, social pragmatics 'is a monster formed by the interweaving of various networks of heteromorphous classes of utterance (denotative, prescriptive, performative, technical, evaluative, etc.'" [LYO 79].

Jean-François Lyotard would continue to prolong and expand on his analyses in *Le différend* [LYO 88], in which he posits that "he cannot comprehend why one should attribute a "mystical" depth to the divide between cognitive and prescriptive sentences [LYO 83]. Incommensurability, in the sense of the heterogeneity of the regimes of phrases and the inability to submit them to the same law (except to neutralize them), also marks the relationship between cognitives or prescriptives with interrogatives, performatives, exclamatives, etc. Each of these schemes corresponds to a mode of the presentation of a universe, and "one mode cannot be translated into another".

Here, as in other cases, communication pragmatics is associated with the deployment of Micropolitics. These communication processes are not only in the area of the metastability of the organization, but are also carriers of risks of disaggregation. That is why (as we have already mentioned, and we will return to once again), there exist simultaneously a policy of languages and narratives of the acceptability of the organization, a study of a relatively complex study of the conflict of languages according to the heterogeneity of the communities within that organization.

The manufacturing of consent as a conflict-based co-construct of the organization's balancing apparatus, runs through the scripts as a whole through a super-political language, a basically scholarly entanglement of organizational "newspeak"[8] and "fairy tales"[9].

And from the manufacturing of consent, establishing a consensus is only a small step away.

And from this point of view, Lyotard notes that the emergence of a "consensualist ideology" comes about in order to counteract the appearance of situations of conflict as quickly as possible, instead of seeking to provide the means of expression necessary for its settlement. Callon, Lascoumes and Barthe have stated that:

> "Consensus is often the mask that hides the reports of domination and exclusion. Democracy cannot expand by seeking agreements on a cost-by-cost basis. Politics is the art of dealing with disagreements, conflicts, oppositions, so why not allow them to arise, to multiply, for this is how the unexpected paths open, as possibilities multiply" [CAL 01].

Lyotard continues:

> "The ideology of consensus at all costs is one of the ways in which the conflict operating at the heart of the scholarly discourse is forgotten. In doing so, it masks the very event which could make possible the epistemic access to the societal transformations, conflict and its power to act as a multiplier. This requires that the relationship with the idea of consensus, first and foremost, be critical" [LYO 83].

Now, let's take a second to move away from studies of conflicts and their issues, from the "Dissoi Logoi" within the organization. With regard to the chronocratic issue, the phenomena of the retention of desire and sublimation are more directly related to the scripts themselves[10]. The conflict of

---

8 For his dystopian novel *1984*, George Orwell invented *Newspeak*, the official language of Oceania [ORW 49].

9 *Contes merveilleux*.

10 These points shall be explored in greater depth further on.

statements in the conflict of collective utterances and mechanistic assemblages (as redoubling, or duplication) of the organization, thus forms part of the search for modes of consensus, the avoidance of the risks of dissensus (a lack of consensus), but also seeks spaces for the futures and creations.

By adopting the classification of statements in a non-critical manner according to J.-F. Lyotard, we will propose to characterize some of the statements (short forms, slogans, micromemes) that play a factor mainly in the field of managerial orthodoxies. They are interventions/translations within the fields of ideas and scriptures, of productive, financial, or marketing forces, which are rather complex.

However, passing through the categories of Lyotard that allow us to account for the roles of the famous "language games" [LYO 79] in the uncertain construction of reality, causes us to momentarily regress in our analysis. While we are establishing "performation and pragmatics" as processes and categories bearing upon and running through the entire manufacture of the organization, Lyotard proposes a classical definition, limited to its own linguistic field. This is quite far from what we are calling for, far from the approaches of Jean-Pierre Faye in his totalitarian languages, far from the proposals of Michel Callon, and farther still from Machiavelli, etc.

Of these language games, Lyotard more specifically states in *The Differend* that we do not "play with language". And he continues:

> "In this sense, there are no language games. There are issues related to the different types of messages. Once they are attained, we may then talk about success. So there is therefore a conflict. But the conflict is not between humans or any other entity, which rather presupposes phrases. At the core, we usually presuppose *one* language, a language naturally at peace with itself, one that is "communicational", for example, one that is only agitated by the desires, the passions, and the intentions of human beings. Anthropocentrism. The relativist and quantum revolution in terms of language remains to be made (*in the Organization and its management as well, we ourselves might*

*add*). Each sentence is, in principle, the issue of a dispute between different kinds of speech, regardless of its regime. This dispute proceeds from the question: how does this develop? That accompanies a sentence."

Thus, according to the categorization of Lyotard [LYO 79]:

– *the denotative statement*: this does not only consist of a description (locutionary act), but of a statement[11]. According to Lyotard, in these circumstances, the sender (the one making the statement), the recipient (the one receiving the statement) and the reference (the thing that the statement deals with) are thus assigned to a specific place. "By means of the statement, the recipient is placed in and exposed to the position of 'knowing' [...], the recipient is put in position of having to give or refuse his agreement, and the reference also approached in a manner peculiar to the things it denotes, as something that must be 'Properly identified and expressed in the statement to which it refers'" [LYO 79]. The denotative statement is subject to criteria for truth, which determine its acceptability. With regard to the deployment in organizations of various apparatus given labels such as "2.0" (whose emblematic applications are social networks, blogs, wikis, etc.), a multitude of statements has been produced. Experts begin to appear, notably from consulting firms, professional associations, or the press... or (an occurrence that is much more unusual in France for professionals) from universities. Among the "diagnoses" they produce, there are radical formulations such as: "Hierarchies are dead, long live the 'digital workplace'"[12], "the era of the company 2.0 is here"[13], "Intranet 2.0: The era of 'peopleware': getting back to the user and e-transformation"[14];

– *the prescriptive statement*: We are within the universe of recommendations, instructions, requests, or even commandments, petitions, or injunctions. "Here, we see that the destiny is placed in a position of authority, in the broad sense of the word (including the authority, a sinner holds over a god who claims to be merciful), that is, he expects the recipient to carry out the action that has been referenced" [LYO 79]. In the managerial

---

11 The denotative statement is closer to that of the confirmation statement described by Austin.

12 The French professional Association *"Observatoire des réseaux sociaux d'entreprise"* [Observatory of Corporate Social Networks], 2011.

13 The Gartner firm, 2003.

14 Title of the professional event, Intracom, Paris, April 2007.

world, as elsewhere, the prescription uses a specialized syntax, "the word of order", and a method for the exposure to high attractiveness, "the event" or "the celebration" of cases of organizations put forward as exemplary (at professional conferences, in the business press, or during the compiling of the "rankings" of the most digital and collaborative company). "ITC and new work environments: myths and realities!" What has changed, what hasn't changed, and what has to change"[15]: This clearly demonstrates the general tone of the mid 2000s, and one that still persists. More recently, we might read from the minutes of a session organized by an association focused on the deployment of internal networks at businesses, and recently (to broaden its area of action), on the "digital transformation", that "digital technology will make it possible to accompany (a) change of position: the whole company is put on the same plane, allowing for the free and responsible expression of the collaborators through collaborative spaces and mobile tools"[16]. Following the interventions of the CEO of Orange, a group that has experienced an unprecedented influx of social problems in recent years, and that has portrayed its "internal social network" applications as one of the possible solutions to the social malaise following its transition from public status to private status[17];

– *the performative statement:* This is characterized by the simultaneous occurrence of its enunciation and its effect, through the capacity to produce a statement jointly with a transformation of a situation (including an action, a behavior, or a perception). And this, according to Austin, is where we find ourselves. Are the "self-fulfilling prophecies" [MER 42] or "creative predictions" canonical examples of the performative enunciations, as theorized by Austin? Given the fact that enunciation and effect do not occur simultaneously, we are inclined not to think so. But the fact that these prophecies and predictions occur, confirms that the fundamental question remains that of understanding and identifying the forces that choose or manufacture certain statements in such a way that they travel, move, have effects, and establish themselves. We will return to these points.

---

15 Title of a plenary of a professional colloquium, Intracom, Paris, 19 April 2005.

16 December 2016, available at: http://www.obsdesrse.com/evenements/les-rencontres-de-lobservatoire/compte-rendu-de-la-17eme-rencontre-experience-salarie-nouvelle-culture-a-lere-du-numerique-4859/.

17 At the beginning of the 2000s, we witnessed the creation of an application prompting every collaborator with public status to "garden his skills" and the future developments of his career in a new configuration of the company. One of the issues was to convince staff members to carry out a conversion, either within the company or outside of it.

*Generally speaking, in order for the performative statements to occur, certain conditions are required.* These statements are sufficiently general so as not to be questionable, but above all, they rely on figures of authority, a degree of confidence, and certain instruments that ensure they have the desired effect. They assume collective assemblages of specific enunciations. For Austin, as well as for Bourdieu and Lyotard, the social position and the power of the speaker is an essential condition for a performative statement.

In keeping with the perspective of ANT[18], it may also be considered that the performative potential of a statement is consubstantial with the forces and the entities that produce it. *For Latour and Callon, the central question is:* "Where do statements draw their strength from?" As we will see later, it is the "collective assemblages of enunciation" of the "mechanistic assemblages" and "concrete assemblages"[19] from which we must examine the various statements, as well as the regimes of enunciation according to Latour. However, since for our purposes the statements are only expressions, under specific, singular, partisan forms, and are expressed from processes of any implantation [SOU 09], such as immanence, the performative statement in the sense of Austin or Lyotard is only of a limited interest.

And even if for Lyotard, the performative statements are *"not subject to discussion or verification by the consignee, which is immediately placed in the new context created in this way"* [SOU 09], all it would take is me changing my assemblage, or moving to discuss it, challenge it, or mock it, so that the initial concurrency of the statement and its effect is broken or chaotic, etc., at the risk of the forces that cause it to collapse. It is essential for the world or organization to be inherent to the assemblage that produces them.

If we continue with performative statements in the trivial sense, two cases are presented for the recipient: either he has the (external) authority to make the statement and give it strength, or he acquires it at the same time as he infers these kinds of statements. The process of legitimation is fundamental,

---

18 *Actor-network theory.*

19 For Deleuze, "the assemblage is not an enunciation, it only formalizes the expression, and only on one of its faces;" with regard to its other inseparable face, it formalizes the contents, it is a machinistic or corporeal assemblage" [DEL 80].

and determines the success of the performative process, namely that it has the capacity to affect the entire mechanism for destination, to achieve the purpose of the statement:

> "The performativity (but not its performative character in Austin's original sense) of a statement, whether denotative or prescriptive, increases in proportion to the information available regarding its reference. Thus, the increase of the power and its legitimation, enters the present through production, memory, accessibility and the operationality of the information" [SOU 09].

This point is important, because it also places the question of the ability to produce data at the heart of the processes of legitimizing knowledge and the statements made in these processes.

In the case of companies setting out on the path towards "2.0", there have been a number of statements produced that function as "significant master concepts", which cut through the uncertain complexity of the actors seeking dominance to reach a higher position, whether technical, financial, organizational, intellectual, etc. This work, consisting of assaulting an unstable reality, offering modes of explanation for processes of chaotization, is a major task. It requires work to manufacture a new order, its acceptability, to develop significant master-concepts for a "simplexity" [BER 09][20] of conquest.

For example, international firms, such as Gartner and Forrester, have for years been maintaining an "overhanging" position, which gives (themselves) the ability to "know the reality", to predict it (in terms of technology or business prospects), attach themselves to it, and make it come to pass. The incessant reviewing of the analyses of these firms by the managers tends to

---

20 "Simplexity, as I understand it, is the entire collection of the solutions found by living organisms such that, despite the complexity of natural processes, the brain can prepare its actions and project the consequences that arise from them. These solutions are simplifying principles that can be used to process information or situations, taking into account past experience and anticipating future ones. These are neither caricatures, nor shortcuts or summaries. They are new ways to pose problems, sometimes at the cost of a few detours, to arrive at faster, more elegant, more efficient actions" [BER 09].

support the idea that a performative process is embodied in the various "repositories" of action, the comparative grids (between such a company and another), or even in the supports given by some university courses (the same professional actors can intervene). Similarly, consultants and project managers, whether or not they rely on "knowledge institutions" or collective figures of authority (such as a professional association), may see their comments being sufficiently appreciated as a "break" from the established orthodoxy, in order to justify an automatic return in the eyes of other professionals[21]. The statements then enter into a kind of sleepless cycle of repetition. These phenomena will also lead us to consider the digital manufacturing of the organization from the point of their "libidinal economies"[22], which are expressed, among other ways, by a fascination with "celebrations".

However, Gartner and Forrester produce "memes" that express themselves in the form of cognitive, emotional, and perceptual behaviors, and their conditions of replication, for the alliance between neo-liberalism, the digital world, and the convergence of NBIC[23] to be implanted. This point will be reexamined later on.

Our examination of Lyotard and especially his work *The Differend* [LYO 88][24] is, according to us, justified by the fact that it opens beyond the reconfiguration of relations on the occasion of a language act to a consideration of "language games" as analyses of the differing relationships between powers of assignment: "[...] To speak is to fight, in the sense of playing, and [...] language acts are generally agonistic [LYO 88]. From this point of view, each protagonist comes under attack, moves (as in a game of chess), and can develop counterstrikes, design other ways to deliver statements (like shooting arrows) and other material and situational conditions that can increase the chances of success. The theater of operations

---

21 One of the current practices in the professional world is to self-impose "reference authority". A practice inherent to the marketing strategy of any professional association or firm, the reflexive self-grounding and narcissism are exemplary of this milieu.

22 Another concept that we can find in the work of Lyotard.

23 NBIC: In French, "*Nanotechnologies, Biotechnologies, Informatique et Sciences Cognitives*", or "Nanotechnologies, Biotechnologies, Digital and Cognitive Sciences".

24 For Lyotard, consensus and dissensus are violent constructs. There is violence in the manufacturing of consensus.

between statements, opening up to pragmatic approaches to communication and the collective[25], is essentially a "strategic act" [HAB 87][26].

## 2.1.1.2. *Autolegitimization and mastering significant words*

Any statement in the managerial and organizational world is continually divided into illocutionary and perlocutionary acts.

However, this could also be said of the army, religion, and politics. The commands in many of these cases are intended to evolve into a quasi-routine script, in procedural memory, into an embodied order. The prescription carries with it a performative potential, so much so that the classes of utterances are blurred. After all, didn't Deleuze and Guattari already tell us that "the watchword" is the fundamental unit of language? In this way, in the "Postulates of Linguistics", is it stated that the orders made by the professor "do not derive from their initial meanings, they are not the consequence of information: the order always and under every case carries other orders with it, for which reason the order is redundant. The machine that is compulsory education does not communicate information, but imposes semiotic data points on each child, with all the basic two-way elements of grammar (singular/plural, noun/verb, subject of the spoken/subject of speech, etc.)" [DEL 80]. And the two philosophers to continue:

> "What we call *watchwords* are not a particular category of explicit statements (for example, an imperative), but the relationship of any word or statement with implicit assumptions, which is to say, with speech actions that are fulfilled in the statement, and can only be accomplished within it. The watchwords therefore not only refer to commands, but to all acts which are linked to statements through a "social obligation". No

---

25 Watzlawick, Habermas, Goffman, Callon, Latour, Guattari, Deleuze, to name a few.

26 On the work of Habermas [HAB 87] and its use in the field of management sciences, advocating the development of "a communication action" to replace the domination of strategic actions: Calori R., "Philosophie et développement organisationnel : Dialectique, agir communicationnel, délibération et dialogue", *Revue française de gestion*, no. 142, p. 13-41, January 2003. "Strategic action" is a teleological action model in which each agent calculates the means and the ends to achieve success (the achievement of his/her goals), anticipating the decisions of other actors, who are also oriented towards their own goals. In strategic action, agents refer only to the objective world and use two types of claims of validity in their arguments: propositional logic and/or efficiency (the empirical evidence of success).

statement exists that does not have this link, either directly or indirectly. Watchwords can be found in questions, or promises. Language can only be defined by the entire collection of watchwords, implicitly presupposed or in acts of speech, in progress in any language in a given moment" [DEL 80].

To return to our organizational and managerial worlds, statements like "watchword" are enough to carry an entire world with them. For example, in its simplest forms, which may include "business-network", "project", "e-organization", "management 2.0", "digital business" or, regarding recent policies based on "data driven" processes. From this point of view, we would be able to re-read the works of Boltanski-Chiapello [BOL 99] and their rich analysis of the managerial books from the 1960s through the 1990s, in light of the functions of the mechanisms driving these watchwords. Just stating them is sufficient to be able to see the entire organizational and managerial script that goes with it, because again, it is the collective assemblage of enunciation that comes first, and the watchwords are merely the expression and the expressed idea of the assemblage that gives them strength and efficiency.

In observing the construction of organizational digital policies, we may also find that the processes of prescription are widely distributed or multilocalized.

Thus, the law is a prescriptive statement that, through its pairing with the judicial system and its institutions, is coercive. However, while the digital project managers do not have their own court of law, they have their evaluative and normative apparatus, from which the requirements formed in this way are redistributed: the rankings, prizes, and labels[27]. Legitimation by

---

27 Thus, since 1998, the objective of the "Prix Intranet" (in English, the "Intranet Prize") – orchestrated by a professional press support in cooperation with a consultancy firm and a professional association – has been "to reward and promote exemplary and innovative intranets". The list is based on a selection of three indicators: innovation, usability, and return on investment. The difficulty of this undertaking is to assess the cases that are presented, so much so, as the officials themselves admit, that these criteria remain eminently subjective (innovation is cast aside as a "novelty" within the narrow circle of organizational ICTs; file analyses are performed via two readings of a document prepared by the candidate for project manager) and unstable (the incessant search for an operational model for calculating the

power also gives the right to administer the evidence (observatories, appraisal surveys for a business classification or manager of the year), categorizations of enterprises into standard ideals, the reports produced, and by increasing this ability to instrument, document, and develop scripts and action programs (which will begin to appear self-evident), we increase at the same time as others, its ability to be correct, and thus its power.

This self-legitimization reinforces the place of the "performativity of procedures" (in the sense of François Laruelle), and their dominance. To follow this last element, we are in a moment where, ever more explicitly, the organizational policy as "the policy becomes truly experimental, and the experimentation finally relays the Marxist concept of "practice" when the distinction of objects, means, raw materials and products fades into one of the differentiated methods, in the generalization and triumph of "means", once we have understood that there are no more contradictions among these things. A generalized strategy puts them in a differentiated relationship and determines one from the other in a continuous "mechanized" chain – outside of any ethical or scientific purpose, whether or not the processes are theoretical – of power" [LAR 81]. Thus, in passing, the absolute dominance of the notion of "governance" arises[28].

Companies therefore increase control over their own contexts of enunciation, control their operating mechanisms, and enhance their ability to legitimize themselves.

EXAMPLE.– If we examine the molecular or micro-political level of the organization, the situation, of a consultant arriving at the stage of a professional symposium on "Digital Companies" or "Best Practices" for intranets (the title is explicit as to the value that everyone has to give to the presentations, we find that three performative processes are initiated. Let's let the consultant say a few words:

– "I am presented as an 'expert' because I was selected by the organizers, who were themselves put in place by the experts present in the room and by the partners of the conference";

---

Intranet ROI is a kind of managerial holy grail). It has developed its model over the years by subdividing its themes. Since 2013, the "Collaborative Business" award has been organized, available at: http://www.prix-entreprise-collaborative.fr/.

28 See the critique made by B. Latour on this master word, which expresses a smoothing of politics and debates.

– "I am announcing the launch of a prize for the best Intranet of the year and the manager 2.0, who has been able to most effectively link internal social networks with the corporate strategy";

– "By organizing this award, the organizers will designate the guidelines to be followed according to certain indicators".

In this situation, a virtuous circle of three performative elements begins: first, the consultant assumes the status and objectives of an authority figure, an illocutionary force; secondly, the "Colloquium" (and the aggregate network of organizations) becomes an evaluation body that has the capacity to designate the model to be followed; third, the companies that make submissions will respond to a number of requirements, including the description of their project and for the others that are not yet ready, to engage (perhaps) in compliance with the criteria requested.

Therefore, it matters that the evaluations are only related to the statements of the project manager, who has a vested interest in seeing the latter rewarded, the machinery is closed and maintained on its own; however, this is conditioned on the circle not being opened, which prevents access to the question of the forces that give meaning to the statements. The dynamics seem autonomous and endless. In this presentation, and in a few years, the dominant signifying word has shifted from "change" (which generates anxiety) to "innovation" (which is unquestionably less political).

## 2.1.2. *On the extension of performation*

Since the time it originated from the philosophy of language and linguistics, the question of performation has been presented in front of the theoretical stage and applied research, more specifically in the political sciences, the sociology of the sciences, innovation (the STSs: Science & Technical Studies), the field of economics, strategy, law, etc. Many articles have been published in recent years regarding what has been presented as a performative turning point[29]. Currently, even the management sciences, and

---

29 *The Laws of the Markets* gave significant momentum to the performativity program in sociology [CAL 98, DEN 06, FRA 06, LIC 10]. This was also the main theme of a conference at UQam, Montréal in 2012: (*Organisations, performativité et engagement*) available at: http:// www. crpcm.uqam.ca/pages/docs/ACFAS2012_Appel_Com_Organisations_Performativite_Engagement. pdf .

especially these previously mentioned fields have seized upon a current that is emerging from critical and management studies[30]. We might say that the excitement of the *performative turn* seeks to depict a kind of management dressed in new clothes. It puts itself in a position of a catcher, or merely uncovers a vague "social constructivism".

There are at least two reasons for this craze, and for this we may follow J. Denis [DEN 06]: The multidisciplinary interest in pragmatic approaches, as well as the consideration given to the performative force of technologies and instruments. Indeed, as recalled by B. Latour in *Inreductions* [LAT 11], the things that may be said of language are true, but they must also be said of every other pipe dream hatched by all other actants.

We have seen many examples in the Moeva scripts, and we have shown how the "speeches" entered into a complex interwoven fabric with the action of interfaces and semiopolitics[31].

Detached from any exclusively linguistic approach, the examination of the performative processes through the anthropology of science and technology has aroused a keen interest in economic sociology. In the continuity of the development of the Sociology of Sciences [LAT 79] and introduced into the economic field by Michel Callon [CAL 98, 13], the "concept" of performation is today widely recognized by many authors, who dedicate themselves to discussing its implications [CAL 02, 10][32]. The awareness of this central process implies rethinking the organizational policies and arrangements, their creation, taking into account the

---

30 See, for example, [ALV 09]. The AIM conferences in management sciences are available at: http://www.strategie-aims.com/events/conferences/25-xxiveme-conference-de-l-aims/com-munications/3336-what-do-we-mean-by-performativity-in-organization-and-management-studies-the-uses-and-abuses-of-performativity/download.
Or additionally: [BOZ 16].
31 This implies that either the trios of "speaker-locutaire-message", as formulated by Austin and later expanded on by Lyotard, should be taken into account to consider regimes of enunciation, each specified by acting entities, materials, transformational processes and formatting, of the "energies" unique to each of them (the "pipe dreams" indicated by Latour), but more generally, by considering them according to the concepts Deleuze, on the basis of the events that occur in the "collective assemblages of enunciation" and "the" "mechanistic assemblages" associated with them.
32 See the critique of the performativity approach, for example [BRI 14].

intervention of a broad mixture of actants[33], bringing about not only "a decentralization of the entire language", but also restoring the full power to material actants.

However, before analyzing the proposals of Callon in further detail, we must indicate some of the difficulties or confusions over the meaning of this shift towards the concept of "performative". A certain number of approaches see performation of the organizational world as a kind of refinement of the conditions that shape human collectives, a way of putting new clothes on a general and rather weak constructivism. This leads to the confusion between performativity and performation, weakening the analytical force of a sociology and political philosophy oriented toward the field of the immanence of the organization. A number of managerial works having long formed part of the camp calling for submission to the norms and values of economic liberalism, bringing about the change (and also being changed themselves) by defeating the issue of manufacturing-performation on the constructual performativity[34] of the organization, as *understood procedural performativity*, which includes within the organizational outcomes themselves. It should be noted that this backsliding and/or setbacks to the potential radical nature of the control of "performation" also sometimes affects the work by Callon that we consider to be seminal.

---

33 See section 1.1. To review, the concept of the "actant" refers in particular to the work of semiotics and the sociology of translation, and in this sense, designates the human and "non-human" entities with a capacity to affect or to be affected. A term preferable to the terms actor or agent, used by sociologists, the term allows us to cover not only human beings, but also objects, as well as theories. An actant corresponds to any entity (technical or otherwise), any intermediary, or any trigger of an action.

34 According to [NOY 17], the constructal theory corresponds to a situation in which the challenge is to find the ideal form of a system in such a way that it delivers the optimum performance. It is relatively easy to perceive that, if applied to human societies, it instead becomes an ideology of absolute control, a moment in which creativity is eradicated as a process and alteration... On the constructal theory and its applications in the world of engineers, see: André Béjan, Professor of engineering and specialist of thermodynamics: what does "optimal" mean, here and in other contexts? What is it about this idea of being "optimal" that would make it capable of measuring our lives and the ways in which we experience ourselves through our future outcomes? "Optimal" like the calculating god of Leibniz? "Optimal" like the engineers of the National Conservatory of Arts and Crafts? "Optimal" like the "algotrading" algorithms, or perhaps "optimal" in terms of the rules of the three great holy books (the Bible, Quran, and Torah)? [NOY 17].

Similarly, we grant that our scope here does not reach far enough in its analysis on the field of orthodoxical immanence, the modes of narrative simplification of which this one is the expression and the material that is expressed. We know, however, that the production of autosimplifying processes (to borrow from N. Luhmann here) according to the levels of scales and the types of inputs considered, such that the organization in its complexity can be used as an instance of these operations themselves, plays a central role.

Their productivity is essential. The scripts, in the broad sense we are examining here, are part of the autosimplifying processes. And the question of "what relevance and efficiency can reference points of action have (carriers of a certain point of view), the crushing of the diversity of contingencies and the complexity of the technical-organizational linkages by strategic diagrams encapsulated in a script repeated as much as is deemed necessary?[35]", should be nuanced. But, one must recognize that in a general sense, the scripts, in their repetition and even compulsiveness, always end up producing the conditions for, if not of their own dismantlement, then in any case the need for themselves to be surpassed under the conditions of both internal and external factors.

At this stage, our analysis sees the organization as a performative assemblage, that is an entanglement of scripts and enunciation schemes, performative regimes and varying paces for performation times, of semiotic – linguistic – non-linguistic materials, grammars of artifacts, modes of propagation of subjectivities, and psychic powers. This leads directly to the fact that a script[36] is never isolated from the collective assemblage of enunciation on which it is based, which allows for the repetition, the

---

35 This further questioning of the "value" of a model can be associated with an evolutionary perspective of the organizations, for which, and in the offshoots of the work of Joseph Schumpeter, the construction of the models is carried out according to a collective learning process, cycles of trial-error-selection-retention of "routines" (internal cycles within companies, or collective cycles). See, for example, [NEL 82]. However, this is an issue of seeing how the "best" elements and the subjective considerations at play are mutually selected within assemblages of "routines", and also consider that a strategic diagram applied in such a company can have a different scope from another, and be totally inadequate.
36 The script as an aggregate and mixtures of complex semiotics, which develops and envelops, deploys its effects to conceal some of its mechanisms (these being the conditions of acceptances and submissions, fluidity and resistances).

regularity, of this particular type of statement. The production process of the statements is therefore always second in relation to this assemblage. But in return, a script as an active entity has the ability to evolve, attract new people and new subjectivity, to set the assemblage in motion.

Take the example of an economic case, or how illustrative the strength of some narratives can be: a script that equates a financial qualification (grade "AA-"), a budget performance of the States and a program of responses (of austerity), comes to disturb not only national economic policies, but rearrange the "narratives" (of governments and commentators, for instance) and the distribution of powers. It goes without saying that the scores given by rating agencies only exercise the power sought to be granted to them by an "economy of opinion" [ORL 00] and the political-economic networks aggregated in their own operation, but, in practice, this script reorganizes the order of the constraints and is brought about in the assemblage, an actant with regard to that which the actors (in this case, governments, for example) did not consider themselves quite so dependent.

The rating agencies are expressions of financial forces, relays, transformers of these forces, and their indicators are fetishes or "faitiches" (or "factishes") [LAT 09]. And as Bruno Latour writes, "This is because (the faitiche) is built in such a way that it is so real, so self-contained, so independent of our own efforts" [LAT 07].

To return to the field of orthodixical immanence, that of speeches and narrations, the medium for the transit, circulation, and transformation of the process of subjectivation, semiotics of energies, libidinal economies, basically, everything that refers to the complexes of passions of the actors, and the micropolitics associated with this, we believe that one of the major issues that has been addressed relatively little by the corpus of management dedicated to the manufacture of consent, is to understand why the actors also act to solidify their own servitude, as if it were their salvation (Spinoza).

## 2.1.3. *Performation: a discussion on the proposed configurations of M. Callon*

The Moeva case is marked by a multitude of trial-events between socio-technical scripts: business scripts, managerial scripts, activity scripts, interface scripts, etc., entering into tense negotiations, confronting their logic and respective legitimacy, sometimes combining to temporarily or locally bring about another apparatus or even ignoring each other, as if they were proceeding forward independently of each other, each one can then find their own account here. As Lyotard develops an agonism of narratives, or "language tricks", he requires us to extend our observation beyond internal communications within the organization.

Here, we will closely follow the approach of M. Callon and F. Muniesa. Of course, discursive activity is essential here, but it is still a matter of taking up the speeches on the use and the digital policies "in their full and complete positivity, not as accompanying speeches, but as constituent elements of the "collective machine" which gives meaning to the technical element. They perform the world and participate in our own self-experimentation; symbolic, imaginary, real" [NOY 06]. There is an entire body of work by linguists in this area, which operates in the midst of processes of transformations between semiotic regimes. We will return to this central point about non-meaningful semiotics[37].

A large array of configurations, marked by dualities, was described in the work carried out by F. Muniesa and M. Callon [MUN 08]. In order to understand the power relationships and tensions that run through the performative assemblages of interest to us here, we attempt to make use of the proposals of these two researchers, to our object, while highlighting the difficulties raised by the perspective used.

First, the authors detect an interconnection between *"theoretical performance"* and *"experimental performance"*. The first is characterized by configurations in which the main challenge is to build a world in the image of a theory, in other words, to insert into a world a set of problems and solutions expressed beforehand in an abstract way into a theoretical body [MUN 08]. In the organizational field that interests us here, in many respects, the examination of a performance, making use of the work of sociology, the management sciences[38] or communication sciences, creating a

---

37 See the approach of F. Guattari, Chapter 3.

38 In this sense, a critical approach to management science has recently been revived. "It questions the nature and purpose of knowledge produced within the discipline, denouncing the "managerialism" of research works which implicitly adopts the same goals as management, and thereby legitimizes them by conferring the "neutrality of technical and scientific status" on them.

"grip" on organizational rationalities (which can function blindly in relation to those of the structures) opens up engaging research issues.

However, these engage in ethnographic works, and the collection of "traces" is eminently consequent, even random: for example, to us, the exercise of a professional association appears too limited, attempting a study on the significance of science of the social human sciences over the course of the training given to its members, their readings, and a collection of this information from interviews conducted with the managing bodies of large organizations. The second, that of experimental performation, is affiliated with processes arising from engineering situations and project designs: "these are more related to engineering situations in which the approach starts from problems and situations" to progressively develop the models, measures, and economic instruments which, if implemented to transform these problematic situations, could provide solutions to the questions presented" [MUN 08]. Forming part of a territory that reaches outside the offices of the company or a sector of activity, this process, as we will see, represents what largely marks the field of immanence of the managerial models and begs an additional question: how do singular projects come to structure the field of analysis and the decision-making of an entire professional body?

Secondly, these authors identify a *"psychogenic performation"* that they relate to beliefs, collective representations or even psychic experiences. In their case, it is a question of considering the economic sciences in terms of "mental, psychological or ideological influence". According to the authors, one may believe in a theory and act in accordance with it, but this is merely a case of influence. We may as well not be interested in it or know it, but be subjected to it through the actions of delegates or special technical apparatus. This is where a *"material performation"* comes onto the scene, in conjunction with the "psychic" processes". The auction market in Plérin-Sur-Mer imposes its logic and prices on hundreds of pig farmers in Brittany who attend each week, who do not question the neoliberal doctrines of the European market; nor do the multitudes of users of the most famous search engine on the Internet wake up every day and question the relevance of the algorithmic model of Google before they surf the web:

---

See the AIMS 2010 conference, Luxembourg, available at: http://www.strategie-aims.com/Events/conferences/2/Round_tables/3/Download_asset and [PAL 10].

"Material equipment is often a vehicle of performativity, as effective as rhetorical conviction" [MUN 08].

The last articulation (or tension) refers to a spatial vision: are we dealing with a "restricted performation", which is confined to a single place (the rules of a company, the rules of a university) or does it apply to a broader assemblage as an "enlarged performation"?

Although this model raises a number of difficulties, we will use it to describe how organizational policies are instilled. But we must quickly specify a few points.

First, the improper use of the term "performation" for the description of processes, which for some has more to do with formatting and a weak constructionism; this is why we preferred to use the concept of scripts in the case of Moeva, like so many framings that act on subjectivities and practices. In our view, a select few of these scripts become organizationally "performative": these scripts "are" the program that they state without being tested to determine whether they are true (scripts of interfaces that impose the "design" of their activities, the project management scripts not queried, etc., on their employees). Others are merely indicators, and run up against one another in discussions and disputes: we have seen, in the case of Moeva, the situation of weakness that injunctions and managerial promises find themselves in.

The second limit, according to us: the configurations are seen didactically [MUN 08]. To us, this seems questionable. In the case of Moeva, we are dealing with several scripts functioning together at the same time, and therefore, to the actions of several performative processes.

Thirdly, the question of time factors and performative paces is essential to be taken into account. And these aren't the only ones – the phenomena of synchronizations and diachronizations are decisive, but the differential ratios between the times of the performative updates make imminent a very strong tension of the effect in the cause (the statements of all Orders). However, according to our authors, the performative sequences appear with a certain simultaneity. Nothing is less secure, and this is itself because of the variations in speed(s) and the slowness of grammars and syntaxes of non-exclusively linguistic statements and the immanent regimes of their effects (internal pragmatics), and the friction of the assemblages themselves (external pragmatics). A few effects of retention and slowdowns are felt; translational effects between the performative paces that stretch and distort the expressions of the transformations operated by the performative assemblages.

The fourth problem of the Callon/Muniesa approach: the agonistic can only then be incomplete, or better yet, can only be a heterogeneity of the fates even if, for them "performative programs intersect and enter into cooperative relations, free or forced, or competitive and sometimes even parasitic" [MUN 08].

On a deeper level, we believe that there are political economies of these scripts, and that it is necessary to examine the global assemblage from which, and within which, the scripts themselves are produced, and therefore create a performative machine that introduces a world to the image of what it prescribes from the various equipments and narratives that it selects and distributes. We cannot rule out that there may be a performation assemblage of the process of producing the scripts itself (for example: how do the theoretical economic models come about?). This is something that may well be questioned in the manufacture of any science [CAL 90]. This is also why the criterion of the territorial scope criterion is irrelevant: the incomplete descriptions must be accepted. As the authors themselves acknowledge, performation "can only be the product of a collective" and it is rarely the issue of a sole figure (perhaps God) that might change the world by its own singular influence.

The intermediate processes, as well as the consideration of the "field of orthodoxical imminence" have been left aside in Callon's perspective. However, the field of orthodoxical immanence must be taken into account. It is here where major productions and transformations with respect to the propagation of psychic powers, the revival of semiotic energies, libidinal economies, and all this participating in the establishment (SOURIAU) of the organizations, etc., occur; without which the "psychogenic" dimensions and the beliefs are, if not misconstrued, then at least misunderstood.

Thus, the entirety of the performative processes is always against the desired assemblages and is constantly open to a possible resistance to alteration-creation processes. Taking after Deleuze and Guattari, it may be said that production-performation is only "the desired production itself under specified conditions" [DEL 72], whether in the case of companies, the struggle of castes, and the specified classes or a study of the conflict of collective intelligence.

By describing that which we refer to as a "general narratique", we are attempting to displace the Callon/Muniesa model and make it more open to other phenomena. The model of expression of the different performations, and thus of the scripts (schematically speaking) is the following.

## 2.2. Digital organizational assemblages: towards a general narratique

### 2.2.1. *Stories: Theorico-orthodox and desirable performations*

We believe that because of the performative processes involved and the difficulties discussed above, the digging of the performative processes (and their heterogeneity) must be supported by a deeper consideration of a general "narratique" such as the context of the conflict of organizational or entrepreneurial narratives.

In order to escape (as much as possible) from the confusion of the "performative turn" found above, this framework relies on specific works, one of which is the analysis by Jean-Pierre Faye on conditions of the emergence of fascism and totalitarian languages, from whom we have borrowed the concept of "narratique" [FAY 72][39]. J. Faye is particularly interested in the effects of narrative: "that which produces the real story" he writes, "may be transformed through storytelling". In particular, we want to show here that *"Narrator and writer" are a single entity and process.*

For Faye, this has to do with going beyond the Poetics of Aristotle, the theory "of the production and circulation of the language of merchandise" called "economics". He continues: "between the registry, closely linked to the birth of linguistics, poetics and that of economics, is the domain of a

---

39 Faye examines the "narratiques" attached to political regimes, their ideas and their role in history, showing how action is engendered by narrative, which he named "the Mably effect".

general narratique: an area of theoretical issues that are those of history itself" [FAY 72][40].

For us, the most decisive part is the description of the techniques of production, the narration of a story (its processes and equipment), the elements of this story given as reality itself, the political economies of this production and their effects, within and as part of assemblages. Introduced in the field of a socio-anthropology of the political economies of the digital domain by [NOY 13], in our perspective, the Narratique stresses the political dimensions (notably agonistic), which one might characterize by an *energetics* of "the collective assemblage of enunciations" [DEL 80].

The different semiotics, taken as a whole, in all their forms and materials (language materials, textual materials, technical materials, digital materials, corporeal materials) are the products of an assemblage that is always collective, which defines the conditions for development, filtering, displacement and updating. The assemblage, in an indissoluble way, is "at the same time a mechanical assemblage for execution and a collective assemblage of enunciation". As such, this principle regulates, using various mechanisms (and not exclusively linguistic ones) the production and distribution of statements, "what is said and exchanged":

> "The statement is the product of an assemblage, which is always collective, and which puts into play, within and outside of ourselves, populations, multiplicities, territories, fates, effects and events" [DEL 96].

The assemblage is a way of thinking of the relationship, the connection, and the composition of relationships "that hold these heterogeneous elements together". The assemblage is defined in particular by the "alliances", "alloys", "attraction and repulsion", "sympathy and antipathy", "alteration", etc., which it facilitates or censors and thus, also by means of the potential

---

40 "Because between the words of the natural languages (through the production and the circulation of keywords, something is designed and is linked to the ideological chaos of languages: the organization of a quasi-language of a political language) [...] It would be impossible to grab hold of this quasi-language through a simple inventory of lexicons. But instead, by introducing itself in this process, in its configurations and its assemblage – its setting – and in the way it transforms itself into different utterances" [FAY 72].

for transformation it allows. It is no longer a question of posing the problem in terms of the spread of technologies, practices, orthodox discourses, cognitive equipment, etc., based on the assumption of a center, but to consider the dynamics, the connections that are aggregated, the relationships between a plurality of actors and localities[41].

These features of the assemblage express a closeness to the phenomena described by the *actor-network theory*, for which we can consider that the approaches have been inherited in some respects from Deleuzian philosophy. Tracing among others in this vicinity, Callon also reiterates the concept to use it as a basis to define performation. It becomes for him – certainly in a very synthetic way – "A set of activities and events that create or modify an assemblage" [CAL 08], a more recently defined perspective in support of several years of research on the economic sciences and which lead him to discuss the potentials for the transformation of the merchant assemblages, the difficult shift of the assemblages, performed by the economy and its equipment, to other configurations [CAL 13][42]. J.-P. Faye also noted, to this effect, "that between the languages of the merchandise and the languages of writing, any attempt to place them into a relationship or correspondence is inadequate if it does not grasp their intersections within the narrative trial. [...] The theory of production in 'The language of merchants' is referred to as 'the economy'" [FAY 72]. Going a bit farther, we will also come across

---

41 To follow Pierre Lévy here, who identifies five dimensions of the machine (and to which we add the organization): "1) *a machine-organization* is directly [...] or indirectly (in most cases) capable of 'self-poiesis' (Varela) or is self-fulfilling (as one may speak of a self-fulfilling prophecy), that is to say, that it helps to prolong the event of the folding to which it owes its existence; 2) *A machine-organization* is capable exo-poiesis: it contributes to producing a world, whole universes of meanings; 3) *A machine-organization* is the result of hetero-poiesis, that is, it is manufactured and maintained by outside forces, since it is formed from a fold. Outside elements are always present there, both genetically and at any given moment; 4) *A machine-organization* is not only formed from the outside (it is the re-folding of a fold), but also open on the outside (these are the edges or the openings of the fold). The machine feeds itself, it receives messages, with several different streams running through it. In short, the machine-organization is desirable. In this respect, all assemblages, all connections are possible from one machine to another; 5) *A machine-organization* is interfacing and interfaced" [LÉV 94]. On these points, see Chapter 3 on interfaces.
42 For his part, Callon states that he reserves the concept of assemblage for the combination of "arrangements + specific actions", the assemblage being "qualified by the type of specific action that is at stake".

the other implications the prism of Deleuzian assemblages has for the analysis of digital pragmatics.

"The general narratique"[43], as Faye calls these declarations, as does Lyotard in some respects, allows us to re-examine the place and function of myths and narratives, in any case, their takeover by a Management class searching tirelessly for narratives like mini-transcendences, weighing on the political and ideological dimensions of the organization over a long history.

Myths, fictions, narratives, and micronarratives operate in the middle of the narrative assemblage as gearboxes-transformers-connectors of legitimacy, and of justification. These are "fabulous" entities, for framing temporal "passersby", the weavers of intensity and desires. It is permissible to think that the work concerning the functioning and effects of narratives and histories in organizations, as they are studied and presented by Yiannis Gabriel, for example [GAB 04], could be reinterpreted in the context that we have just mentioned. "Narratives and histories (as) essential elements of the apparatus for detecting the meaning of the individual and the organization; as characteristics of the organizational policy representing attempts for control and resistance; (like) individual and collective identity elements; (like) symbolic artifacts expressing profound mythological archetypes; finally (like) means of sharing, disseminating and challenging knowledge and learning,"[44] they must be evaluated within the framework of the collective assemblages of enunciation and the mechanistic assemblages that we have mentioned[45].

---

43 "The theory of the production of the writing language, first with Aristotle, and then again, with the Russian formalists, was given the name of "poetics". The theory of production, in the "language of merchants", is named the economy. Between the registry, closely linked to the birth of linguistics, poetics and that of economics, is the domain of a general narratique: an area of theoretical issues that are those of history itself" [FAY 72].

44 [GAB 04] available at: http://www.yiannisgabriel.com/2015/11/narratives-and-stories-in-organizations.html.

45 Here, the works of Foucault and Gramsci are essential, showing the disciplinary power of the narratives, and that still others hold hegemonic power. The organizational and collective identities and their psychic and collective individuals are also narrated, and the narratives that concern them are part of the weaving together of the organization. The circulation of "memes", their phenomena of transmission and percolation, and the substances of expression which serve them as vehicles, play a key role. Similarly, it is important to note that, working more directly on the psychic powers of the actors and mingled with the other narratives, the

All this is fitted, transforms, and differs in the middle of the operational field (professional associations and presses, experts, business advisors, project managers, study organizations, etc.), therefore, rather on the side of the dogmatic constraints, general and normative prescriptions, which tend to define an info-communication and organizational model, based, for example, on the paradigms of "Web 2.0". The result of this performation, which can be described as *theoretico-doxic*, describes an organizational world and helps to bring it about. As we have already suggested, it is already embodied in a collective codification of knowledge, in the repositories of action made available and instituted by various opinion leaders. The operations of "problematization", the "processes of interest", enrollment and "mobilization of allies" (according to the perspective of the sociology of translation), will involve many intermediary entities, including professional associations, "contests"[46], consulting firms, professional works, and other press articles.

### 2.2.1.1. *An example of production on social networks of companies*

Over the period from January 2003 to March 2010, and in relation to the specific actors in magazines for professionals, we have identified more than 800 articles (originating in France) concerning the use of DSNs (digital social networks) by employees, with a very significant growth starting in 2008 (80% of items are produced on or after that year). The "Intranet 2.0" becomes an emerging topic addressed in the corporate or general press starting in 2006[47] and, at the same time, several works intended for managers

---

organizations manufacture narratives using proven forms (also borrowing them from a repository of myths and classic works), playing an essential role in this production. They are great attractors who "precipitate" energies, even if they are abusive to the actual facts. Different gurus and leaders feed their will to power through regrouping their energies acquired from these areas, and the procession of the infinitely small narratives that accompany it.

46 One illustration of this is the Intranet award, organized by Entreprise & Carrières/Les Échos/Cegos since 1998. This apparatus carries the autoconviction of its performative power. In particular, we studied this process in our thesis work.

47 A selection "L'électronique de loisirs se décline dans le monde du travail", *Les échos*, n° 19586, January 18, 2006; "BlueKiwi met les entreprises au Web 2.0", *L'expansion*, May 25, 2007 ; "Le travailleur nomade fait sa migration vers le "mobile 2.0", *Les échos*, May 21, 2008; "Le Web 2.0, un outil de gestion RH", *Silicon.fr*, June 12, 2008; "Les services RH se mettent au Web 2.0," *L'entreprise.com*, April 28, 2009; "L'utilisation des outils Web 2.0 est encore timide dans l'entreprise", *La vie éco*, August 3, 2009; "Comment les entreprises apprivoisent le Web 2.0", *Les échos*, October 13, 2009; "Les réseaux sociaux raniment les intranets", *Usine nouvelle*, March 26, 2010.

address the subject[48]. It is also a heyday for organizing professional symposia and seminars that seek to promote this "Intranet of the future"[49].

We have seen that the social position, the authority, and the power of the enunciator were essential conditions for a performative statement to achieve its ends. It is therefore not the intrinsic quality of the technical innovation that makes it necessary to impose itself, but the value of a set of intermediaries-mediators speaking on behalf of other entities. Thus, theoretico-doxic performation is closely interwoven, in our case, with what Callon and Muniesa call *psychogenic performation* and that which they relate to beliefs, collective representations or even psychic experiences. As opposed to these notions, we prefer the prospect of an assemblage crossed together with subjectivities, intentions, strategies, forces, passions – basically, desires (in the sense of social and desirous production, as considered by G. Deleuze and F. Guattari), thus feeding into a techno-politics of the so-called intranet 2.0 projects. We refer to this process using the term of *desirous performation*. It mobilizes a multiplicity of watchwords, slogans, diagrams and indicators (the spokespersons administer the elements of "evidence" and evaluation apparatus). All of these elements contribute to excavating "temporal and strategic chreodes" [NOY 02], points of passage required from organisational action and nourishing a desire for "revolution" (which nevertheless remains subject to the illusion of control) that is continuously revived.

The commentary made by Deleuze on Foucault's power apparatus should be recalled here. *From the perspective of the assemblages, there is a primacy of desire over power*: "It is not the power apparatus that are trying to form power," but the assemblages. "Inciting, inducing, diverting, making them easy or difficult, broadening or limiting them, making them possible, or more or less probable ... this is a listing of categories of power" [DEL 86].

And these are categories that we can see in action in various places: the offices of a project team, the ranks of an assembly legislating on a law about

---

48 Here's a precursor: "L'Art du management 2.0", *PriceWaterHouseCoopers*; *Les Échos*; *Financial Times*, 2001 [NON 06, ROU 07, HAM 08, CRE 09, JAR 09].

49 "De l'intranet traditionnel aux perspectives de l'Internet 2.0", *Intracom*, Paris, April 2006; "Intranet 2.0 : L'ère du *Peopleware*: retour à l'utilisateur et e-transformation", *Intracom*, Paris, April 2007; "De la révolution dans l'air ; web 2.0 état de l'art", *Intracom*, Paris, March 2008; "Intranet 2.0 et e-Transformation" Intracom, Paris, March 2009; "Entreprise 2.0 Forum : première édition parisienne", March 17-18, 2010, on the suggestion of Bertrand Duperrin.

digital technology or computations and algorithmic treatments of the work applications of an employee. Power apparatus is only one component of the assemblage (and there are others). This permits Deleuze to ask the following question: "Why is power desired?" And similarly, we could question the organized digital policies as follows: "Why are the scripts desired?" And all their procession of prescriptions, injunctions, the flow of imitation between organizations... it is still necessary to include the serrations of desire, not merely at the "molar" level, but to consider – and this requirement is even more imperative in the digital environment – the action of Micropolitics:

> "The semiotic formation of the collective labour force, within the framework of capital-intensive systems, does not depend solely on a central power imposing by the constraint of the operating reports. It also implies the existence of a multitude of intermediairy operations, machines for semiotic initiations and facilitations that can capture the molecular energy of the desires of individuals and human groups. These machines, which come in all kinds and sizes, compete with the same productive-semiotic-libidinal function that we will call: the general function of collective equipment" [GUA 11].

The coupling between the specific language of organizational innovation and the narrative of the digital world produces powerful effects. This coupling immediately becomes a generator of the scripts themselves. This again raises the question of the couplings between the conceptions in the actions of ICT projects and "organizational theories", the need for a re-assembly between "saying so and doing so".

As stated by Jean-Pierre Faye, "between the language of the merchandises and the languages of writing, any attempt to link or match is inadequate if it does not seize their intersection in the narrative trial" [GUA 11]. In passing, a phenomenon is expressed here with strong resonance, a subject of intense discussion in recent months[50], on the performance of economic theories, the capacity of the languages of the

---

50 See for example the controversy created by the book by Cahuc and Zylberberg, their new "scientism" [CAH 16].

economy (theorems, econometrics, etc., stock prices, and the ratings of financial agencies!) to create a world in their image. The perspective of this "general narratique" must also reinforce the exit of the difficulties of all linguistics; "the imperium of the linguistic meaning", as it was described by F. Guattari.

The "stories" that the managerial world generates and give themselves regarding the digital domain are therefore to be examined in view of the assemblage of the desires that run through them. Therefore, the narratique carries particular intensities and presents itself in the form of an "energy machine", which acts at the heart of what could also be described as a "libidinal economy" of management and organization. It is therefore still the reason why we cannot isolate a "psychogenic" character (and a specific performation process), the interpretation of the intermediaries and the recipients of a numerical strategy, the assemblages of desires in which they are already taken and actively involved in other processes.

Borrowing from this intervention, there are standardized modes, with exposure to the narrative, easily identifiable for those who regularly attend seminars and professional events and also, specific processes and narrative regimes. This narrative is a translation: it is an articulation, the creation of relationships between elements that are captured, isolated and converge towards the same purpose of valuation. Each element of enunciation (technical objects, slogans, numerals, etc.) is mutually reinforcing, and taken as a whole, they all constitute a combination of subjectivities, of supports, an association of "localities" (the company in which the project was conceived, the places and situations where the apparatus is used, the other companies brought together as examples, the teams of designers of the technical solutions, the offices of the CNIL or the ISO, etc.). A professional event thus becomes an assemblage of the enunciations-translations by which the filtering and the discrimination of narratives, the process of passage and assembly of narrations, and the simplified and partial presentation of scripts are performed.

Thus, itself taken in a broader assemblage, the narratique is inherent to the digital manufacturing of organizations, and thus consists of the apparatus (the actors, the inputs and processes), the production of the scripts (more) of the contents of these scripts (more) of the actions of the scripts. Depending on the intensity and the combination of the forces circulating within this narratique, it is considered that certain scripts will be of a fully performative nature, and others merely of a *perlocutory* or non-performative nature, the second of these having a propensity to give rise to effects on the interlocutors, but to be scripts that can fail or become exhausted, because the conditions do not allow them to incarnate fully, to update themselves as performative and have to spend Alliances and compromises to achieve their full and complete performative capacity.

---

**An intervention in a professional colloquium: a narrative of innovation at work**

We will now take the example of a presentation that a manager of a large company makes on his intranet apparatus. It is intended for peers as part of a professional event that aims to present "selected" apparatus for their exemplary purposes. The narrative of the digital project carried out (accompanied by the obligatory Powerpoint actant) and from which the achievements are highlighted without real tests (because there are very few arguments). We may observe a script of the production of the narrative (because here there are routines as well), which in this case may mobilize the following elements:

– an organizational environment, a contingency (activities, clients, trades, cultural "markers", project organization, etc.);

– screen copies, online demonstrations of the intranet home page, specific spaces and features, through which the scripts on technical objects are expressed;

– genealogies and schedules (the dating of the "versions" of the Intranet and breaks from the strategy, the project calendar, etc.);

– institutional, prescriptive or coercive norms, laws (which compel or participate in the decision-making, with the law having its own narratique);

– slogans (and there will be plenty of these) and opinion leaders (a quote from a major international firm or other authoritative source);

– other cases of the completion of ICT projects (brought together within the narrative of different companies, evaluated as examples);

– justifications expressing the managerial imperative and the internal rationality of the project;

– statistics (for example, from consultations about its intranet or from study results);

– evaluations (which, in the context of these events dedicated to "cases of excellence", leave little room for the presentation of any malfunctions or self-criticism), etc.

---

**Box 2.1.** *Example of a narrative for the gallery*[51]

---

51 This presentation is reminiscent of the many rules of speech and political technique of Machiavelli, and that we see taken a step further by L. Sandra: The rule of *credibility*, the rule of *similarity or resemblance*, the rule of *the accumulation of examples*.

In both cases, the narratique "sets things in motion," creates "its own associated medium"[52] (we enter the script, it is challenged, it is actuated). It opens up a potential for refreshment, transformation, a kind of interior of the organization, but as an incomplete state within the production process, always subject to its environment. All organizations *are what they do or can do* with what their environments make of them (Von Foertser, Maturana).

### 2.2.2. The narratique: self-referentiality and autopoiesis dimensions

What we are facing here is an environment that is constantly being enticed by the construction of "the theory of its own practice and the practice of its own theory" and proceeding to the "formatting of its own formatting" [CAL 99].

Self-referencing is the key process for describing a situation where the action models are produced by the actors for which they are intended. These programs operate on the basis of an observation and a selection of practices by the environment in which they are established, and they create a "loop" in which the apparatus feeds back into itself. The referential phenomena have an important place at the heart of the general narratique that is at work. And this is especially the case within what we have defined as "Theoretico-doxic scripts", all things that are attached to the narratives and doxas of the professional worlds that "self-institutionalize" themselves as part of seminars, symposia, the activities of associations, or in the interests of professional press articles.

Self-referential phenomena are instead studied in natural or formal languages when a sentence, a statement, refers to itself. Douglas Hofstadter, for example, has insisted in particular on self-referential sentences. Luhmann defines self reference as "the idea that systems are capable of their own operations, of constructing a description of themselves and of observing themselves" [LUH 91][53]. However, the self-referentiality that we indicate here is closer to the process of "experimental performation" of

---

52 With the meaning used by G. Simondon.

53 "Communication et action", partial translation of Chapter 4 of *Social systems* [LUH 95, 11], Réseaux, no. 50, pp. 131–156, November-December 1991, available at: http://louisbasle.unblog.fr/2009/04/14/introduction-a-la-theorie-sociologique-de-luhmann-note/.

Callon/Muniésa in which the processes begin from situaitions of the engineering and design of projects, and conclude by establishing themselves as a model of framing that overhangs other projects. This self-referencing does not have the same characteristics as those possessed by natural languages or formal languages. The self-referencing that is referred to by our approach or that taken by Callon-Muniésa refers to the processes of self-founding and self-legitimation through the performativity of procedures, which feed back into themselves and which are conditions for the emergence of the organization, the conditions of its metastability and permanence. This provides the rationale for our preference of considering autopoiesis as a more relevant concept[54]: this concept of autopoiesis [MAT 80] has been applied very quickly [WHI 95] to the field of companies and organizations. Here, we are effectively facing a situation characterized by multiple feedback loops that ensure the stability of what we may describe as a "machine-organization".

According to our perspective, because of the coexistence of several systems or tools, the relationships of experimental self-reference with other means of expression of the narratique, open to tests that we must consider. And as we have seen from the works of Callon on economics, it is not only a matter of studying the configurations where the academic works on management (and the digital policies of interest to us here) format the managerial practices and subjective factors – (when a project manager builds their world "on the image of a theory") – but also *to examine situations where project managers call for an the attempt at theoretical performation as a possible aggression*. This can therefore be rejected (the theoretical scripts become a-performative, that is, they become sterile). Indeed, what we have seen from the long observation of practices of professional associations, is the never-ending investment of the managerial world in works of legitimation: of course, a researcher can be "invited" in an exceptional way to the gallery of a professional event; of course, these people may be there to provide an intellectual assurance for the observatories of "digital transitions" or "e-organization". But this does not in any way interfere with the work of affirming a position which is intended

---

54 For living systems, Varela assigned a high priority to the concept of autopoiesis, with all others being considered by him as a kind of allopoiesis [VAR 89]. See this question again in Chapter 3 on interfaces.

as self-founding for its repositories of actions and its "good practices". It is thus considered that the recruitment of the researcher, as someone potentially critical and therefore dangerous for the maintenance of its legitimacy, can form part of the interplay between the relationships of power between narratiques: the academic world is integrated into its own apparatus to better reassert the power of that apparatus.

On the other hand, the examination of a performation of the management sciences operating on organizational rationalities (which can function blindly in relation to that of the structures) allows for ambitious research to be opened. Some works related to the current *Critical Management Studies* are attempts to analyze the effects of the production of intellectual grids and multiple instruments on the practices and functioning of organizations[55]. One programme on the performativity of science and organizational transformations even involves a much broader disciplinary approach: the relationship between information and communication sciences (in France, this is the field known as "Organizational Communication") and management practices, neuroscience and behavioral marketing, the sociology of work, and the management of human resources, even between the business world and philosophy (since this area sees a reliable interest in every "crisis")[56]... are very much involved.

However, such research involves ethnographic work and the collection of "traces" that are very clear consequences of these. Once again, we could argue for an empirical approach, and for research that would have the advantage of not assuming that the only analysis of "academic" quotes and references in works "classified" as professional would be sufficient to learn about the pragmatic efficiency of theoretical bodies. It should be noted from this point of view that approaches using complex infometrics, intended to

---

55 We can refer, for example, to the critical analysis of *New Public Management* in the public sector [BAR 09].

56 "After the attacks last January [in France], many patrons also challenged philosophers on the issue of secularism," notes Isabelle Barth, director of the EM Strasbourg. With issues in the background such as freedom of religion in the company, intercultural management, the expression of individual singularities within the teams... "Philosophy can help managers take a broader view on their practices, and manage situations of conflict," says Isabelle Barth, in "When philosophers meddle in businesses", 2015, available at: http://www.capital.fr/Carriere-management/dossiers/When-les-philosophers-make-barging-in-les-entreprises-1063355.

free up sociocognitive structures, internal pragmatics, and the internal-external system of relationships of these fields would be particularly useful. They alone may make it possible to understand the connections between the internal pragmatics of the field and the external pragmatics of other fields and other actants. And therefore, to give autopoietic approaches their full consistency, the strength of the phenomena of translations and the role of borders as interfaces with their productivity.

If such (rather complex) reflections have already been carried out on some of the major structural programs of the twentieth century (i.e. Fordist models, quality approaches, approaches to knowledge management and its procession of translations in *Knowledge Management*, innovation approaches, etc.), in many ways, they still have yet to be carried out in the area of digital policy. The implementation of such research can be very random if we do not stick to what the actants say. Indeed, at no time during the Moeva project, largely described over the course of its years of development, was there any reference made to any academic theory or "great thinker".

We have already referred to the limits of a case of internal communication managers engaging with a researcher in a reflexive exercise, in order to identify "their sources" of inspiration in the humanities. Such a weak expression of the theoretical performativity reinforces our hypothesis of a self sufficient managerial narratique and is also related to the functioning of the decision-makers, who are partially blind to the factors that shape their choices (even after having graduated from the major schools of management or universities).

It is, therefore, necessary to turn once again to equipment, apparatus for evaluation, standards, procedures, and micropolitics to follow the "traces" that these connection lines leave. The skepticism of some works in the management sciences also confirms the self-founding *temptation* of the organizational world. In this sense, the researchers are given the task of being alert to "the nature and purpose of knowledge produced within the discipline, denouncing the "managerialism" of research works which implicitly adopts the same goals as management, and thereby legitimizes them by conferring the "neutrality of technical and scientific status" on them."[57] This reversal of forces, favoring the managerial scripts, operates on the feedback enclosure of the desired narratique[58].

These phenomena show the strengthening of a general movement over the past 30 years, which is no longer just a matter of the self-imposed professional convictions in the legitimacy of their own knowledge, of the influence of professional expertise on entire areas of public decision-making[59], the blurring of the border zones between laymen and experts, and between "opinions" and "scientific knowledge" (in all cases, these are gathered within the same space), but more generally, the observation that has already been made a long time ago, on the complication of roles and statutes, of a science that has lost its institutional character and has become less trusted [LAT 11, LAT 12][60].

And the rise in power of professional associations is not the only culprit[61]. Countering the "managerialization" of research and higher

---

57 See the AIMS 2010 conference in Luxembourg and [PAL 10]; see the issue of the magazine *Sciences de gestion* on the impacts of its research, 2016, available at: https://www.cairn.info/revue-francaise-de-gestion-2016-8.htm.

58 Example from the CIGREF, which for five years has been asking researchers to provide white papers, either through studies or interviews – and the same holds for the observatory of corporate social networks becoming "think thanks of the digital transition" and their numerous academic guests and reading advisors – see the "business sector that mobilizes ECs to do seminars for managers", the "Digital renaissance" with Christine Balague of Telecom Management ... Thus, what we are addressing are "hydrides", which change themselves to create linkages between businesses and the university (the subject is no longer the inverse relationship).

59 For Robert Castel, "Mandated expertise" is used to describe the use of specialized knowledge to break through a problematic situation" and the expertise that is established, the situation where "the assistance expert becomes a partner and even the principal partner in the decision process" [CAS 91]. See these questions in the case of the transformation of universities, their cost-cutting measures and the affirmation of expertise as a new method of university regulation [GAR 08]. On the "managerialization" of the University and the implementation of *New Public Management* [MER 12].

60 For Latour, there is a need to examine objectivity (or "rationality") starting from its concrete conception. While we were heirs to a conception of objectivity that involved "the suppression of one aspect of the self, and that was 'opposed' to subjectivity", Latour indicates that we can no longer think of them as one against the other: our situation is one of "subobjectivity". See [DAS 12]. See also [LAT 12].

61 Not content with having mobilized an army of "practitioners" who represent the majority of the actors among the masters, we can only find the blindness of some senior curriculum

education, the critical approaches of the organization, labor, communication apparatus, and recently, the management sciences themselves (under the label of *Critical Management Studies*[62] and their educational component, *Critical Management Education*) warn of an increasingly subordinate relationship of theory with regard to practice, or even a submission to solely financial ends[63]. The construction of these strategic narratiques (the problematization and the creation of a repository of decisions) is a script that runs through the managerial realm. If they can build a base of "academic" theories, from relatively extensive networks, it is nonetheless difficult to see their explicit mobilization[64] (whether in the field observations made on the repository of a project group or within professional events). Some researchers in the management sciences and in information systems themselves recognize the difficulty for the works produced within their discipline to extract themselves from professional narratives on such issues as the modes of conduct and the assistance for reorganization of the organizations associated with technologies:

"[...] The academic literature has its own ambiguities in this area, because it is reluctant to engage in the debate on the strategies of organizational transformation, as if the answer to this question did not fall under a scientific approach, and that only the practitioners had the standing to give their point of

managers to be deplorable, going so far as to mock the supposed "jealousy" of teachers and researchers of their professional colleagues.

62 "Critical Management Studies (CMS) has become remarkably successful in establishing itself as an alternative voice among management scholars; so successful, in fact, that it now has its own well-attended conference, a division within the Academy of Management and numerous handbooks; with the publication of a collection of "classic" readings" [ALV 11]. See also [CLE 11].

63 Sociologist Vincent De Dasarraju, in his work, criticizes a form of management based more on efficiency than on the relevance of ideas; management experts present themselves as the prescribers of normative models. "Management in itself is not flawed, but it perverts itself as soon as it positions human beings as a resource for the enterprise. The ideology of management is characterized by a series of beliefs and a certain worldview that present themselves as rational; however, this ideology maintains an illusion, and legitimizes profit as its end goal" [DEG 05].

64 Instead, we find traces here of another movement, one already developed in the nineteenth century, for example by J.B. Say (1767–1832) who, on the basis of the experimentation of "the industrial or manufacturing economist", promotes the creation of theories based on solutions for managing the company found upstream and on the ground.

view. Based on assumptions about the nature of organizational inertia, research only sees fit to make general policy recommendations" [BES 11].

In our view, there is less urgency to  point out the risks – which are nevertheless very real – of "the alignment of education and its institutions with nothing more than the interests of private enterprises" [HUA 11][65], that is to say, a search for operationality and "placing students on the market" who have instrumental skills that are supposed to be able to be directly mobilized, than to refuse the displacement in which academics are defined as laymen and professionals have earned a supposed expert status from a sudden "reflexive modernity" [HUA 11] and by the contradictory debate (to which very little is added by the unions, in particular regarding the digital issues that concern us here). Rare but stimulating proposals, following the work of J. Rancière and the placing of the challenges in a political economy of knowledge, propose to "escape from the self-referentiality of the discipline [of management] to open it up to the divergences brought by other disciplinary fields [...], and then the issue would only be that of pedagogy, the place of management in society, its role as a tool of control, [can] then be questioned through the creation of controversial spaces" [HUA 11]. We may agree that while the scenes of the managerial praxis remain unfavorable to the dissensus, the scenes of the university amphitheatres would be at least as unfavorable (and become so again).

## 2.2.3. *Narrative and celebratory practices (examples of intranets)*

The practices of events, conferences, contests and charts are characteristic of what we call a celebratory apparatus, in which desirous productions also run through. Here, as elsewhere, we have seen that the work of adoption, distribution, updating, of one model or the other, is partly supported by a production of narratives and watchwords that move, with help in particular from the translators equipped with a strong visibility (governmental bodies, opinion leaders, professional associations, suppliers of technological solutions, business managers with visibility, other managers, etc.). In the sociology of translation, translators are actors in which a large number of connections relate to each other, and whose interactions with other actors

---

65 On reflexive modernity, see the works of Ulrich Beck, Anthony Giddens, and Scott Lash.

materialize through a varied mixture of *intermediaries* that they put into circulation[66]. The intermediaries are both "supports and agents of the definition of the actors".

To illustrate, at this stage, another expression of the self-referential nature of this digital policy manufacturing, we reconsider the case of intranet strategies, the model that adopted the name "e-organization" and the role of the professional associations, the powerful intermediaries in this area. Urged on by the demand to break away from earlier models, "digital organization" has equipped itself with its own promises, slogans and "valuers". Its juries and its celebratory bodies have intervened.

In this way, in the 2000s and in the past, the Intranet award was designed to "reward and promote exemplary and innovative intranets"[67]. The ranking was done by a selection process based on three indicators: innovation, usability and return on investment. The winning companies, and therefore the "exemplars" (a title to which the project leader of Moeva laid claim) are of course featured in press articles and at conferences and other professional events. The difficulty of the apparatus in evaluating the cases presented from a single file provided by the project managers is rarely noted, considering that, as the officials themselves admit, these criteria remain eminently subjective (innovation is renamed "novelty" within the narrow circle of organizational ICTs; the analyses of the files are carried out based on two readings of a document prepared by the Project manager) and unstable (the incessant search for an operational model of calculating the ROI[68] of the Intranet is a managerial holy grail). Similarly, "The Intranet Observatory" develops classifications widely promoted to members of associations, at conferences, and of course, is a "theoretical" reference figure for intranet prices. The encouragement to adopt new managerial and technological scripts, and thus new intranet policies, is repeatedly associated with the standardized categorizations of the e-organization proposed from an "evolutionary" perspective. It is not just a simple metaphorical process. We have seen many cases in which the principle of the deployment of intranets

---

66 From the perspective of ANT, each intermediary describes himself as a network: a set of human or non-human, individual or collective entities and relations between these entities, "the actors inter-defining themselves by the intermediaries they put into circulation; "The social aspect is read in the inscriptions that are healed by the intermediaries".

67 Conceived by the professional newspaper *Entreprise & Carrières* and the firm Cegos.

68 Return On Investment.

for presenters has been used, leading to an automatic transformation in the organizational worlds, since the latter result from the numerical tools that are deployed there. The appearance of any new item or event, in terms of applications and digital management, becomes a reason for a "progressive push", without this push ever being questioned.

During the conferences, the modes of exposure and the mechanisms of narratives are repeated (there is a script of the narration itself). As L. Sfez recalls from Machiavelli, for whom all politics is fragile and must be constructed following an optics of artificialism (and not from Nature, according to him), it is necessary to give consistency to actions and organizations. The following stated rules are just as much an effort to create this consistency as soon as the politics take effect. Among these, we may note the rule of *credibility*, which requires Machiavelli's Prince to ensure his actions are within the framework of the plausible; the rule of *similarity or resemblance*, which requires any act or speech to base its credibility on similar and well-known actions or speeches from the past; and also the rule of *accumulation of examples*, examples that are taken from history and therefore absent, but a large number of which allows for a demonstration; and finally, the rule of *passion*, which suggests that the Prince should be passionate about the content of his speeches, in order to strengthen their credibility, even if this passion is not genuine [SFE 02].

The effectiveness of a script and its desirable level of power are thus ensured by:

– the power of the instances that act within and through the assemblage by the links that unite them;

– the process of self-simplification they propose, in response to the complexity faced by decision-makers (the delegation and legitimation of decisions based on scripts);

– the drawing down of innovation processes and organizational strategies to substantial, typefied ideal forms. Determinism and probabilities are the law.

The narrative is still mirrored by the evolutionary ideal (of which we have not discussed the principle of selection which predominates here, namely within itself)[69] by the development of a genealogy: the 1st, 2nd, 3rd and 4th generation intranet. Starting in the mid-2000s, this last category is characterized by the "participative web" and "2.0 technologies" which were called on to be established by 2010 (which did come to pass partially, but the overpowering interest in corporate social networks beginning in 2012–2013 was not sufficiently taken into account).

On this basis, a general criteriology of intranets is established. The formation of classifications located on a time scale in this way establishes reference scripts, "standards", in relation to which typefied ideal organizations themselves will be located ("They're late"/"They're early"; "Precursors, stragglers, the wait-and see crowd")[70]. After being established and becoming benchmarks, these classifications have a propensity to direct the memories, to act as decision supports and, as Mary Douglas points out, are part of dynamic processes acting on the psyche: for Douglas, institutions "direct our emotions to a standardized level, on subjects that themselves are standardized." We may add to this the fact that they lay claim to being righteous and they propagate their respective influences (which are corroborated) through all levels of our information system. Thus it is no wonder that they train us to follow their narcissistic self-contemplation [DOU 89]. Thus, the evolution of the e-organization is described by this repression of the generations as they become obsolete and the order of innovation as uncertainty, which goes through datings presupposing an isomorphism between the organizational form and the technological form. In addition, it was not uncommon in the 2000s to see collections of companies establishing themselves as "pioneers" and *precursors* in the field of digital apparatus, ignoring the passage of an entire line of creations and practices beyond the scope of companies (many of which do not understand the already long history of collaborative apparatus within the networks of researchers, for example).

---

69 At the end of the 2000s, a blog for Intranet managers (B-rent) asked its contributors to pick out who had been the "big players of the intranet". Apart from the collective itself (quoted first), the result of this process shows how professionals attribute significant value to associations, prices (Ujjef, Cegos/Entreprise & Carrières), consultants (active members of the network), projects and achievements of their "peers" (other intranet managers (France Telecom, Elyo, Groupama, BNP Paribas, the United Nations Intranet manager referred to by an English consultant, etc.)).

70 Classification of organizations by type of intranet, according to the findings of the Intranet Observatory of 2006.

By organizing the retentions and filtering, by prescribing redundancies within normative and honorary apparatus, the activities of professional associations create this imperative for the adoption of one standard or another, a recurring and legitimizing imperative (used in order to obtain budgets from its management, for example) with strong powers of "sympathy" and seduction. The actors build stories that compensate for the weakness of critical analyses, substitute for a relative complexity, in order to provide themselves with a world that is tailored to their own desires. The stories of the e-organizations or the digital enterprise create a collective cognitive map enriched with generic scripts, and are criss-crossed by watchwords which then proceed with as many projections of a managerial universe that seeks to break with a previous model.

As we have shown on many occasions, the manufacturing of digital policy is therefore inseparable from the manufacturing of its own story. Here, the most notable parts of the story are the cases that assume the status of "good practices" and those that recognize them, value them, bring them into a fiction where the digital component (regardless of the unique aspects of each project) paves the way forward for the models to come. The affectations themselves of a desire for models and to relocate processes of imitation at the heart of the processes of innovation are engineered by various "evaluation" and "institutionalization" apparatus.

Sometimes, it's true, professionals call for a distancing from "charming speeches" and then the model that is taken up becomes a topic of questioning, a topic for the next conference: "Intranet 2.0 and blogs: should we succumb to this temptation? What are the risks of corporate blogs? Should everyone be allowed to take the stage at the company?[71] "In this case, detaching from the collective standard becomes a condition for the acceptance of the projects: an argument is made for the necessary adaptations of the technical choices to the specific contingency of the organization, as in the case of Moeva, where at the time of defining a strategic bias and a choice of solutions, the project group said they wanted to "think for themselves"! But the scripts march on, the scenes and imagery from professional events continue, supported by an endless parade of case studies and 15-minute testimonies, "and there's always a Powerpoint to back them up!"

---

71 New tools and old threads, conferences with an intranet manager during the program of the University of the French Association of Internal Communication, Paris, March 21 2006.

Similarly, an entire assemblage has been established around the watchword of Enterprise 2.0, where the same actors of the "intranet" world of the 2000s and new professional associations that find the opportunity to occupy a specific media space, and one that, for some, will be extended in a few years (as the "2.0" niche was narrow and going out of style) to a more holistic reflection on the strategic transitions in a digital context. The same processes and performative equipment do their job: the narratique regime remains in place. What we are addressing here is a codification of knowledge, the establishment of repositories of action carried out by new events, "barometers"[72] and a multitude of spokespersons, instituting, at a minimum, opinion leaders, or even "Organizational transformation thinkers". Each grouping of professions can claim the right to be the custodian of this expertise, and to speak "on behalf of organizational assemblages". Here, the Association of Information Systems' Director says: "Our network of large companies has the mission of promoting digital culture as a source of innovation and performance" and the ambition to be "a crossroads of information, reflections, exchanges, and orientations on the company at the heart of the digital world"[73]. In this area, on *digital project managers*, "managers 2.0" or managers of intranet and digital policy portals: The Association "addresses, among other things, large companies, ministries and organizations confronted with internal digital transformation issues. A true 'think tank' in the digital age, the observatory aims to promote the sharing of good practices with a group dynamic. Its goal is to shed light on the digital transformation of organizations, going beyond any commercial or technical approach"[74].

Under these conditions, the scripts continue on to filter a simplifying and foundational reflexive process of a managerial machine that selects its *best*

---

72 The dominant methodology: self-reported online surveys given to project managers themselves. The barometers used by the Observatory and studies on social networks, available at: http://www.obsdesrse.com/category/publications/etudes-sondages/.
The barometers of the Intranet Observatory and E-transformation are available at: http://www.etransformation-intranet.com/.
73 Businesses 2020 in the digital age: Issues and challenges, report of the Cigref, Association of Information systems directors and large companies, 2016, available at: http://www.cigref.fr/publications-numeriques/ebook-Cigref-Enterprise-2020-issues-challenges/files/assets/common/downloads/entreprise% 202020.pdf.
74 The observatory of corporate social networks, 2017 presentation, available at: http://www.obsdesrse.com/category/articles/management-2-0/.

*practices* (its benchmarks), which tends to reduce innovation to its most essential forms of the ICT/organization pairing. Translated in this way, the script operates within the realm of opinion, in the field of the immanence of orthodoxy, and becomes no longer the expression and expressed material of an assemblage open to the future, but of "apparatus" organizing the redundancies and replications that are prescribed. But *the desire is for imitation or "normative and mimetic isomorphism"*[75]. *The "experimental performation", the storytelling of experiments, the filtering of cases (feedback from experiments), and the production of theoretico-doxic scripts all form part of a single process.*

It would be appropriate give a more detailed examination of the replications, redundancies, constraints, and combinatorial actions that the scripts carry out, and examine them in terms of the capacities of alterations and transformations that they may generate, the place they offer for future outcomes:

> "Becoming something new can never be an act of imitation, neither doing something like something else, nor complying with a model, whether of justice or truth. [...] Future outcomes are not phenomena of imitation, nor of assimilation, but of a double capture, of non-parallel evolution, of a marriage between two kingdoms" [DEL 96].

This perspective implies that all the lines and tensions found in performation/creation should be taken into account as early as the microprocesses of innovation and micro-outcomes in the assemblage that generally favors their distribution.

The narratique becomes consubstantial to the apparatus of organizational capture and the words associated with it (the design of such an application, the requirements of the editors, the applications and programs of these

---

75 In the theory of organizations and neo-institutionalist approaches, Powell and DiMaggio have described situations of convergences of behavior between organizations forming part of the same *field, processes defined as institutional isomorphisms. They distinguish normative* isomorphisms (involving the professionalization of the actors); mimetic isomorphisms (the tendency by which different things imitate one another to be perceived as more legitimate); *coercive* isomorphisms (operated by the state, law, public funding, etc.) [DIM 83].

applications, the practices of different users, the successes and internal debates, etc.). The connections between these worlds that have been brought into play, as seen in the case of Moeva or in the case of the experiments highlighted here that testify to the reciprocal relations, of the "effects of the presence of certain places transported to others" [LAT 06]. Professional associations then present themselves as one of the bodies that code over the spaces of the offers involving technology, engineering, experimentation, knowledge, and subjective elements, which leave lines running through the plan of the reflexivity of the actors on their digital policies and on the organizations they bring in according to the value they attribute to them at a given time.

### 2.2.4. *Hetero-poietic narratives connected to outside forces*

In the case of Moeva, we have identified the formation of the scripts inherent to the organization at the same time, and linked them to their "foreign policy", the policies that give rise to them and feed into them. It is in this sense that we envisage these formations from a point of view of heteropoesis. Here, we adopt both the perspective of Pierre Levy as quoted earlier, and that of the sociology of translation, for which the translation expresses the gradual transition "from local negotiations between micro-actors to more stabilized sets of macro-actors". Similarly, the development of strategic scripts based on the evolution of the practices and functionalities of the internet, as well as the digital experiences and practices of employees, their learning, as "experiential performance", will serve as points of support for us.

As we have already indicated, the assemblage (as a case of cooperation between varying actors) is, on one of its sides[76], a collective assemblage of enunciation, and this is responsible for settling, under various mechanisms (and not exclusively linguistic ones), the production and distribution of the utterance in a given organizational field. In this perspective, the script is a complex actant of performance, which forces us to think about the processes of standardization as objects or border areas, such as capturing devices, ensuring the translation processes, the processes of variation that accompany them, and opening up the possibility of bringing together a varied mix of people.

---

76 As Deleuze tells us, an assemblage "is both an assemblage of execution and a collective assemblage of enunciation", with these two being inseparable [DEL 96].

The problem of any organization and any collective (of any assemblage) is thus that of creating neighboring zones between several varied apparatus, taken together within a block of outcomes on their behalf, and more or less controlled. And it should be addressed in the midst of the broader assemblages within which it is included, and of which it is also the expression and the material that is expressed. This, therefore, gives rise to a study of the conflicts between the scripts, the processes of alteration-creation that inhabit them, and they can be caught in the turmoil of the controversies and the outlying updates that are generated against them, but with everything against them as well.

The scripts are vehicles and paths, producers and trajectories. We have already noted that they produce the surrounding area associated with them. And it is their own actualization and meeting with other scripts/micro-worlds that opens up the possibility for variations, innovations, and also sometimes the possibility for the conditions of their own dismantlement. The question at hand is not whether the managerial, organizational and more broadly speaking, the sphere of info-cognitive capital, promotes the expression of new lines of individual and collective subjectivation at the heart of the most localized innovation processes, but regarding what nature this expression would be, and what cognitive and libidinal economy would be activated?

We have presented the script as producers of apparatus of capture of varied actors, affectations, and different desires that confront each other at the very center of design projects. The effort that should be made would be that of observe the movement of scripts by considering the resonance between levels of scale, the association of "the local and the global", and therefore, to envisage the potential capacity of the project actors, their individual subjectivity, to confront the available scripts and to alter them to create new ones. Or, as considered under the perspective of G. Tarde, the submission of individual representations is not "from the top down", through a collective consciousness, but "from the bottom up", at the infinitesimally small level of beliefs and desires. These "imitate each other, and in this imitation, they combine with or oppose each other, neutralize or strengthen themselves" [TAR 01].

Basically, a morphogenesis should be done in order to have a grip on mechanisms of techno-political individuation of the scripts. This would then make a real political economy of management possible, an exit from the concept of governance. But we still have a long way to go for that.

To further illustrate these extended trajectories and convergences within the narratiques of heterogeneous elements, let us take other examples that show that the fundamental nature of the policies and apparatus designed is one of heteropoiesis.

---

**The software offering: technical performation is distributed and celebrated!**

As we have seen in the Moeva case, the unique practices and desires of an organization can be registered, solidified and distributed in the technological offerings of the publishers. Based on their client references, they will be able to demonstrate (and strengthen) the legitimacy of their solutions: the cases that are presented are, of course, "cases of excellence". Choosing one or the other of these offers means espousing the organizational model embodied in the functional characteristics of the tool (in its programming lines).

This program of professional actions, this script of activity assisted by the Intranet system, is the result of an aggregation of contingencies and heterogeneous practices of other organizations whose publisher derives a temporarily established "consensus" from them, and offers the optimum level of commercial potential. This consensus (which can be said to be the embodiment of a meta-stable state) allows for the establishment of a "standard" offer to respond, after some iterations, to the configurations and requirements most frequently formulated by future clients. The Moeva intranet would then achieve an unprecedented participation in the enrichment of the technical-functional script: the choice would apply to the offering of a publisher, but this one would be subject to a long specifications list, demanding specific developments. Thus, by appropriating the activity scripts from other locations, via the standard established on the basis of projects previously conducted, the intranet scripts in this part become "isomorphic" to those of other organizations, and at the same time, by in return allowing the publisher to capitalize on the specific developments that will be made for the Moeva Intranet, those being the contexts and practices related thereto that are put into circulation and available to other potential customers.

In the same way, the project manager will participate directly in the apparatus for the Moeva case to be prescribed to its professional environment: it will conduct conferences within professional associations and present its apparatus to the "rankings" of the best intranets organized by the magazine *Entreprise & Carrières*. These actions are explicitly subject to a search for the legitimation of organizational practices, based on instances identified by "experts". We are in a situation of inter-couplings between performation processes that are experimental (the design emanating from a project), technical, and celebratory. These recovery approaches will be marked by an intentional erasure of the many tensions and criticisms that have stood out in the Moeva project. The debates then become about the three dimensions described above. From a political point of view, the integration of the various subsidiaries into the scheme, which is legitimized by a speech on the effectiveness and sharing of an "intercultural" richness, runs up against a question of the inclusion imposed on the system in a context where each subsidiary claims its specificity and where the intranet plays a symbolic role in the group's real formation (the project is launched during a period of reorganization).

While order-words invoked are "autonomy" and "decentralization", a system of direct or delegated control (on directors by subsidiaries) and for the tacit evaluation of users (with the headquarters taking the opportunity to be able to monitor the practices offered by the tool), is also put in place. Since the strategic and political challenges cannot be envisioned, the controversies essentially involve the functional aspects, the operational gains (it then becomes much easier to challenge them since no one evaluates them over several years), on the relevance of the standardization of practices (the script of the tool that imposes the design of common repositories, weakening business identities, which necessitates the creation of management processes perceived as contradicting the "realities" on the ground).

On the margins, the requirement for the sharing of informational capital between users is also criticized in terms of its feasibility: the end-user does not want to think of the technical apparatus as a delegated manager of an entire array of varied, untraceable processes, that had previously been processed by "humans" (a controversy that expresses the negotiation of a transfer of skills from the employee to the technical object).

**Box 2.2.** *Technical performation celebrated and distributed in the case of Moeva*

### The movement of Web 2.0 within the company

The importation within the organizational digital spaces of Web 2.0 apparatus thus marks the advent of what has been described as a new disruption. In the 2000s, only a few months separated the recommendations of the *Work Foundation*[77], favoring the adoption of a *social software* within organizations and popularization of the concept of "Web 2.0" by Tim O'reilly[78]. In 2007, the celebrated American firm Gartner proclaimed that "the era of Enterprise 2.0 has arrived"[79] and the economic forecasts, which were attached to this

---

77 "You don't know me but... Social capital and social software," Work Foundation, British Institute of researchers and Practitioners, January 2003.

78 The expression *social software* was widely adopted over the course of the year 2002 in the United States, referring to a significant growth of the "user-oriented" applications on the Internet and their social dimensions, but it was launched in earnest at the techno-economic networks in April 2003 at the O'Reilly Emerging Technology Conference, held in Santa Clara. By 2005, the concept of "Web 2.0" appeared to have become preferable and was instituted by Tim O'Reilly [ORE 05]. Far from stabilizing, there would then be a certain neglect of the term "2.0" (among large firms such as Gartner or Forrester) today.

79 "Predicts 2010: Social software is an enterprise reality", available at: https://www.gartner.com/doc/1243515/predicts--social-software-enterprise.

industry of the "social web", whether on the Internet or in business, were presented to us as a market with very high potential for the operations of "Problematization", the "process of interessement", enrollment and "mobilization of the Allies" (from the perspective of the sociology of translation), will involve many intermediary bodies; including professional associations, "contests", consulting firms, professional works, and other press articles[80]. As we have seen, each entity works in its position of authority and then ensures the conditions for its performativity to prosper. They put one of the key processes of innovation to the test, namely, that it is not the intrinsic quality of the technical apparatus which makes it necessary for it to impose itself, but the value in which a set of intermediaries/mediators is found to be invested, which speak in the name of other entities. Thus, the movement within organizations of Internet-network apparatus (blogs, wikis, digital social networks, etc.) seems to be accompanied by an emphasis on the illocutionary domain, and unlimited marketing.

In France, the conferences and works have largely been carried out on this subject, and "visionary" speakers continue to format the perception of a socio-technical era, of the coupling of "technogenesis" and "sociogenesis" [STI 96], advocating the archetypal model that forms the "organization 2.0". Deterministic promises determinists and normative genealogies of intranets, glorified rites of "good practices" carried out by associative actors or media bodies, order-words relating to the breakdown of management strategies and info-communication: all of this helps to contribute to building a state of emergency. However, the strategies and practices branded as "social software" or 2.0, as part of their integration into a normative digital territory (the intranets), still continue to be discussed at length for a few months. Behind the apparent consensus, and within the project management and teams, a lively debate is held on the adoption of solutions 2.0 and the socio-technical scripts that accompany them (the "Facebook" model).

This debate was also driven and constrained to a large extent by the "free exposure" of employees and professional communities on digital social networks, blogs, or discussion forums (the last of which continues to be used). The social web in business has a fundamentally political nature: the establishment of a "corporate social network" is a question of testing the hypothesis of a possible movement of employees from the web to the intranet, where debates on working conditions would be less exposed. For other projects, this is an opportunity to reinforce possible collaborative dynamics, or to initiate a new way of sharing knowledge[81].

**Box 2.3.** *Narratique of Web 2.0 in the organization*

---

Prediction for 2008: "Enterprise 2.0 will become a $4.6 billion industry by 2013 and social networking tools will garner the bulk of the money, according to a report by Forrester Research", available at: http://www.forrester.com/rb/Research.

80 See section 2.2.1.1.

81 See section 3.2.

The formatting systems are always in a state of tension brought on by the combinations of closings and openings, though not symmetrically: creation and innovation can no doubt be carried out only against these constraints, even by phenomena of "resistances" (so decried by management), by the expression of relationships of forces that they will engender. The latter constitute the collective assemblage of subjectivation, where the forms of powers slip by being too inclined to clog the lines opened in this way. It also implies accepting that the "technical innovation" and the "leap" (whether radical or marginal) that can result, are consubstantial with the emergence or association/imitation of deviations and other workarounds. If these phenomena are as much recognition of the margins of autonomy of the actors and their free spaces, they also operate as a forum that tends to make the actors themselves the managers of their own submission or domination. These points are delicate, and should be addressed in a more vigorous way.

Indeed, from a synthetic point of view, our approach, always in line with the way digital networks are deployed, affirms the conclusions of Peter Sloterdijk (and a few others), that the technology is – always – opportunely and effectively, "a mode of unveiling"[82] social, cognitive, and political developments. The German philosopher asserts as "a basic philosophical and anthropological theorem, that man himself is fundamentally a product, and can only be understood if we look, with an analytical mind, at his mode of production" [SLO 00].

It is therefore impossible to define or characterize the power of the performative process from a more or less adequate incarnation in relation to a model or a potential of this same process. Performative productivity is expressed within the same movement of its actualization, an updating process that is constantly differentiating itself from this movement. When we ask ourselves whether one performative process or the other is actually followed and carried out, we have, in *stricto sensu,* completely missed the mark. Our judgement is thus based on the belief that the performative action, in being updated, is transparency from one self to another.

To ask the question of whether such a model, such a technical script, or whether such theories or "prophecies" meet the conditions for success necessary for its effective self-realization [MER 49], is tantamount to giving up the radical nature of our approach, which consists of thinking and

---

82 Heidegger, cited by Peter Sloterdijk.

analyzing the Performation as Immanence. Whether something works or not, that our intentions and desires are found to conflict, the dissonance with the power of the performative vortex, this is ultimately included in this power. It is the same with our "polemology" in the study of the conflicts between the scripts. *Ad infinitum.*

The technogenesis-socogenesis coupling actualizes and differentiates itself as a "milieu" where there is, in a sense, an identity between organic and non-organic individuals, registration machines, desiring machines. Following that, the *Anti-Oedipus* – we could say, at the limit – that the performation in the sense that we understand it, "is only desiring production itself under specific conditions" [DEL 72], that is according to the scripts in the same movement of the codetermination of technogenesis/sociogenesis that they express, and from which they are also derived!

And the minor innovations are based on the assemblages within which they are included, and the coupling of autopoiesis, the latter regulating the relations with the outside (their environment) and defining the modes of activation of a particular state that is internal to the assemblages. There is a close connection with the internal processes of alteration-creation that sometimes create favorable conditions for the powers of innovation and their modes of propagation. Without a guarantee of their strength, their percolation, without a guarantee of seeing them switch to a new assemblage.

All this leads us to expand on the empire of innovative reason.

### 2.2.5. *"Revolutionary" narratives and innovative reasoning*

Since the beginning of this work, we have explored the characteristics of the processes of innovation. Since management is constantly laying claims to them, it is necessary to clarify some points briefly.

"Each invention reveals reality, at the same time as history," said Michel Serres. As soon as the invention emerges, and with it potential innovations. The understanding of our being in the world, of this "already-there" that bubbles up, that calls for this passage through history, by the codification of the time spaces that situate us and clarify, perhaps, the complexity of the anthropo-technical processes of societies (Silex, Codex, printing, steam engines, railroads, etc. to information technology today and Nanotechnology tomorrow.)

Without these temporal markers, embodied in an object-link or object-break, the socio-technical ruptures would have trouble expressing these ruptures. If Jean-Baptiste Say wants to be a witness of the first industrial revolution and explain the growth of industry in Britain, he remembers that it was industrial and first attributes it to the invention of the *mull-jenny*: "These are two small rollers, one inch in diameter, and a notice is given to lay one on top of the other, in a small town in England, which then had an effect on global trade, this revolution was nearly as important as the opening of the seas of Asia via the Cape of Good Hope". The complexity of the assemblages on which the anthropotechnical transformations are based, which is to think in terms of political, economic, social and philosophical co-evolutions, the techniques are successful in their synthesis. However, it is only one of the actants, but can nonetheless be shown as "a totally social phenomenon" [MAU 73]. According to Simondon, studying the technique is therefore a discovery made by the one who uses it, mobilizes it, confronts it[83].

---

83 From the first page of the introduction of his doctoral thesis, Simondon tells us that "culture must incorporate technical beings in the form of knowledge and sense of values," and further, "to give the culture back the truly general character that it has lost, it is necessary to be able to reintroduce in it the consciousness of the nature of the machines, their mutual relationships, and their relations with humans, and the values involved in these relationships [SIM 58]. The understanding of these processes implies a formal description of the temporal elements of innovation, as well as the forms of production of the collective cognitive grid that are developed. Forming the sociogenesis of the Internet, backed by the technogenesis which precedes it, requires this study of the modes of apprehension of a anthropo-technical calendar and its various normative expressions. Chronos is in itself a "monstrous" machine which the spokespersons for innovators appropriate and constantly feed. These traces of a perception of the socio-technical times lend themselves to seeing how time is engineered, either to rationalize it and make it "controllable" or to extract the benchmarks that serve the particular strategy of each instance or even to make it a constraint to dissolve locally. Making time an ally by mobilizing it becomes the condition of the desired influence on the environments, on their present dynamics, and the evolutions to come. While it may seem easy to do, after the fact, the genealogy of technical inventions and the environment in which they are hatched, produces technical couplings in the short term, societal and political transformations – in short, the process of innovation itself becomes a much more delicate business. In fact, how can we account for, say, the diversity of technological apparatus, managerial policies, collective working practices "of their relations with man" for organizations? [SIM 58].

When organizations present us with very short genealogies, these are new informational processes (mostly procedural ones), within the immediacy of their movements (supposed movements toward enhancement). Moreover, these genealogies must confront the acceleration of the cycles of innovation that we have known of since the end of the 20th Century, particularly in the field of digital technologies. To be sure, from a global point of view, "we have entered the era of permanent innovation" [STI 08], but our grounds show that it is difficult to go beyond the watchword in the organizational framework. In the midst of the digital productions of the organization, it is clear that everything begins to blur together: the smallest new feature on an internal application has the potential to be revolutionary, and lead to a radical innovation. While it is much more likely that these are only, in the best possible case, a transformation of a process, or in the worst case, a reassertion and reinforcement of that process:

> "Change is now an objective within itself, or at least it is perceived as so difficult that we forget about everything else. The qualities of adaptation tend to give more consideration to the skills and unpredictability of tomorrow than to the incompetence of today" [DUR 97].

Understanding the powers and frontiers of innovation in the managerial field has led us not only to question the modes of production of the "models" and the codifications of collective action, but also, as a result, the propensity of the organization to "create all over again", to update itself and defer. It would therefore involve espousing, follow the avenues where the singularities express themselves, where the prescriptions part ways, where the repositories of action are associated and transformed, the expressions of the imperium of innovation compensate "for the limits".

But it is therefore appropriate, within this narrative, to think at the same time of the way in which we have an art of manufacturing visibilities. What we are addressing here is a grammar of innovation, carrying cognitive effects and which should itself be considered as a "discursive event" distinct from its proposal, resting (as we have already said) on a series of (not exclusively linguistic) narratique processes, a connection of specific argumentative components. What we refer to as the narratique constitutes all the equipment, the writings that create the conditions of association between them by themselves, a kind of "Boostrapping narratique"[84]. Indeed, the general grammar of innovation must allow room for the varied nature of subjectivities and situations, local strategies and intra-organizational variations that also produce language games and specific argumentative logics. Majoritarian grammar[85] can therefore be reconfigured at various levels of scale and according to new problems that can feed into it, revive it, or even annihilate it.

---

### Narratique of the decade 1990–2000

   The rupture, which in many cases is celebrated (each conference or Intranet award bears witness to a "mutation"), has its rhetoric: the sense of urgency facing the necessary "acculturation" and adoption of "this new world outside our door" [GER 97]; the excess of myths and the acceptance of a change ("ICT and new work environments: myths and realities! What has changed, what has not changed, what has to change")[86]; the revolution of ICT *business models* (convergences of "B to E, B to B, B to A and B to G" within an extended organization)[87]; the new era of *Peopleware* or organization 2.0.: "after a decade (1995–2004) of deployment of information and communication technologies in labor organizations, the advent of Internet 2.0 (2005–2010) has reached a new milestone. It has opened up prospects for shifts that are even greater than those we have experienced[88]". What was referred to as *e-transformation* was irreversibly in motion

---

**Box 2.4.** *A "revolutionary" reason*

   As in the case of normative prescriptions and models, the contract between the company and the dominant reasoning available is unstable and temporary:

   "We thus orient ourselves towards multiplicities of finite meta-arguments, by which we mean: arguments concerning meta-

---

84 We borrow this expression from [NOY 10a].

85 In this case, "majority" is to be understood in the sense used by Deleuze: "The majority assumes a rule of law and domination, not the other way around" [DEL 78]. It is therefore more a matter of an expression of the potential performation power than of homogenizing cognitive processes.

86 Title of a plenary, *Intracom*, Paris, 19 April 2005.

87 The 2005 Intranet Observatory aims to show the increasingly tenuous and enhanced articulation of ICTs from *Business to Employee* (intranet), *Business to Business* (extranet clients/suppliers), *Business to Administration* and *to Government* (Interactions between organization and administrative, associative, and governmental bodies).

88 Program of the Intracom event, 2006.

prescriptives, and limited in space-time. This orientation corresponds to the evolution of social interactions where the temporary contract in fact supplants the permanent institution in professional, affective, sexual, cultural, family, international, and political matters" [LYO 79].

However, the processes of argumentation applying to ICTs, in their various semiotics, are indicative of the current innovative reasoning, and its technical, social and political determinations. It would thus be necessary to be able to conduct the analysis to the systems and fields of forces that form the condition for the actual and singular formations.

The continuous innovation movement, where mobility and plasticity carry out a general mobilization, one that even leads all the way to the brain, is expressed in the order of discourse as the basis for new regimes of desire, regimes that define a "managerial epithumia" in the folding into a "neo-liberal Epithumia", and vice versa[89].

For a clearer understanding of the meaning of our effort, we will briefly state the storyline of history, of which we are the "children". Through the tangle of inherited forms (which Sloterdjik would have us to replace as soon as the rupture occurring in 1492 occurs – the event that set off a seismic shift in the world and its economic operations) and forms of actualization, are sometimes expressed as "naive rationalities", but which are also deliberately instrumental[90].

They then translate into creating messages, built to be irrefutable and already fed into by the fictions put in place by the new electronic capitalism as a whole: they are part of the communicational engineering designed to support the project. Indeed, without any slogans, there is no way to mobilize the project. To borrow a shortcut – if you may pardon our audacity – we might observe that what was effective for the "messianic" undertaking

---

89 Here we use the Greek term, meaning "lust, desire, passion". For his part, F. Lordn, uses the term epitome in the non-anthological sense, which however is not very far from a desirable/desirous precision [LOR 13].

90 The founding actors often recur to a logic in which the future will provide the "benefits" and the merits of the *socio-technological choice. They may also be aware of the limits of their rationality.*

carried out by Columbus (according to Sloterdjick, the explorer was an agent with a propensity for madness common throughout Europe) was just as much for "evangelization" as managerial spirit. From the perspective of imitation, and as stated by this German philosopher, it will therefore be agreed that the "fever for success" and the "project" are closely linked: "without a project, there is no chance that other people would catch the same fever they have" [SLO 06]. The emphasis, to the point of becoming enthusiasm for absurd reasoning, is a recurring process that we have encountered in the process of institutionalizing e-organizations. In this context, operational targets become secondary to the risk of becoming irrational in light of the organizations' short-term effectiveness and profitability objectives. "Enchantment" refers to the result of a process that allows for supporting "a surplus of effects in relation to the cause" [SLO 06].

There may therefore be some sort of "decoupling" between the political rationality of the project (the symbolic integration of all the managers of subsidiaries into an intranet, as in the example of the Moeva case) and the operational rationality (to reduce costs of operation). This is also the domain of self-persuasion and the self-motivation of project managers. As a reinforcement, they can appeal to consultants, associations, and various managerial celebrations, which provide them with as many additional resources as are necessary for their belief: these actants remove their doubts and give "forgiveness"[91] to the latest hesitant managers, or put themselves at risk in the adventure of the e-organization. As a last resort, the project may also be driven by the sole personal interests of the bearer of the project and, on a purely selfish level, be fundamentally rational in relation to the specific purposes and subjectivity of this project bearer (which, as an example, may be reflected in the games played between actors of a project). From this point of view, what is it then that is rewarded? Can we say that such a project leader is still an author, an innovator, when in fact it is his adherence to the status quo, his compliance, which are celebrated? Drawing again from the work of Peter Sloterdijck, with everything already being so integrated "into the post unilateral forms of action and thought", the resonances already so thoroughly

---

91 Over several pages, Sloterdjick develops an analysis of consultancies, as a process of forgiveness for the decision-makers.

proven, that to claim the originality of a project or a creation would be no more than a concept for the "people of yesteryear" [SLO 06].

In the contemporary world, innovation is thus defeated by the role of the author, according to this philosopher, and instead refers to the notion of the collective assemblage of enunciation and that of psychic and collective individuals [DEL 09, DEL 16, DEL 77, GUA 80, SIN 58]. The major innovation would then be expressed by the transition from one assemblage to another with the disruptive effects that go with it, effects that manifest during or through the movement of emergence. Therefore, a major innovation has an essential link with the "virtual-actual" circuit, and the process of performation is the manifestation of this passage, of this "coming and going" taken together as a whole (*of mediations – we ourselves would add*) of activities and of events that establish or modify an assemblage.

### 2.2.6. *From a "network-centric" narrative to a "data-centric" narrative: the breviary of recent years*

"The technological *a priori* is political in as much as the transformation of nature involves that of man, and in as much as the 'man-made creations' issue from and re-enter a societal ensemble. One may still insist that the machinery of the technological universe is 'as such' indifferent towards political ends–it can revolutionize or hinder a society. An electronic computer can serve equally a capitalist or socialist administration; a cyclotron can be an equally efficient tool for a war party or a peace party. This neutrality is contested in Marx's controversial statement that the 'hand-mill gives you society with the feudal lord; the steam-mill society with the industrial capitalist'. And this statement is further modified in Marxian theory itself: the social mode of production, not technique is the basic historical factor. However, when technique becomes the universal form of material production, it circumscribes an entire culture; it projects a historical totality – a 'world'" [MAR 68].

Already mentioned in various examples, we will summarize what we believe to be some important markers of the digital managerial organizational policies of the last 15 to 20 years. From the beginning of our work, we have been particularly interested in intranet policies and their progressions.

Here, we support our positions not only on the Moeva case, the observations of professional conferences, but also an analysis of an observatory of "intranet policies" in public organizations [CAR 13a][92]. The Moeva case showed us the tangled web of broadly varying scripts, each of which brought back a set of forces and mediations into itself. In this context, we wish to describe the assembly of a digital narratique and its shift from a perspective of "communication", based on the role of the "network" to a current data-centric perspective. One of the last embodiments of this capture, from elsewhere to better align it within itself, may be the "spirit of the maker" [LAL 15], which is unique to the current aspirations of the models of innovation and internal management, or even "the common goods" that we will find to be related to approaches of "governance".

---

92 Embodied in the policies of e-administration, the "modernization" of public services, internal digital apparatus, and more recently by *Open Data* and *Open Gov,* authorities at the local level participate in the establishment of an increasingly complex assemblage of new processes for work, communications, collaboration, and engineering. A continuous reconfiguration of organizational digital spaces, which have become the federating agents of a multitude of applications and information systems (for process management, interaction, publication, and the economic operation of content, etc.) and in which all or part of the collaborators, entities and organizational structures, are entitled to participate. While the evaluation of the "ambitions" of these policies often still tends to point to a delayed response by local authorities in relation to private enterprises, it is appropriate, in our view, to go beyond this postulate and the macro-visions that flatten out these broad variances within the apparatus created here. Similarly, it would be wrong to consider that the communities in France had been sensitized to ICT only long after private enterprises. Indeed, professional associations, specifically from the world of local authorities, have played a role as an early warning for the need to think about the issue of ICTs in terms of targeted digital policies for citizens/users of the administration, or targeted at the community's internal practices. An analysis of the associative activity has shown us the fabric of a very rich network of actors who, since the end of the 1990s, have constituted a significant force for influence [CAR 08]. These all present themselves as particularly active spokespersons of a new techno-political model within the territorial communities, a model forcefully affirming the necessary shift from a vertical logic of bureaucratic administration to a "transversal logic" to which ICTs could contribute.

In the case of the community observatory, project managers have been put in a position in which their narratique is exposed[93]: this does not imply that individuals are capable of expressing the reasons for what they do in a comprehensive and "enlightened" manner, with the file rapidly moving from "writing for work" status (as action writings that occur during daily activity and participate in the structuring of this activity [FRA 01]) to that of the "organizational narrative" [ALM 01, GIR 05] or "ventriloquism" [COO 10]. Just as with the stages of professional conferences, but here in a version in which this is expected to be put into writing, the project is "documentarized", to fulfill its needs regarding the observatory and its evaluators. These combinatorial scripts present themselves as strategic cherodes[94] that have been at work within digital media for about 15 years in the field of digital policy. The chreodes are mandatory points of passage for the organizational action: they are the expression and the expressed materials of the problematization, which for B. Latour presents itself as "the operation by which various elements are captured and articulated in a system of interdependencies, and eventually called on to act as an integrated group, whose forces, instead of neutralizing themselves, converge in a single direction by relying on one another [LAT 06].

Each domain here is described based on a problematization (the mobilization of the same diagnosis and necessity[95]), on recurring order-words, on a directory of responses and action prescriptions, an organizational apparatus that frames them. Some critical elements from our analyses on various fields have been indicated.

---

93 The 70 files analyzed here consist of a document prepared freely (presenting the strategic framework of the project, its mechanisms for design and governance, the related managerial actions, the transformations and difficulties that are perceived, the policies of interfaces and editorials, the proposed features, and various added materials: screenshots, connection statistics, editorial charters).

94 The chréodes, terms derived from René Thom and taken up in the analysis of the morphogenetic fields of R. Sheldrake, can still be seen as attractors. Chreodes are "valleys" that increasingly deepen as the information installing itself is confirmed.

95 Here, we may observe one of the fundamental mechanisms of Translation, which, for M. Callon, consists of "proposing relationships between different activities, interests, problems, and concerns ..." [CAL 86] and for B. Latour, it presents itself as "the operation by which various elements are captured and interconnected in a system of interdependencies" [LAT 06]. In addition to the problematization, the operation of translation is accompanied by processes of interest, enlistment, and the "mobilization of allies".

## 2.2.6.1. *Organization-network*

Many works of sociology in recent years have sought to propose a general characterization of the new forms of the capitalist economy by focusing on the very object of the transformations following the appearance of the form of Network Organization [DOD 95 DAT 98, VEL 00, DUR 97]. Of course, the synthetic description made here should be made in harmony with the very thorough work of Boltanski and Chiapello [BOL 99][96] whose analysis of managerial works has highlighted the emergence of the "city by project" (and the imposition of the conception of the "network"), which according to the authors is characteristic of the late 1990s, and examined the integration of their critique of capitalism.

The network, whether it is hypostatized or used to break up the messages of essences, is the focus of theoretical reflection, the focus of organizational production, the focus of the collective as a problem. It is also at the crossroads of reflections concerning a set of notions, such as those of milieus, territories, relationships, topology, and trials. At the core of the Latourian associations and the sociology of translation, and supporting works as diverse as they are stimulating (such as those of Burt, Granovetter, Galloway, etc.[97]), it can be found running through many theoretical fields. In some way, it runs against the concept of "rhizome" found in the philosophy of Gilles Deleuze and Félix Guattari. It is still active in the question of software and documentaries, at the level of the algorithms of the linguistic-semantic treatment of the corpus and all these titles; it plays a major role in the question of politics and geopolitics. And thus, with a seemingly limitless level of enthusiasm, management has seized on it.

But it must be noted that the reticular figures and implications – as far as internal information systems are concerned – have mostly been reduced to non-complex forms and most often brought into an orthodox figure of the organization, in which the "network" would be substituted for the "hierarchical tree", and one that nevertheless remains in place. Thus, in a few years, from *top-down* communicational apparatus (a digitalized internal communication), intranets have gone on to become indispensable spaces for

---

96 [BOL 99, p. 46], here, capitalism is not seen from the viewpoint of a Marxist critique of the forces of domination and subjugation, but as "a set of beliefs associated with the capitalist order, which helps to justify this order and, by legitimizing them, to support the modes of action and the provisions that are coherent with it".

97 In this regard, see [CAL 06].

any employee (working on a computer): by bringing together a single point of entry to the applications of professions, cross-information systems (such as HRIS)[98], collective working tools, document databases, couriers (which have made intranets into obligatory waypoints), etc.. In short, by ingesting all streams of information that may be present, they now position themselves as a *digital workplace*. Since the end of the 1990s, the deployment of digital technologies within the engineering of info-communication appears as a privileged goal of the construction of models relating to what has been referred to, successively, as the "business-network", "extended business", "e-organization", and "digital organization". Based on the massively developed linkages between the intranet and an increasing set of work practices, the "e-organization" is the condition and the product of the placement into a reticular form and an integration of flows[99].

According to [BOL 99], the last 30 years have thus been marked in the organizational world by an "increasing interest in relational properties (and relational ontology) as opposed to properties substantially "attached to beings that they would define within themselves". In fact, in "cognitive capitalism" [LAZ 04, MOU 07], it is the ability to link, to associate, to "hypertextualize", to "put brains into cooperation", which tends to replace the political questions of the division of labor and of professional classes, to instrumental visions of qualifications and the normative repositories that previously prevailed. This comes about, in the context of uncertainties and mobility that is thrust on us, together with the logic of competence, flexibility, and employability (as constraints), with the register of "belonging" losing all its relevance for some managers. Memberships would even be conditioned by their registration in the business directory! Favoring the development of ICTs, the organizational assemblages have therefore been heavily supported through the metaphors of networks, the first of which is the brain: in its displacement within the managerial world, the connectionist model of the brain, also supported by the interest in knowledge management, which has carried out a naturalization of the social and is, based on a neural network model pared down to the forms contested by some cognitive scientists [MAA 04][100]. But all this matters very little, in the

---

98 Human Resources Information System.

99 For example, the Xnets or One NET projects are some of the digital apparatus characteristic of "the extended organization".

100 Drawing from the works of the neurosciences, Catherine Malabo criticizes the instrumentalization of "cerebral plasticity" in the business world. She summarizes Boltanski and

messages transmitted, the effectiveness of "neuro-organizational plasticity" and of a generalized connection within networks described as "a-centric" (and thus a-hierarchical), there is no longer any doubt: for management, the employee has become a " connector", highly flexible and only counting for the extension and correlatively, the control, of its connective power.

### 2.2.6.2. *Digital connectivity and integration*

Allowing extended access to digital workspaces (intranet, messaging) appears as a logical first step, but will take a political turn from the very beginning. This vertical integration of employees is coupled with an integration of applications into the universe of the Intranet. Sometimes linked to a justification of the category of "strengthening the sense of belonging", this is a script that responds to an integration issue through an infrastructural response. The objective is to extend the possibilities for the connections of "de-localized"[101] agents or employees, agents not exercising a trade and requiring the shared use of a computer (in local entities, family assistants, agents at nurseries and technical services, etc.) and to expand the locations for consultation (from home or on the go). In the public sector, the specific case of the elected officials is also envisaged in some projects: it is thus a matter of providing them with a service for information and organization (management of agendas, meetings) accessible from anywhere. The watchwords are: "dealing with internal digital exclusion"; "Associating staff members traditionally excluded from the digital system"; "Equal access to information for all agents". A linkage is sought between professional identification processes and "connective identities"[102].

Given the user population and the dispersion of the entities involved, extranet versions can be proposed, along with terminals, computers with free access, and increasingly via smartphones, which complete the different possibilities of access. While the necessity for widespread connectivity (through its technical assemblage) is a strong political symbol, at the same

---

Chiapello in her analysis of a close correlation found today between the descriptions of the inner workings of the brain and the forms taken by management, the contemporary spirit of capitalism [MAL 04].

101 In the local community, for example, TOSs (technicians, workers, and service professionals). Following Law No. 2004-809 of 13 August 2004 on local freedoms and responsibilities, ninety thousand TOS workers in national education were transferred to the territorial authorities.

102 See section 3.1.5.

time, this "digital integration" requires us to consider digital divides from the point of view of individual learning and collective abilities, which go beyond technical access[103]. Charters of access and use are implemented (including accessing the internet at work, a rather controversial subject). This narratique is imbued with an "ecosystemic vision" of the organization, where the structural vision for a "organization-network" (referred to at the end of the 1990s as "extended business") is left out, requiring a hyperconnective infrastructure, integrating all the entities with which it interacts (infrastructures of linkages between internal and external entities, localities, and immediate environments). In doing so, the network will transition from addressing infrastructure issues (linking a disperse array of points) to becoming a socio-cognitive entity, whose "corporate social networks" are emblems.

The main criticism in response to this concerns "digital discrimination" (the rights of access to devices, the lack of training and assistance for different uses), with the new surveillance and hyperconnectivity seen as a syndrome of "the company-network". As we will see in Chapter 3, these tensions will be more broadly linked to an interface policy.

### 2.2.6.3. *Standardization and industrialization of informational processes*

As in the case of Moeva, there is a focus on automating various processes of information processing. The clearest testament to the managerial rationality of private or public organizations, the idea of these digital and intranet policies seeks to attain organizational and economic performance through the standardization of processes and optimization of information flows (in terms of time and human resources). As described by V. de Gaulejac in particular, management is thus seen as the set of techniques designed to streamline and optimize the functions of the organization [DEG 05]. The construction of narratives is carried out largely according to the benchmarks for efficiency and effectiveness, then evaluated in terms of time savings (for employees dealing in particular with the transversal and administrative processes) and economic gains. In the public sector, this argument is explicitly reinforced by coercive provisions in relation to

---

103 This joins together with a perspective of "e-inclusion" developed strongly by some public administrations for citizens.

subsequent laws for the modernization of the State[104]. For example, as early as 2003, the electronic administration plan gave organizations the objective of "making their exchanges with administrations paper free, thereby increasing processing speeds and the transparency of procedures while optimizing the services provided"[105]. In this case, an eco-societal justification was used: the digitization of documents associated with a sustainable development issue[106], the reduction of the ecological footprint of communications exchanges. The order-words are: "simplification", "automation", "homogenization", "paperless" and "process industrialization". At the level of operational responses, many applications and various *workflows* of processes were offered. Apart from business or specialized applications[107], this approach can involve very many different processes. The forms backed by a *workflow* frequently concern the reservation of a vehicle, computer equipment, rooms, requests for computer assistance, supplies, etc. Unlike large private sector companies, the "e-HR" orientation (mobility

---

104 The French organic law on finance laws (LOLF) promulgated on August 1, 2006, has imposed new accounting procedures on French administration since 1 January. The key words are "performance", "budgetary transparency", "public management", "responsibilities", "indicators", "a logic of results", "management control" and "audits". The model is put into use explicitly: "With budgetary reform, the accounting of the State becomes a real instrument for directing public action." It is based on corporate accounting, while taking into account the issues specific to the public sector," accessed in 2006 but no longer available today, available at: http://www.finances.gouv.fr/lolf/6_1.htm.

105 Nevertheless, according to the reports by F. Riester (2010), there was still much progress that remained to be made in order to "improve the digital relationship with the user". Countless reports on the digital transition and its various incarnations are no longer considered (see the example of Open Data, section 2.3). All this revolves around multiple organs, including the emblematic secretariat general for the modernization of the state (SGMAP), that are presented as conductors of the orchestra that is technical-institutional performance.

106 A normative prescription may also take part along the lines of Agenda 21, in terms of reducing paper consumption. Each community is responsible for development, for its territory, and for implementing an action program that responds to the principles of Agenda 21. In October 2011, eight hundred and eleven community initiatives were listed, accessed on October 10, 2011 and available at the following addresses: http://www.Agenda21france.org/e and http://www.developpement-durable.gouv.fr/Agendas-21-locaux,14252.html.

107 A broad catalog of possible applications can be found here, ranging from "webises" business tools to information systems that may be potentially usable by all or part of the services: geographic information systems, map, base and management of the deliberations and orders, software for managing school enrollment and extracurricular activities, social action management, purchasing management, etc.

management, leave, training, payroll) is far from systematized (with only one-third of the files), though it is an important investment axis. The management of mail has been handled by some localities, sometimes smaller ones, communities that rely on internal resources to develop specific applications. Under these conditions, these localities manage to invest in the orientation of "e-administration", a community that has developed an online re-registration management application for school services, accessible to the parents of pupils, or an application for the management of the planning of recreation centers. The development of such apparatus is passed through the technical integration of all applications (known for a time as a "webization" movement) and a design of the "federating" workstation of informational and communication practices. The criticism has less to do with the traceability of the procedures (from the ichnological scheme to the work, which can be assumed to still only be perceived by a small number of employees) than the permanence of the flows, the acceleration of the time at work [ROS 10] and a feeling of being swallowed up by a "consuming chronocracy" [HAR 10]. In the public sector, a confrontation occurs specifically between the script-business and the activity from the point of view of the public official and the national-level indications taken over by the internal management [CAR 13b]. Considering the increasing role of the Internet in an ever-greater number of administrative procedures, irrespective of the social, cognitive or economic difficulties of the citizens, the agents (in particular, social services) call for an urgent reflection on the right balance to be devised between digital processes and oral interactions, requiring a consideration of the persistent inequalities within a part of the population.

The design of information architectures and modes of navigation requires a reflexive work on what is presented as a semiotic means of piloting, namely as apparatus for identifying and staging "collective acts" (to indicate only its most significant mechanisms). From the point of view of problematization and legitimation, the apparatus highlights two imperative needs: the requirement for an exit from the hierarchies reproducing a structural logic and the requirement to adapt the interfaces to the specific context of each agent. The incessant growth of data/pages/documents within digital spaces, the multiplication and dispersion of thematic spaces, the cognitive overload and the criticism of the users (mainly related to the search for information), and the "past-ist" impression of graphic design, are all motivators that lead the project managers to initiate a "redesign" of their interface policy. This action is systematically referred to as a "version change" of the intranet. The communities that have adopted an ergonomic repository from the public web, develop and evaluate "the main possible scenarios for navigation done by agents" for the Intranet to become "the virtual office of all internal audiences". This orientation, which tends to position the intranet as the sole interface on which professional practices take place, seeks to respond both to a demand for adaptation to user practices and to an objective of optimization, growth, and uses. The keys words are: *"federation"*, *"personalization"*, *"better orientation"* and *"virtual office"*.

### 2.2.6.4. *Collaborative, "community" and "ad hoc-cratic" injunctions*

The records of participation and collaboration (terms given very little nuance in the managerial world) refer here to various policies and apparatus that describe the organization from the viewpoint of a "social network" (the reticular figure being confused with project management as envisaged by [BOL 99]). Here, the concept of a network allows for the transition from an organization characterized by procedural rationality to a community-based rationality (see the widespread distribution of the work in management sciences on the organizational communities) [WEN 02, COH 10]. By focusing on the principles of "mutual adjustment", this reticular logic would tend toward the replacement of hierarchies by borrowing the well-known "adhocratic" model of management [MIN 82, TOF 70, WAT 90][108]. More recently, this model has shed its feathers, becoming "holacracy"[109], another term forming part of the recent managerial newspeak and presented as "a social technology", referring to a horizontal management (without pyramidal authority, but with "governance") which, pushed to its maximum, can transform autonomous teams into "real internal start-ups". The deployment of network applications (from the first collaborative spaces to existing corporate social networks) within organizations is part of a context in which the need for creativity has been in place for several years from a requirement for the *"disinhibition"* of the employee (to publish, share, interact, formalize their experiences, etc.). Widely celebrated during various

---

108 Inherent to the approaches taken by project management, the "adhocracy" is a configuration "that, within a context of unstable and complex environments, mobilizes multi-disciplinary competencies reaching across various areas to carry out specific missions." Available at: Https://fr.wikipedia.org/wiki/Adhocratie.

109 "Holacracy": a term created in the US in 2007 by three business creators. *The word Holacracy is a trade mark owned by http://www.holacracy.org/.* "The traditional hierarchy is reaching its limits, but 'flat management' alternatives lack the rigor needed to run a business effectively. Holacracy is a third-way: it brings structure and discipline to a peer-to-peer workplace".

professional events, corporate social networks are an update of these perspectives, and for their spokesmen, they present themselves as a break from previous organizational models [GAL 10].

These apparatus are therefore part of an engineering of knowledge whose dominant perspective is "socialization": linking individuals and their professional problems; sharing and cooperation following a "peer-to-peer" logic; the development of communities of practices, of expertise, of interest, with these "partly retaining their self-organized dimension while being interconnected with the formal organization" [BOO 13]. This would be a transition from an engineering of the knowledge stock (preservation, codification, classification, views from the lens of a documentary engineering) to a logic of "sociocognitive flows" (which is presented as being without hindrances), a logic that is nevertheless inseparable from any process of "collective intelligence" and at the heart of the Anthropology of Knowledge [BRA 07]. Thus, in response to a requirement of "decompartmentalization" between services, the imperative need for a flow of resources against hierarchical routines of information management has been established: the principles of decentralized publication have been adopted (the distributed engineering of communication and internal information backed by networks of "contributors" on the intranet), of documentary sharing, of project management (each of which can be endowed with a portfolio of projects that are as much of activities that are added to its core activity), endowment of spaces dedicated to "communities" (driven or not by the directorates). The watchwords are: "cooperation", "transversality", "communities", "Organisation 2.0" ("social networks against the corporate organizational diagram"), "participatory innovation" and "entrepreneurship"[110].

In addition, the participatory narrative is associated with the idea of new social interactions, and in this case, digital projects call for the enhancement of the possibilities of the direct expression of employees from interactive tools (forums, which then gave way to blogs and social networks). These approaches have had to confront for many years, in this case, "the inhibition" of management and the fear of losing control over the expressions of employees (hence the perpetuation of moderators, administrators and other Community Managers who oversee their screening).

---

110 Intrapreunariat, or in a situation of entrepreneurship within the company, valuing the creativity of the employees and helping them to carry out their projects.

Some companies have begun to undergo a reflection on digital apparatus and social dialog: firstly, this involves equipping the unions with tools and means enabling them to participate in the intranet, and secondly (and much less commonly), to contrast different viewpoints by allowing "interaction between directorates and agents"[111]. It may be noted that most of the time, the topics of discussion do not concern labor organizations, large internal transformations, social conditions, etc. Both in the private and in the public sectors, subjects minimizing the risk of criticism or controversy are given priority. As far as spaces for unions[112] are concerned, this subject has rarely been imposed in the first version of the Intranets, but instead after a redesign. The objective is to give the unions a dedicated space, as well as tools (document management, page administration, couriers, etc.), while framing the mechanisms of usage. This union-oriented expression is negotiated within the framework of the charters. Also, in 2016, in most organizations, the communications of unions remain rather lacking in innovation: the intranet acts as an electronic billboard (for the reproduction of leaflets and press releases) and the challenges for mastery are also always a factor. The perceptions of employees associated with these dimensions are clearly differentiated according to the recent histories of the organizations, the managerial routines, and in particular, the practices of the local management, but there are a number of points of convergence, particularly in the public sector. In the particular case of local authorities, the expected model for socialization and cooperation carried out by the digital (if we take what the agents state literally) is based on principles of:

---

111 The ambitions on display in this area still struggle to take root. At the beginning of the 2010s, in areas such as local communities, the discussion forums were, for many, the first sign of a willingness to open up the possibilities of expression. However, it is usually only applied to a restricted area of subjects. In fact, the discussion forums are, in the large majority of cases, deployed within the project areas or spaces dedicated to business communities. However, we stress that the orientation toward "communities of practices" or "professional social networks" are of increasing interest, or in addition, the approach of the CR of Brittany, which has opted for a blogging solution designed to promote trade following four strategic focal points: professions (they now have a blog for the cooks at schools), "project" blogs (the collective restoration in high schools, the regional schemes of innovation, the project of the administration, the regional Agenda 21), "debate" around internal subjects (new provisions for the day of solidarity, the evaluation of the agents), and related blogs (friendly, athletic).

112 As part of our field studies, we have also been able to observe the tensions between management and unions regarding the staffing of these unions in terms of communication tools, and exchanges with employees, as well as with management.

– free interaction (excluding hierarchies) between selected colleagues;

– the creation of enriched directories (with identification of the professions and skills of agents, integration of external bodies);

– greater efficiency of research tools and classifications (with an indexing scheme stemming from of a top-down approach being evoked);

– spaces dedicated specially to self-organized microcommunities;

– autonomous management of the degree of visibility and the boundaries of these networks/groups.

And all this is done for the initial purposes of the exchange of practices, experiences and advice. Critics can then focus on an instrumentalization of "collaboration", on the declaration to carry out less inhibited messaging, paradoxically coexisting with the controls on "words", on the requirement for inter-departmental collaborations within organizations "continuing in their state of being", one that is deeply bureaucratic. In many respects, the narratique of the employees-users of the digital spaces is interwoven with the words used by the management that they put to the test of concrete transformations and their own repository of practices from their experiences from the Web.

### 2.2.6.5. *From "cognitive capital" to its connection with data*

Over a period of 20 years, the orders have hardly changed. They now come dressed in a new wardrobe of a never-ending procession of updated features, to dress up their strategy, to announce a rupture and new words. Because, ultimately, what the digital narrative within organizations continues to re-publish, over and over again, is an ongoing and repeated attempt to reposition itself in what has been presented by Negri, Boutang, and Gorz (among others) as "cognitive capitalism" [BOU 07], by Sloterdijk, a palace for "hypercommunicative constitution" [SLO 06], and by Guattari, "an integrated capitalism". The narrative and narratique of the organization and its "digital" assemblages require us to examine the new production reports that are proposed, reports that for some analysts and researchers present renewed figures but the same operations (including those on the Internet), and forms of "cognitariat" or factories using digital labor[113].

---

113 See current developments on the rise of what was described by A. Toffler in the 1980s as the "cognitariat" [TOF 83], [NEW 09]. On the digital labor in the process of intensification

The interest firstly in "human" capital, and thus in "informational" and "relational" capital, and secondly in the anchoring of digital technologies as a key feature of collective work processes, have gradually led organizations to reconsider the digital workplace as a condition for the development of "organizational collective intelligence". All this requires an examination of the problematics and the newspeaks that have seized on the opportunity presented by digital technology to reinvest in the *General Intellect*[114]. This perspective is much more pronounced in private organizations and even in some large public organizations than it is in, for example, the territorial authorities in France. Is it a simple rediscovery or questioning of the stakes involved with the couplings between "intellective technologies"[115] and the transformation of collective work processes? In the narratique of e-organization, it is no longer only a matter of considering digital workspaces as large silos of documentary storage, but as a tool for conservation (a logic referred to as *defensive*) and enrichment (a logic referred to as *offensive*), potential for an "organizational memory", and the creation and capitalization (sharing) of knowledge[116]. At the core of this, and while the vast variations and volumes of information flows continue to grow, the question of the relevant utilization of innovative resources and search engines persists and comes back, but since the mid-2010s, has been

---

[SCH 13, FUC 14]. A. Casilli defines digital labor as a "low-intensity and low-expertise contribution, profited on by means of data algorithms and data mining", in [CAS 15].

114 It would be worth remembering that Marx, in his time, spoke of the *General Intellect*, during a time that was hardly Marxist. "Abstract knowledge – primarily scientific knowledge, but not exclusively – tends to become, by the very same means of its autonomy in relation to production, no more and no less than the main productive force, relegating broken and repetitive work to a marginal position. This involves objective knowledge in the fixed capital, which was incarnated (or, to put it more precisely, has solidified) in the automatic system of machines. Marx uses a rather suggestive image to describe the entirety of abstract knowledge (or of "epistemological paradigms", as it would appear today), which, at the same time, form the epicenter of social production and organize the entire context of life: He speaks of a *general intellect*, of a 'general brain'", [VIR 92].

115 A term proposed by J. Noyer to refer to the synthesis of intellectual and cognitive technologies. Documents, web pages, microcontents, etc., are embedded within a long chain of cognitive processes (writing, evaluation, interpretation, transformation, description, association, classification, filtering, orientation, etc.).

116 We will spare the reader all the literature related to Knowledge Management. For a summary and a critique, see Cohendet P., Héraud J., Llerena P., "La dynamique de l'innovation : une interprétation de l'approche de Michel Callon en termes de communautés de connaissance", in [AKR 10, NEW 09].

confronted by the deployment of Web 2.0, released to great fanfare, that will benefit from an initial "Agenda setting".

This *social software* is presented as the driver for future transformations of organizations: social software not only gives us the tools to understand these social networks, it can potentially empower individuals, communities and organizations to better manage networks, and to build social capital"[117]. As we have already pointed out, social networks thus assume the burden not only of "spontaneous" participation, but also of the unveiling of a relational capital presented as a new performance resource and a condition for the objectivity of "Ordinary Innovation" [ALT 10] which the collaborators may show. Currently, as we will see, it is data that has universally become the center of attention.

In terms of its coupling with *Knowledge Management*, what are the watchwords on digital technology that have been implemented since the 2000s? "Human capital", "Intangible capital", "Participatory Innovation", "Social Intelligence", "Learning Enterprise", "Organizational training", etc. And therefore they can partner in a semantic cluster with those used for collaboration and *social software.* All these concepts benefit from a rich theoretical backing[118]. Though we won't be revisiting the various obediences of knowledge management here, we will take time to point out the prescriptions that link these questions to digital apparatus.

All these years have been characterized by a clash between organic metaphors (the organization as a living body) and neuroscientific metaphors (the company as a brain), thus enriched by a "holacratic" ideal of community embodied by the shift of companies toward Web 2.0. In the 1990s, H. Sérieyx, a management researcher, defined knowledge management as the key to "a strategy for change that would lead to the transfer of a

---

117 Huton W., in Davies W. (ed.), "You don't know me, but... social capital and social software", p. 2, available at: http://theworkfoundation.com/default.aspx. In the document, the expected benefits of *social software* are related in particular to its contribution to *Knowledge Management,* to the objectivization/exploitation of collective interactions and social networks (tacit or formal), to the possible recomposition of hierarchical and managerial forms.

118 It was at the beginning of the 1950s that Simon proposed to transpose the concept of learning to organizations, which had the capacity to acquire, store, process and use information. In this perspective, the spreading of new knowledge and practices, as well as the linking of pre-existing capabilities, represent two means of learning for the organization, which then expands its capacity to tackle issues left unaddressed up to this point. See [DEL 98].

mechanistic organization into a living organization" [SER 00]. One of the conditions for achievement and efficiency is the extraction/objectivization of "tacit" knowledge and the conversion of this knowledge to "explicit understanding". The theoretical explanatory model of the managers, which has now become "canonical", is that of Japanese theorists Nonaka and Takeuchi [NON 85][119]. Composed of a simplifying matrix, it is still considered to be highly operational by the professionals of knowledge engineering and can always be found in courses. Using metaphoric processes, technologies cause the nature of the company to change from inert and mechanical to biological: "It is sustained by information exploited by its nervous system, which takes advantage of NICTs."[120] In his book on the Intranet, consultant Ryan Bernard did not hesitate to make the analogy between the latter and "a self-governing organism, which maintains and governs itself [...] The spirit is in the machine" [BER 97]. "The spirit" does not get down there alone, but it doesn't matter... As opposed to strategic planning (determination in relation to a goal), the principles used are those derived from cybernetics: offering degrees of freedom, the mission of the organization is to avoid mistakes and minimize risks. The SOPRA company, specializing in the publication of Human Resources software, stated in its commercial brochure from 2001, "The changes of the staff managers, now becoming directors of human resources, and tomorrow, managers of 'intellectual and cultural' capital[121]", leaving open the question of the relevance of these steps[122]. "There's nobody left today who disputes that innovative ideas come as much from the ground up as from the circles of upper management." Yet, some believe that what is propelling this

---

119 The model used by the Japanese identifies four types of possible conversions of knowledge into the organization: from tacit to tacit, it involves *socialization* (knowledge is directly transmitted by interaction between individuals through learning that is implicit and therefore not utilized at the collective level); the movement from the explicit to the tacit corresponds to the *internalization* (the rooting of the explicit knowledge expressed by automatism, reflexes that enrich the tacit knowledge of individuals); explicit to explicit involves a *combination* (explicit knowledge is combined to constitute new explicit knowledge); the *externalization* or *formalization* will characterize the transition from tacit to explicit (where the individual tries to explain his art and convert his experience into explicit knowledge).

120 *Les Échos, op. cit.*, March 17, 1998.

121 Société Sopra.

122 Seminar of the AFCI (French Association of Internal Communication).

emergence is a simple exercise designed "to give employees the feeling that they are being listened to"[123].

It remains to be determined whether the company may truly be seen as a *living system* (naturalization) or as an *organizational computer* (informatization). In fact, these two approaches appear to be quite different, and are handed down dominant organizational conceptions[124]. This would involve revisiting the narratiques on knowledge management in terms of the development of organizational theories and accurately examining the borrowings, continuity, and real movements that occur. What's more, these entanglements are essential to consider, since you can sufficiently "bend" the postulates of a cognitive approach of the organization to better integrate them into a kind of Neo-Taylorism[125].

Closer to us, and this time in an assemblage that concerns both the workplace practices and at the same time the marketing strategies of companies, or also public organizations and various policies of management of territories and cities, the industries of "transhumanism" – in short, the assemblages of the associated digital media in their entirety – the major bifurcation consists in how desires are invested in data. We will see in Chapter 3 how the horizons of *Data Management* applied to the socio-digital practices of employees and their cognitive behaviors (in particular, with the example of digital social networks) may be profiled. This will involve questioning the populations of data that come into existence and the regimes of desires that go hand in hand with them. Our interrogation focuses on the following [CAR 15]: data production, the digital folding of the world, the rise of algorithms and artificialization as a continuation of the living being by non-organic means, are all essentially linked. Data populations and their forms of existence sketch out cosmopolitanism of hybrids; uncertain, and associated with new forms of being together, and

---

123 *Ibid.*

124 We can consider at least five lenses used for a reading on the organization: a machine (characteristic of the classical theory and the first approaches of management), a political and institutional system (critical approaches, neo-institutionalism), a social organization (evolutionary approaches, environmental approaches), a "concrete" action system (action theory, etc.), a cultural system (analysis of cultural influences, sociology of identity, etc.), a cognitive system (theory of limited rationality, organizational learning, approaches by the company doing the learning, the "waste basket" theory, etc.), to cite just these few currents. See a summary in [CAB 05].

125 See the expert systems.

new ways of performation by collectives and their governances. Prediction, a tool that is inherent to the process of the metastability of hybrid collectives and occupies a central position, to the point of being "arched", now maintains a grip on the self-manufacturing of humans – post-humans and its related areas.

In these conditions, how will the chance marriage with these future outcomes be possible? What is the strength of this immense gap that never ceases to grow and fill itself with data, while creating the conditions for its own collapse? Will it be "Data all the way down?" We summarized this movement in the exploration for "*Désirs de données*" ("data desires"). And in the following section, we will provide an illustration of it.

## 2.3. The case of *Open Data* public policies: the processes of performation at work

The incarnation and implementation of Open Data policies is an extremely rich example for examining the linkage coupling between Data Management being deployed and its organizational dimensions. This connection is essentially techno-political. It is also the medium for expressing the many processes of performation that we propose to describe in the case of public Open Data.

From a methodological point of view, it is again a question of examining the Open Data/Big Data in the public sphere from the concrete assemblages within which these approaches are conceived. These assemblages include bureaucratic semiotics, and the apparatus of Open Data are enveloped in a vast field of legitimizing narratives and watchwords. In this way, they aggregate not only technical devices, but also a whole series of prescriptions, laws, actors, and models, which are involved in the expansion and formatting of practices. All of these factors fuel the performation of digital public policies and take form within new practices, new professions, new names, such as Open Government, Chief Data Officers, Smart Cities, etc. This apparatus characterized by various interfaces, methods of data production, formats, and processing programs. They are brimming with technical procedures and legal regimes. They are inhabited by educated actors in the bureaucratic manufacturing done by the elites. These apparatus fuel the performation of digital public policies. In this section, we will examine some of the emblematic features of the promises of "transparency" made by Open Data:

the opening of the data on public procurements. Our field of observation concerns both the international recommendations and a project involving several territorial entities (regions, departments, and cities) involved in the same scheme. We show how the various different actors negotiate, and how they constrain this updating process. And once again, this is a case of observing how a political project emerges, a project which is fundamentally overdetermined by the dominant forms, and never questioned by the underlying economic rationality.

### 2.3.1. *On maintaining the desire for data and barometers*

Data have long been a major actant in public policy development; they act at the heart of the decision-making processes, the semioticization of practices, subjective elements and strategies, and "collective intelligences". Digital data, as well as the public programs which currently promote its utilization, thus undeniably form part of the alliance between statistical reasoning and the emergence of the nation state, as demonstrated by A. Desrosières [DES 93, DES 08]. Gabriel Tarde had also highlighted certain promises about the power of this reasoning, which was necessary for the modes of governance that he thought could be improved. Today, their proliferation, their heterogeneity (with qualitative and quantitative traces), the mechanisms for their treatment and their intricate interweavings in order to give life to new assemblages of territories, all raise the question of the possibility of a questioning of the leadership that is inherited and perhaps the forms of government, without any damaging effects to the political leadership that may be put in place, or the socio-political scratches that come into maturity. It is impossible for the way these issues take shape to be written in advance. This continues to be a hotly debated topic [KIT 14, MOR 14].

This abundance of reports and laws is a testament to this digital and "data-centric" viewpoint taken by public sector actions[126]. And of course, all

---

126 In France, the last few months have been marked by a series of laws (to the point where they border on causing confusion or even contradicting themselves) that put the issue of data within public action at the forefront: the Macron I and II laws, NOTRE, Valter, Lemaire pour un Republique numerique (enacted on October 5, 2016); the Fouilleron or AGD (General Data Administrator) reports, to name some of the more recent ones, whose focus moves us from Open Data to "governance by data". At the European level, the rules of Open Data were updated in 2011 and 2013 to supplement the PSI directive on the re-use of Public sector information (Directive 2013/37/EU). Similarly, the regulation on the protection of

of this is accompanied by the production of articles by a multitude of experts, current and former elected officials, and press articles that stir up this environment. The obsession with digital data is far from being exclusive to the public sector: we have already had the opportunity to analyze "this investment of desires" in data [CAR 15][127].

In the future outcomes of the pairing between technogenesis/ sociogenesis [STI 96], the manufacturing of the law [LAT 02] occupies a strategic but uncertain place in the manifestation of powers, which is to say, the actants (private or public), in the regulated adjustments of their strength ratios. From a certain point of view, it consolidates prescriptions that may still seem fragile, and indicates arbitrations which in this case affirm one of the first key aspects of a data-centric public action: the requirement to open the data. After the wave of e-administration measures starting in the early 2000s, the opening of data became not only the indicator of an "innovative" potential, but also the rule.

Another expression of data-centrism in the public sphere: the interest in the use on a mass scale of data produced by sensors and various digital practices "outside" of the administrations. The processing of these data using data search methods ("data mining"), characteristic of "big data", invites us to critically examine the algorithm as a medium that is characteristic of "data-centric territories and cities" and more generally, of our digitally saturated societies. Generally speaking, what is referred to as *Open Data* can be seen as a set of processes that converge on a common objective and *modus operandi*: the dissemination and use of information resources, irrespective of the context in which they were originally produced. This implies the free access to data and the absence of enclosures that would restrict its re-operation (enclosures which may be of a technical, commercial, legal, cognitive, and political nature) [CAR 12, ERT 15, PEU 13] . This issue of persistent enclosures and power relationships is just one of the aspects to be questioned within the current digital political economy. We may also be able to include an array of very diverse "movements", apparatus and actors under the label of Open Data (which historically includes actors involved in

---

digital data takes effect as of 2018, in addition to the standardization of legislation and strengthening of the sanctioning powers of the Cnil, with a new mission profile: the *Data Protection Officer*. For legislative clarification, see [CAR 16].

127 From the evolution of SHS and digital humanities, continuing on through various "Open" movements, to various forms of transhumanism and marketing, see [NOY 14, 17].

free software, free licenses, and open research archives at its forefront)[128]. With regard to "public" data relating to States, communities, administrations and other entities whose data may be considered "in the public interest"[129], the first prescriptions date back to the mid-2000s (although in the case of France, we may consider, for example, that free access to administrative documents has been enshrined in French law since 1978)[130]. At the same time, private Open Data is also in development. More broadly, the pairing of Open Data/Big Data/data mining characterizes what is presented – regardless of its sector[131] – as the chreode of our digital futures, and as a fabric woven from multiple expressions [CAR 15]. The programs of Open Government, the first incarnation of which was proposed by the Obama administration in 2009, present Open Data as one of the three pillars of its approach: it adds support for citizen participation through consultations or through the mobilization of certain Civic Tech actors[132], and intra and inter-organizational transformations taking place under the banner of "interdisciplinary actions" and collaboration between the stakeholders within the territory [LAS 10].

---

128 The works of Lawrence Lessig, Richard Stallman, Steven Harnad and Paul Ginsparg have been seminal in this field. In the science domain (*Open access*), ArXiv (in physics), made in 1991, is the first platform for access to data sets. In France, Archivesic was launched in the SHS in 2002 (later integrated into HAL). *Open Access* covers not only open access to scientific publications (open archives and open journal platforms such as Revue.org), but also the raw data for research, with *Open Data Mining* being an extension of this.

129 In February 2015, the Macron law required companies, such as public transit companies, to put all information relating to their timetables and stops online, in a free and open format. However, the Lemaire law of early 2016 has added a limit to the opening perimeter for the SPIC and the EPICs (SNCF and RATP) whose activities are subject to competition.

130 Law No. 78-753 of 17 July 1978 on the right of access to administrative documents. Or in addition, the Declaration of Human Rights and Citizens' Rights - article 15: "The company has the right to hold any public official in its administration to account." In the United States, the *Freedom of Information Act* was adopted in 1966 in the context of the Vietnam War, and obligated federal agencies to release their unclassified documents. It has since been regularly reviewed.

131 A characteristic pairing between science and, more recently, programs for *Smart Cities*, but also *hypermaketing*.

132 According to a report by the Knight Foundation, the areas in which Civic Tech intervenes are: collaborative consumption, crowdfunding, debates (including social networks, online consultations), organizing collective actions, public data (exploitation, access), *The Emergence of Civic Tech*, 2013. See also the works by MIT on the subject, available at: https://www.media.mit.edu/research/groups/civic-media.

The narratique of public Open Data is also based on sets of celebration[133], the production of grids of intelligibility translated into barometers (which are, for the most part, quite weak) and in doing so, the establishment of repositories of actions are, at a minimum, put to use in speeches. As in the case of the digital policies inside the organizations, the project managers have their evaluative, normative and legitimizing mechanisms, from which the requirements formed in this way are distributed.

Through the promises of Open Data once more, and by defeating the various (widely differing) national/territorial incarnations and policies for standard ideals, fictions, narratives and micro-narratives will be distributed in the midst of the narrative assemblage like gearboxes/connectors of justification.

An analysis of the policies and apparatus carried out around the world on the opening of public procurement data shows the legacy of the complex interconnections between non-governmental associations, public bodies, and economic actors. To summarize briefly, the prescription can develop according to a bottom-up or societal dynamic (as can be seen, for example, in the Anglo-American world)[134], according to a more top-down model (for example, in France with the massive investment of government and legal action), or in a decentralized manner (based on local agency initiatives) [BOU 13, GRA 14]. Generally speaking, the opening of public data is one of the pillars of the Open Government[135]. It is a means of achieving it in the same way as the steps aimed at promoting the participation of citizens and those aiming at greater organizational efficiency (internal to the administrations but also with various other organizations and

---

133 See the DataConnexions "contest" organized by Etalab (an entity responsible for opening public data for the French government), but also the celebrations and labels of associations of the interconnected type, available at: https://www.etalab.gouv.fr/dataconnexions and http://www.interconnectes.com/.

134 In Great Britain, the Open Knowledge Foundation was created in 2004. In March 2006, *The Guardian* launched a campaign called "Free Our Data", asking the government to open up public data. In the United States, created in April 2006, the Sunlight Foundation is an American non-profit organization that acts to promote the transparency and the openness of government data on the Internet.

135 See the eight techno-political principles of *Open Government Data* presented by L. Lessig in 2007 at the Sevastopol conference in California, available at: https://opengovdata. org/.

stakeholders). Although they can take on very different forms depending on the countries involved, these programs explicitly connect the watchword "transparency" to Open Data [LAS 10, RUP 13]. The opening of data on public procurement is thus, *a priori*, one of the emblematic features of Open Government and public Open Data. In the area of public finances (including procurements), we may distinguish between two main types of actors (citing here only the main ones), the instigators of what we call, along the lines of the sociology of translation, "processes of interest" [AKR 16][136].

### 2.3.1.1. *Processes of interessement carried out by non-governmental bodies*

An American non-profit association created in 2006, the Sunlight Foundation, along with the Open Knowledge Foundation in England, has been engaged in the first movements for Open Government. It is involved in the fields related to Open Data at the local, federal and international level. Presenting itself as a citizen watchdog group, and also benefiting from a unique context of campaign financing in elections and access to a relatively broad array of public data, the association has adopted the mantra of political and financial transparency. One of its emblematic areas of action in the US has been the production, analysis, and recommendations made with regard specifically to public procurements[137]. In addition, the Sunlight Foundation is associated with the analysis group *Open Contracting*[138]. This group works on standards and practices relating to public contracts, including calls to tendering procedures, contractual arrangements, and other such apparatus. *Open Contracting* also carries out various analyses and recommendations on the topic by developing a more economical approach to the opening of public procurements than the Sunlight Foundation. At

---

136 A few processes of note: as in the case of the adoption of a technological innovation, an idea, etc., the commitment to such an action or policy depends on the problems, needs and interests that characterize the parties. They can only become "involved" if they are "concerned" in this way by the problematization that has been constructed, argued and are engaged with the same desire (or against it, and the formulation of the problem and its solutions). Apart from coercive situations, it therefore becomes a question of evaluating the power of the forces and the networks that act there and the performative processes that are activated and activate these desires (one of the conditions for this will be the formation of a coalition – such as the creation of a new power relationship – around the same goal).

137 Available at: http://sunlightfoundation.com/issues/procurement-government/.

138 Available at: http://www.open-contracting.org/global_principles.

European level, the nonprofit organization OpenTed[139] promotes the development of data formats and the enrichment of the perimeters of data on public procurements, while developing innovative analyses (going beyond simple infographics), doing so by utilizing the data from *Tender Electronic Daily* (TED).

### 2.3.1.2. *Intergovernmental interessement processes*

In 2010, the leaders of the G20 created the Anti-Corruption Working Group (ACWG). With the support of the World Bank, the governments involved sought to reaffirm "the negative impact of corruption on economic growth, trade and development". In addition to various transformations to be made to public procurement processes, budget analyses, etc., the 2015–2016 G20 anti-corruption plan stressed the importance of the actions to be taken in favor of Open Data:

> "The ACWG has identified Open Data, public procurement, whistleblower protections, immunities from prosecution, fiscal and budget transparency, and standards for public officials as issues affecting the public sector which merit particular attention in 2015–16[140]".

In addition, launched in September 2011 by eight founding countries, the *Open Government Partnership* (OGP)[141] is an international initiative, which

---

139 Available at: http://ted.openspending.org/ and http://ted.europa.eu/TED/misc/choose Language.do.

140 Available at: http://star.worldbank.org/star/about-us/g20-anti-corruption-working-group.

141 The OGP is in favor of the transparency of public action and open governance, public integrity, the fight against corruption, and the growth of digital and new technologies. The countries that founded it in 2011 were: Brazil, Mexico, Norway, the Philippines, South Africa, the United Kingdom, and the United States. The last world summit was held in Paris in 2016. This event was characterized, in particular, by a force for massive enrollment, since it was the occasion for government representatives of more than 100 countries, NGOs (some of which were fighting against corruption within those same governments and the public sphere, or against laws judged to be destructive to basic freedoms), donors (the French Agency for Development, US Aids, the Hewlett Foundation, etc.), local authorities, private actors, etc. to all be brought together in the same place. In this regard, see the boycott of the event by some French associations: "Participatory Democracy: The Paris summit begins, surrounded by controversy", available at: http://www.lemonde.fr/pixels/article/2016/12/05/democratie-participative-le-sommet-de-paris-s-ouvre-sur-fond-de-polemiques_5043813_4408996.html# 6CZG5oE2IFWdcVYu.99.

seeks to promote transparency and the integrity of Governments. According to the body, it is supported by the widespread use of digital technologies and the Internet[142]. Here, political openness is synonymous with communication and Open Data.

Thus, it is a doctrine that aims to improve the effectiveness and accountability of public governance by advancing the necessity for citizens to have a right of access to the documents and the procedures of their governments in order *to promote greater transparency and accountability*, which would involve giving citizens the means to monitor, oversee and participate in government and local decisions. The partnership now comprises 76 member countries, including France since 2014 (with France being assured the presidency in 2016). Its mission was to promote "access to information on government activities" as well as practices of transparency, democracy and citizen participation (to control, oversee, and take part in decisions), the use of the Internet and technologies that would allow for "an Open Government". The arguments and promises made are:

> "Beyond OGP's normative arguments for opening government-held data, there are three common instrumental arguments in favor of opening up data held by the Government (Center for Data Innovation 2015):
>
> 1. Economic: Potential economic impact;
>
> 2. Social: Improved public services;
>
> 3. Political: Better accountability through reduced fraud, waste, and abuse[143]".

For its part, the OECD is also developing an international analysis on innovation and public procurement as part of the fight against corruption[144]. Its "performance indicators" in this field are: the efficiency of the public

---

142 In the OECD recommendations from 2014, we can see the major role given to ICTs in this sense: "Capturing the value of digital technologies for more open, participatory and innovative governments", available at: http://www.oecd.org/gov/ Digital-government/ recommendation-on-digital-government-strategies.htm.
143 Available at: http://www.opengovpartnership.org/.
144 Available at: http://www.oecd.org/gov/ethics/public-procurement.htm.

procurement process, the openness and transparency of the process, the professionalism of the actors, the management of contracts, and the monitoring of achievements.

For these actors – in particular the non-governmental associations – the strength of the prescriptions and the construction of a power relationship with government authorities pass through the creation of very powerful "communication" apparatus: barometers. Acting in line with a general narrative about Open Data, the barometer – a ranking of different countries based on their level of commitment to an OD policy – like many other mechanisms for evaluating digital strategies or practices, is presented both as an intelligibility operator (to give itself a criteriology), a normative operator, and performative operator (if the ranking is favorable, this may be seen as the occasion for celebrations, and if it is less so, it can spur on calls for a new "mobilization"[145]). The main criteria for these barometers (created between 2012 and 2014) are: the data-related subjects referred to in data released by States[146]; technical characteristics[147]; the rights for use[148] and for certain apparatus, with government incentives also taken into account[149]. In addition to those of the OECD mentioned above, we have at least three apparatus, taking into account as of recently the field of public procurements. These are the Sunlight Foundation, the Open Knowledge Foundation[150], and the W3C Open Barometer (which ranked the UK in first place in 2015, which has

---

145 France fell from 3rd place in 2014 on the OKF barometer to 10th in 2015. In April 2016, the government site modernization.gouv had not yet updated its messages on the subject.

146 For the OKF and its *Open Data Census* apparatus, a list of 15 key data sets at national level has been defined. These data sets have been chosen because they represent an interest for citizens and economic actors. They are regularly cited in the consultations as emblematic data sets of an Open Data approach. Of course, the importance of a data set also depends on the country's context, its level of development, its infrastructure, its political structure, etc. This incomplete list may be completed later. Open data is data that can be freely used, reused and redistributed by anyone – subject to, at most, a requirement to indicate that sharing under identical conditions be allowed. Open data will meet the technical, legal and economic criteria that are evaluated by the *Open Data Index*, using an *Open Definition* as a reference.

147 Digital formats, machine readable and non-proprietary. Update frequency. Full data sets. Level of detail.

148 Availability free of charge and/or involving licensing fees. Open license. Searchable license.

149 Legislative framework of the country. Assessment and case analyses. Accompanying initiatives.

150 Available at: http://global.census.okfn.org/.

since been bested by Taiwan and Australia as of 2016)[151]. The general criteriology retains a high level of convergence, as well as the methodology based on self-reporting by representatives from each country (depending on which association is involved, further investigations may be carried out)[152]. With regard to public procurement data, it is worth noting that these are not completed – in particular, in the case of the OKF and W3C barometers – until a later period (in 2015), with other data relating to public finances (completing the budget and expenditure data sets). However, despite the significant investments made in the subject by many actors, according to the barometer of the World Wide Web Foundation, in 2015, less than 10% of the countries on their barometer (nearly 100) proposed an Open Data approach to public budgets and procurements.

We may consider that, based on these barometers, often self-reported by the actors who are supposed to be evaluated (and even if certain methods and criteria change)[153], a self-legitimizing by the power occurs, and this is also the reason why narratives obtain their strength.

### 2.3.2. *Visualizations and format pivots: techno-political writings*

In this period, when each area of public action is given the order to "release data", and summoned to register itself as part of the data-driven movement, on a global scale[154], in the following section, we give preference to an analysis of the co-determination of enunciation assemblages and practices, statements that are not summed up merely in general recommendations and injunctions, but which take particular semiotic forms: interfaces, data, features, and treatment programs are considered as the most important instruments for performance, and as the most important

---

151 Available at: http://opendatabarometer.org/.
152 A comparison of the Open Data barometers [SUS 14].
153 See the changes in the *Global Open Data Index* in the OKF index: "The Global Open Data Index (GODI) is an independent assessment of Open Government data publication from a civic perspective. GODI enables different Open Data stakeholders to track government's progress on Open Data release. GODI also allows governments to get direct feedback from data users. The Index gives both parties a baseline for discussion and analysis of the Open Data ecosystem in their country and internationally. We encourage all interested parties to participate in an open dialogue to allow for ownership of the results and to make the Index as relevant as possible." Available at: https://index.okfn.org/methodology/.
154 See the Mc Kinsey reports from 2011 and 2013 on Open Data and Big Data.

instruments of a public government that extends across various levels of scale. Thus, there is a need to consider the co-determination of professions, practices, and technical skills. Following M. Foucault, in this case, we understand "governmentality" to refer to "the rational forms, technical procedures, and instrumentation through which it is exercised, and on the other hand, the strategic issues that make them unstable and reversible" [LAS 04].

The case studied here concerns an approach initiated in 2014–2015 by certain actors in the same region (regional councils, cities, departmental councils, economic development associations, companies) for the opening of data on public orders and the design of a related web communication platform. It proved to have two separate interests. First, although the regional council's prescription was very strong (it was also one of the main funders of the project), the design process is polycentric: the approach was not decreed by the state, the communities are free to engage in the regional project (on the other hand, the obligation that had just been decreed by the legislator would obligate them to release certain data), the associated actor sets out with him on undertakings and enrollments (progressive and specific), other entities are promoted (the enlargement of the project group to include new participants). The second phenomenon distinguished in this case: the initiative precedes the legislative framework for the opening of public procurement data specified in 2016[155] and even aims to act as the power for the development (and ongoing adaptation) of the national doctrine in this area (the entanglement of the levels of scale is seen here as an additional force, since there are two levels of proximity between the pilot of the project with the territorial actors and the actors of the ministries in charge of regulations on the modernization of the state and *Open Data*). In order to show the co-determination of the scales and the socio-technical dimension of a political instrument such as Open Data, we present an overview of the main topics of discussion of the project group observed over the period from September 2015 to May 2016, by linking these debates with the configurations of the emerging political project.

---

155 Public procurement codes.

## 2.3.2.1. *Justification: economic and organizational optimization as a virtue*

An initial goal, in this case economic, is necessary from the outset: it is a question of promoting the access of small and mid-size businesses to public markets by balancing legal constraints, for which the burdensome nature of the processes is often criticized, by providing them with mechanisms for research and more efficient monitoring, the knowledge of markets and their competitors that would promote a more efficient "territorial intelligence". In this case, it is the association initiating the apparatus that supports this orientation, positioning the project in alignment with the *Small Business Act*, passed in Europe and elsewhere[156] (a course of action that was implemented notably in the US in 1953). A second justification appeared primarily after the introduction of a pilot site: it involved the gains that appear in terms of leading the public action. Open data, applied to public orders by requiring for work to be done on the data collected and its formats, opens up the possibility for new analyses to decision-makers ("measurements of territorial attractiveness", "measurements of the competitiveness of local companies"). This new knowledge of economic dynamics, the commitment to a new reflexivity with regard to their purchasing practices, however, is not without political questions. The interest in charting the different procurements held by the communities of a region and tools such as infographics/data visualizations (we still can't really call this stage advanced data mining) is indicative of the challenges of mediation (in this case, we have allowed screening panels to be crossed together with another semiotic representation). For the actors, this visualization is also an example of the application of the "data science", even though this only requires us to use simple cartographic tools. A fundamental tension is created by the sharing of this mapping, and by extension, the new possibilities of knowledge and interpretations of public procurement practices with the general public. It could be said, in the sense that the teams and decision-makers are prepared to recognize the internal reflexive gains (giving themselves the conditions for new structural visibility), that the mastery of semiotic control is not something they can avoid.

---

156 The SGAR Midi-Pyrénées and the communities have designed SBA apparatus by revising certain practices (revisions within the limits of the legal framework), such as increases in the advances, the simplification of administrative procedures, etc., available at: http://www.action-publique.gouv.fr/files/files/PDF/2015_rapport_innovation_territoriale.pdf. Similarly, the OECD also stresses the consideration of other measures favoring the equity of access to public procurements, particularly for small businesses.

In addition, the project's passage through a phase of identification of available data reveals the differences in the practices (within administrations or between administrations), the existence, non-existence, or differences of perception (procurements in their value after sales tax, or otherwise) or redundant information[157]. The Open Data project thus becomes an issue of optimizing internal apparatus (questions about the configurations of the databases of the few dominant management software programs on these subjects, the need for these to carry out transformations of formats, to consider the automation of certain processes, the obligation for the agents to complete missing data fields and therefore a temporal load to consider, etc.). This issue of data processing, of "working on the raw formats" is recurrent [DEN 14, RUP 13] and resonates with the formula presented by B. Latour, for which, instead of data, it would make more sense to talk about the gains made. This allows us to interrogate the processes of the capturing, filtering, and treatment of this formula.

Another point that becomes established relatively quickly, also with regard to the prospects of the gains to be obtained by the communities: *Open Data* would thus be associated with a learning loop for the buyers. Here, more than a real observation of this (which must be done over a long period of time), we assume possibilities of improvement to the purchasing practices that would also be obtained in this practice, to the search features, and to alerts: the companies' sourcing could be facilitated, the monitoring of the procurements and the establishment of order groupings. At this point, though the consensus on the economic purposes of Open Data for public orders is clear, tension remains for those within organizational areas. This has to do with determining the level of constraints that will affect the agents (and to a lesser extent, the publishers). The obvious differences between the desired (projected) analyses and the actual data is a major issue. This point opens up a discussion on the legal aspects and the format pivot.

### 2.3.2.2. *The format pivot as a zone of strategic and political determination*

Techno-policy and regulatory policy are thus closely connected, and will participate in resolving the differences between the desire for "increased knowledge" (this notion merits discussion) and organizational constraints. At the beginning of the project, the legislative framework is not yet stabilized,

---

157 In particular, this includes extraction and mapping done in the format pivot.

and the international standards are hardly known, if they are known at all. Thus, the team initially sets out on a phase to define a format pivot (already existing at European level), which requires several weeks of negotiation and discussions with the pilot communities. As of March 2016, section 107 of the Public Procurement decree specifies that "essential data" must be made open to the public[158]. It states that: "By no later than October 1, 2018, the purchaser shall offer, on his buyer profile, free, direct and complete access to the essential data of that public contract, with the exception of information whose disclosure would be contrary to public order." The list of essential data is as follows:

– no later than two months from the notification date as defined in article 103, the unique identification number assigned to the procurement and the data relating to its attribution:

- the identification of the purchaser;

- the nature and purpose of the public procurement;

- the procedure by which it was passed;

- the primary location in which the services or works forming the subject of the public procurement are made;

- the duration of the public procurement;

- the amount and main financial conditions of the public contract;

- the identification of the responsible party;

- the date of signature of the public procurement by the purchaser;

– the data relating to any changes made to the procurement:

- the purpose of the change;

- the impact of the change on the duration or amount of the procurement;

- the date of signature by the purchaser of the change in the public contract.

---

158 Available at: https://www.legifrance.gouv.fr/affichTexteArticle.do?idArticle= JORFART I000032296716&cidTexte=JORFTEXT000032295952. The essential data on public procurements are published in accordance with the terms set by the minister responsible for the economy.

The first format pivot of the regional project focused on the allocation phase, and did not take into account the changes in the procurement that are specified in the decree. On other aspects, corresponding to the decision makers' desire for analysis, it indicates elements such as the need for the company's SIRET number[159], information on subcontractors and contractors, or on the salaried staff of the contracted company. In any event, the scope of two formats is nonetheless much less demanding than the international standards mentioned previously, which apply over the entire lifespan of the public procurement, and which insist on the need to integrate documents from the procurement for a more thorough semantic analysis. Now entering a new phase, the regional project has given itself the objective of being a space for the contribution to and enrichment of this format pivot by mobilizing other actors, and in fact is currently a place for experimentation from which a national recommendation (which may possibly be enriched) will be formulated. A question asked by a purchasing services officer indicates a certain degree of uncertainty as to the dynamics of the approach: "What are the obligations and penalties involved, in particular, the risks for my election if I do not openly provide this procurement data?" At the end of these phases of discussion, the data driven perspective seems to shed its immaculate image, or to be in the process of reformulating: the word "data science" becomes more commonly used, providing an outlook combining both traditional screenings together with *DataViz*[160], and in this shift, predictive algorithmics seem to only offer a vague possibility and very fuzzy practices.

This process was still underway in May 2016, the date that had been set for a political phase made up of recommendations to the government, the interest of local elected officials, the requirements within organizations, and the enrichment of data and features of the regional platform. As a result of the work done by the project group, a quite unprecedented chain of performations has been expressed, which has led to the creation of a national decree for public procurements that applies to all public organizations.

---

159 This allows for the entity that carries out the mission, and not its parent company, to be accurately located. This has a fundamental impact on the analysis of the level of solicitation of local companies and the impact on elements such as employment.

160 See, for example, this graphic on public procurements available at: http://www.dataplazza.com/pres-de-10-milliards-deuros-de-marches-publics-en-2014/.

The example of the pivot format shows how much semiopolitics and molecular performations are closely linked, and that their characters have the ability to redistribute themselves by molar forces, in a kind of "performation down to the bottom". This is also done openly, in a state of permanent incompleteness[161]. The next chapter will focus on clarifying the actions of these semiopolitics, and the methods by which they are formulated, by examining other political economies, and more globally, the political economies of interfaces created within organizations.

161 See [STE 10, CLI 86].

# Monitoring Assemblages and their Semiopolitics in Action

## 3.1. Interfaces and semiopolitical regimes

In the previous chapters, we examined the organizational fabric, through the lens of multiple dynamics: the instauration of sociotechnical scripts deriving from various conflict relationships and relations of strength; the development of complex, generalized *narratique* giving rise to the desire for constant innovation; and the shift towards a data-centric approach. Performation as a process has played a central role, and we have looked at a number of phenomena in which it manifests. We have briefly shown how this affects what could be called the "organizational epithumia"[1].

It is in this context that we turn our attention to organizational semiopolitics. Particular attention will also be paid to the status of interfaces, to the digital methods involved in this "regard", and to analysis of new organizational empirical corpora.

Among other things, the aim is to step into the arena of praxis and creation of new sociocognitive and technopolitical ecologies offered by "online socialization platforms" – platforms which can be used simultaneously for different purposes, by the employees and by the management. Along the way, we shall put forward a number of proposals to develop – founded on the concept of "assemblage" advanced by Deleuze and

---

1 See section 2.2.5.

Guatarri – a renewed outlook on ethno-graphic approaches, including the digital traces, produced or left by the actors in the course of their activities.

### 3.1.1. *Machines and interfaces: some pointers*

Like Leroi-Gourhan, Simondon and Latour, Guattari sets out the principle of indissociability of the object from the milieu in which it exists, and to whose existence it also contributes. Thus, Sauvenargues focuses on this technical issue as described by Guattari:

> "A machine is no longer a subset of technology, and certainly does not represent technical progress over a tool."

Rather, it is the issue of technology which is dependent on "machines", as Guattari views it:

> "Machines are the prerequisite for technology, rather than the result of it." [GUA 91a]

Basing his arguments upon those of historians and philosophers of technology including Leroi-Gourhan, Détienne, Mumford and Simondon, Guattari states that an individual technology, tool or machine – a hammer, an airplane, etc. – cannot be studied in isolation, without taking into account the milieu of individuation which surrounds it and makes it work. No machine or technological tool exists on its own, because these items only work within an ordered milieu of individuation, which is its possibility condition: there can be no hammer without a nail. Thus, there is an interaction between a multitude of technical items facilitating the manufacture of both hammers and nails, but also the conditions of their uses and usages. Simondon [SIM 58] puts it thus:

> "Any individual technical item contains reference to its associated technical system, which acts as a transcendental condition of possibility." [SAU 12]

In Guattari's view, machine assemblages are not limited to "the functional set which combines the machine with man". Account must be taken of numerous components:

"– material and energetic components;

– diagrammatic and algorithmic semiotic components (maps, formulae, equations, calculations surrounding the machine's manufacture);

– components of organs, influx and mood of the human body;

– information and mental representations, both individual and collective;

– investments in machines with the goal of producing subjectivity in adjacency to their components;

– abstract machines[2] which are instaured transversally to the hardware, cognitive, emotional and social machine levels discussed above" [GUA 91a, 91b].

Here, more than ever, interfaces have a major role to play.

"An interface lends ontological consistency to something which happens between two heterogeneous layers of coding or semiotic expression" [GUA 91b].

Interfaces act as mediator or passage between two milieus[3]: they handle and "facilitate" the passage between the different components of the assemblage. Depending on the case, on the basis of a variety of semiotic systems (a computer program, a software application, a smartphone screen, for instance, but equally a political spokesperson, money, music, etc.),

---

2 The term "abstract" here refers to extraction, as Guattari points out: "When we speak of abstract machines, 'abstract' could be understood as 'extracted'. These are setups which bring into contact all the heterogeneous levels that they pass through, listed above". In the case of organizational politics, we can therefore consider to be phenomena of the abstract machine, not only any entity or process which contributes to the filtering and interweaving of scripts, digital policies deemed exemplary, but also any milieu giving consistency to a digital machine which selects paths on the Internet, capturing them and weaving them together, and by combining them, creates a strategy (scientific strategy, marketing strategy, etc.). In that sense, datamining is a powerful abstract machine as understood by Guattari, always in relation with the other listed components (material, semiotic, desire-based, etc.).
3 "In computer science, the idea of an interface denotes any apparatus, be it hardware or software, placed at the man–machine intersection to allow them to communicate" [SER 98].

interfaces express the flows passing through that assemblage, linking together the points, actants, behaviors and subjectivities, and in doing so, transforming them, enacting them (which, once again, is somewhat reminiscent of the very idea of "translation").[4]

Thus, a socio-technical set is both the manufactured and the manufacturer, the expression and the expressed, or to put it another way, "a machine is interfacing and interfaced" [LÉV 94]:

"It expresses, betrays, unfolds and refolds, for a downstream machine, the flows produced by an upstream machine. In itself, it is made up of interpretative machines which split it, multiply it and harmonize it. The interface is the 'foreign policy' aspect of the machine, which can insert it into new networks and make it interpret new flows" [LÉV 94].

In that sense, the *organization as a machine* (as understood above) is also interfacing and interfaced: the digital applications which it designs, its various information systems or any other device and semiotic equipment, do not only shape the relationship between human beings and their working praxes, the internal and external organizational environment, and the different human and hardware components which make it up; the *organization as a machine* is performated, traversed, modeled by flows over which it only has partial control (think, for example, of software programs, data security protocols or labor law).

If we go a little further in defining the conceptual framework, we can say that we are dealing with something similar to the autopoietic dynamics described by Francisco Varela and Humberto Maturana. In *Autonomie et connaissance* (Autonomy and Knowledge), Varela puts forward the following definition:

"An autopoietic machine is organized (defined as a unity) as a network of processes of production (transformation and destruction) of components that produces the components which: 1) through their interactions and transformations

---

4 See Chapter 1.

continuously regenerate and realize the network of processes (relations) that produced them; and 2) constitute it [the machine] as a concrete unity in the space in which they (the components) exist by specifying to the topological domain of its realization as such a network. It follows that an autopoietic machine engenders and continually specifies its own organization. It carries out this constant process of replacing its components, because it is continually being subjected to external disturbances and constantly forced to compensate for them. Hence, an autopoietic machine is a system with stable relations where the fundamental invariant is its own organization (the network of relations which define it)" [VAR 89].

This means that sociotechnical ensembles[5], considered to be autopoietic, are characterized by multiple feedback loops ensuring the stability of the whole. The interfaces in this instance act as filter-and-capture membranes, translators, transformers.

However, as pointed out by F. Guattari as regards machine autopoiesis, we can just as easily consider a "machine-organization" to be characterized by imbalance rather than stability

"Its emergence is shadowed by the threat of breakdown, catastrophe and death. [...] The machine always depends upon external elements in order to exist as a machine" [GUA 91a].

In that sense, it would undoubtedly be more fruitful to envisage the proliferation of the interfaces (digital interfaces, in particular) as the expression of "machine-organizations" subject to a type of tension, a dual movement which pulls as strongly toward autopoiesis as towards allopoiesis. The challenge for interfaces, then, is to get around the simple phenomena of homomorphy and self-reference seen in the previous chapter, and become

---

5 Note that Varela reserved the concept of autopoiesis for living systems; non-living systems, in his view, were the product of allopoiesis.

open to creative potentials fed by the outside world and its ontologically unstable condition[6].

Again following on from the work of J.-M. Noyer, based on the concept of continuity of thinking of assemblages, we consider that the concept of *machine interfaces* must be envisaged from an extensive standpoint. The description could apply to a number of intellectual technologies: search engines, mapping tools, automatic language processing software, immersive apparatuses, intranets, socio-digital networks, etc. In an organizational context, "they define and feed into the internal and external pragmatism of socio-technical machines", characterizing and equipping the modes of existence at work:

> "They translate, filter and determine the types and numbers of possible connections and relations within the autopoietic system constituted by each specific apparatus or organization. They also serve as mediations, such as membranes that regulate the evolution of the system–environment couplings and are involved in the filtering of the environment events that will activate specific internal states within the organization, be they beneficial or not" [NOY 17].

In that sense, they act at the center of what Alexander R. Galloway, and others before him, describes as a "zone of indecision" between an external and an internal [GAL 12]. Thus, "they again define or lend consistency to the interstices, the zones of indetermination, of shifting or elimination of the boundaries which populate the existential realms at work and which traverse (constantly disturbing it with their disruption) the molar organization, the entrepreneurial and administrative desire of collective intelligences – desire which is exhausted by the incessant striating of the energies and economies of the libido" [GAL 12].

---

6 On metastability: a system is in "metastable" equilibrium when certain variations might bring about a departure, a transformation of the equilibrium. Death is a stable state (as it no longer allows for any possible transformation). A collective (e.g. a company) is in a metastable state: it is full of variations, tensions (even slight), which are the condition of its perpetuation, the precondition for its shifting towards other systems (themselves metastable). See also [STE 04].

This question obviously goes beyond the organizational environment, and also characterizes the set of digital milieus. Such is the case of the IoT, which J.-M. Noyer states is "at the heart of all modern technological developments, whereby any object, any living being, any plant or mineral (with its associated data) can instantly be related with any other, through unprecedented semiotic elaborations and through the proliferation of interfaces and their software applications (smartphones, tablet computers, captures, CCTV cameras, etc.). Meanwhile, the consumerist vertigo finds therein new raw material to explore and exploit." [NOY 17].

We have described the instauration of organizational milieus coupled with semiotics and digital machines, collective assemblages of utterance which serve as a milieu for strategic model selection devices, libidinous economics of the technopolitics of organizations, local adjustments stemming from local pragmatism and interface pragmatism, with the scripts being both the vehicles and the conditions for them.

To go into greater detail about the manifestations and conditions of this fabric, we need to more fully explore the layers of action of the interfaces – layers examined through the lens of the case of Moeva and its political economies, for which we propose other expressions characteristic of what we define as a "semiopolitic".

The terms "political economy of interfaces" and "semiopolitics" denote all the rules, constraints and decisions occurring in digital interfaces or delegated to those interfaces. Such delegation is done partly blindly, because it is instantiated beyond any control and rational choice on the part of the decision-makers and users, stemming from programs designed elsewhere. Semiopolitics places emphasis on the coupling between signifier/a-signifier semiotics, on the action of non-linguistic semiotics, on the exponential growth of digital data-plots and automated data processing, on the movement of semiotics as major actants in the performation of praxes and an organizational political economy.

### 3.1.2. *Molar/molecular and D/T/R*

At the heart of the digital fabric of organizations, digital semiopolitics is simultaneously the product of social, cognitive, desirant machines (of the action of multiple adversaries that are more or less close to the concrete working praxes)[7] and material and ichnological components[8], hard and soft. All of this mobilizes forces of varying intensity, more or less associated, coming and going (because the movements are reversible and the connections are multiple), for example in the case of construction of digital politics of public organizations, state institutions and legislative bodies at the offices of agents, and the data processing programs that they use, by means of a crowd of prescriptors which we have seen act as a vast performation machine. One of the requirements for organizational studies, therefore, is to be able to identify the forces and consequences of the micropolitics and macro-politics and, which is more, the links between them.

As described by F. Guattari in *Lignes de fuite* [GUA 11], here as in other situations, we distinguish between molar and molecular processes. The philosopher puts forward possible combinations of the two, based on a criterion of size and a political criterion. For each possible combination, there is a specific corresponding "revolutionary potential" – that is, a capacity to transform the assemblage in question. The simplified model presents two domains which are dependent on the size of the social sets in question: on the one hand, *infra-individual and microsocial sets*, and on the other, *macrosocial sets*. Two politics of desire apply to these social sets: *a politics of molecular power* – that is, *social de-stratification* or *"micropolitics of desire"*, based in a collective assemblage of production and utterance; a *politics of molar power* which sets up and stratifies the *socius* and spreads over formations of power, engaging a function of setting up and implementing a collective equipment network (see Table 3.1) [GUA 11]. This standpoint seems interesting to us to examine in further detail in a specific ethnographic work which describes the "molar/molecular cycles" where each enters into exchanges, transformations and complex futures. We have seen this in the case of Moeva's politics, Open Data in the public sector, and will examine other configurations and situations below – in particular, the development of business social networks or that of the establishment of the Internet by employees. With respect to these latter two phenomena, we can say that we have a situation of destabilization or conflict (1-4-3) between managerial macro-equipment (the appropriate internal

---

7 Management, consultants, action standards, judicial rules which apply to organizational politics.

8 Ichnology: science of traces – a term applied to digital apparatuses by L. Merzeau to describe the development of a political economy of the trace (and the associated data).

information system) – itself based on operating systems of traces of praxes (micro-equipment of power) – and utterance micro-assemblage (multitudes of expressions of employees on the Internet). Similarly, and to simplify, we can consider that the macro-assemblage of utterance Facebook (1) has disturbed the macro-equipment of managerial power (2), which then dealt with the problem by adapting the social network to its own milieu and making one (3).

What appears essential in Guattari's reasoning, at this stage, is the emphasis placed on the combinations and passages between each of the states, combinatory in movement, which redefine the assemblage to which they pertain.

| Size / Politic | Microsocial | Macrosocial |
|---|---|---|
| Molecular powers of desire | 1) Micro-assemblage of utterance | 2) Macro-assemblage of utterance |
| Molar power | 3) Micro-equipment of power | 4) Macro-equipment of power |

**Table 3.1.** *A rhizome layout [GUA 11]*[9]

"Indeed, by graduating the sizes of the sets under consideration, modulating the powers and strengths, we would achieve a political map, a rhizome whose fundamental compositions would be infinitely richer" [GUA 11].

From a general point of view, we must constantly bear in mind the fundament of sociocognitive and sociotechnical transformation of organizational configurations. Based on the new cross-linked dimensions, a new onto-ethology of individuals is being rolled out, and the schools of labor and thought are being profoundly restructured. The world increasingly seems like a vast set of relational systems in which new maps are needed to live.

---

9 Guattari stresses the simplification of the table, and asks for forgiveness for the formal nature of this presentation. He then describes various possible compositions.

This resonates with a more or less accentuated evolution of the "politics" as a generalized experiment and as a problematic treatment of the means and performativity of procedures for ethical and political purposes. Still following the reasoning of J.-M. Noyer, this research aims at taking account of a semiopolitic of interfaces, signaling that the "new relations of production as well as the new forms of subservience signifying semiotics have a function of subjective alienation, of 'social subjection'; a-signifying semiotics have one of 'machinic enslavement' (in the machinic sense) and subjugation. It also aims at derailing their hybridization and implementation both by and central to various apparatuses. These subjugating apparatuses are informational and digitally communicational. They are apparatuses to create, store and exploit data, but they also involve existential patterns, temporalities and the breaches pierced through the suffocating texture of intelligence societies. This generalized interfacing and therefore normalizing strategy is one of the major pillars of the contemporary transformation of the governmental essence, especially when it is understood in the framework of the 'becoming empire' as defined by Negri and Hardt [NEG 00]. A relative weakening of centralized control systems is indeed visible, in parallel with the strengthening of distributed systems of control and intelligence that are immanent to the production system of networked urbanity. There vast and complex systems of [a-centered] networks are managed in a multifractal mode that involves many recursive loops and local rules implemented on increasingly elaborate digital machine interfaces" [NOY 10b].

Whatever their destination milieus, digital apparatuses, from the organization through marketing industries to the processes of globalization, are immanent to the assemblages in which they are contained. We still need to know which types of passages, transformations and leakage lines may be opened up from that point.[10] These passages (Guattari's multiple combinatory dynamics) manifest in the presence and strength of the molecular and molar powers, semiotics as a major politico-strategic issue, micropolitics and singular feeds. Under which conditions, by which channels and by which new relations, do state, organizational or military assemblages

---

10 Transition from the Nation State to the Market State (in the context of the attempt to force the establishment of a global market); transition from conventional forms of sovereignty to new decentralized forms; transition from neo-Taylorian forms of organization and of work to a societal form, where the concept of work is reinvented.

have the ability to shift, to bring about other configurations, to engage in a well-known loop of *Deterritorialization/Territorialization/Reterritorialization*?

Let us briefly recap some of the characteristics:[11]

> "Deterritorialization is a process which releases some content (multiplicity or flow) from any code (form, function or signification) and channels it along a release line" [VIL 03].

Reterritorialization consists of remaking a territory on something else:

> "Reterritorialization (as defined by Deleuze and Guattari) is an original operation (which) does not express a return to the territory, but those differential relationships within the D. (Deterritorialization) itself, that multiplicity internal to the flow line" [DEL 80].

"To deterritorialize is to abandon a custom, a sedentary manner. More clearly stated, it is to escape alienation, specific processes of subjectivation" [DEL 72] and reterritorializing corresponds to the moment when "consciousness comes back into its own domain, but in new modes [...] before deterritorializing again" [DEL 72].

In the movements of DTR of assemblages, therefore, semiotics is of particular importance. Deleuze and Guattari already made this point in the 1980s:

> "As matters of expression take on consistency they constitute semiotic systems, but the semiotic components are inseparable from material components and are in exceptionally close contact with molecular level. The whole question is thus whether or not the molar–molecular relation assumes a new figure here" [DEL 72].

Thus, when we envisage the constitution of a "digital spatium" for an employee of that organization or for the organization as a whole, it is always envisaged not (only) as a space delimited by administrative boundaries or as a molar hierarchical space, but as an associated and rhizomatic milieu, from

---

11 It is worth remembering that in the eyes of Deleuze and Guattari, the process of DTR has very little to do with the idea of delocalization or administrative territories.

which new connections can be established (e.g. sociocognitive networks), relations and unprecedented, unique explorations, molecular praxes which tend (possibly) to shift the specific assemblage that is the workplace. Thus, a web-based forum for employees stems from a micro-assemblage of utterance and the molecular powers of desire, which bring the company out beyond its own walls, extend the times and spaces of the organization, and bring it into connection with other milieus. Similarly, we can observe (and inquire about) a movement of deterritorialization of neotaylorian organizations for reterritorialization in other regimes of utterance and desires, such as the data-centric organization currently being consolidated.

### 3.1.3. *Organizational semiopolitic regimes*

Thus, semiopolitics affect the potentials for digital praxes, their extent and their richness. They are rolled out and customized to fit a variety of regime types: *a regime of signs* which becomes a regime of "capture" and intensive encoding of the relational, cognitive and behavioral processes; alongside that, there is *a regime of connectivity* which defines the rules of association/severance and therefore access; and finally, we have *a regime of reflexivity*, from whence it is possible to define the fields of visibility and scaling. We quite deliberately employ the term "regime" in keeping with M. Foucault's biopolitical outlook and highlight the fundamentally political nature of digital assemblages: in new incarnations and unprecedented confrontations, politics is at the heart of the process of design of the apparatuses, the recompositions of working praxes or indeed the definition of new "existential territories" [LAT 12].

#### 3.1.3.1. *A signifying and an a-signifying regime*

In the field of management, the profusion of performative exercises (discourse and other language elements mobilized in a quasi-ideology of "community")[12] is associated with the constant extension of computer

---

12 In passing, by espousing this *"community"-type outlook*, the business or organization *no longer appears to be a space of discipline or imprisonment* (Foucault), a place of fixation of manpower (Taylor) or a space of capturing of a workforce (Marx). The organization has become a constellation of communities (of practices, of interests, etc.) which are the subject of numerous research publications, notably in management sciences. These previous publications, in our view, have taken too timid an approach to criticizing their postulates, the

interfaces, which also contribute to the implementation of projective solidarity: the design of the homepages of intranet portals or "internal social network" platforms are amongst the possible examples of this.

The constitution of the "we" is, of course, crucially important. As is pointed out by Sloterdijk:

"Elementary foyer solidarity, if it can be so called, is a basic layer of the ability to say "we": the first person plural pronoun is not the term for a group object, but rather the performative evocation of a collective constituted by self-excitation and self–spatialization. This does not rule out trans-local solidarity on the basis of empathy with absent strangers – the Christian churches, when not denying one another salvation, and the Buddhist *sanghas*, to name only these two, prove quite clearly that love can form a *rex extensa* of its own kind as long-distance attention and coherence in the disapora" [SLO 06].

Thus, organizational digital spaces are established on the basis of a semiotic system (not just linguistic) devised by the management (a molar reflexive and performative function) and evolving with the praxes and distributed participations of the employees, but this takes place at the same time, based on a non-representational process combined with a-signifying machines (molecular process)[13].

praxes, norms and values which they carry, and thus their own performative actions in the managerial world [PAL 10].

13 "The semiotic components of capital always operate on two levels. The first is that of 'representation' and 'signification' organized by signifying semiotics (language) with the goal of the production of the 'subject', the 'individual', the 'I'. The second is the machinic level, organized by a-signifying semiotics (such as currency, analog or digital machines of production of images, sound and information, equations, functions, scientific diagrams, music, etc.), which "may involve a set of signs which have a symbolic or signifying effect, but whose specific function is not symbolism or signifying". This second level does not relate to the constitution of subject, but the capture and activation of the pre-subjective and pre-individual elements (affects, emotions, perceptions) to make them work as parts, as cogs in the semiotic machine of capital" [LAZ 06].

Without going into great detail about the principles and consequences, we shall follow in the footsteps of F. Guattari and M. Lazzarato in exploring the modes of coupling between different types of semiotics, working together in digital devices. Even partial understanding of these modes is clearly of crucial importance from a managerial standpoint. We shall focus mainly on signifiers and a-signifiers, leaving aside energetic semiotics, presignifying semiotics, etc., and passing over the consideration of the various regimes of utterance put forward by Bruno Latour and their mixing and hybridization in organizational pragmatism. This task is a complicated one [LAT 98].

Signifying semiotics, to begin with, "perform" the order of the identities and roles, beings, man–machine systems, territories, in accordance with the ratio of forces inhabiting the same collectives of utterance of the dominant political and libidinal economies.

In Lazzarato's view, they stem from a process of *social subjectivation* [LAZ 06]. This semiotic overcoding contributes to the creation of the map of organizational territories, and prescriptively defines the navigation and exploration of the resources. It is at the heart of knowledge–power relations, and operates in what could be referred to as the field of doxic immanence of the relations of production. It constantly feeds into the creation/objectification of the boundaries and ratios of strength. It is expressed in large organizations, for example, through the definition of lists of websites that employees are allowed to consult (which can be viewed from their workstations, in specific conditions), through the definition of sections and navigation menus, through the production of document descriptors (metadata and structuring of resources by taxonomies, thesauri and predefined ontologies).

According to Lazzarato, "if signifying semiotics have a function of subjective alienation, of "social subjection", a-signifying semiotics have one of "machinic enslavement". A-signifying semiotics synchronize and modulate the pre-individual and pre-verbal elements of subjectivity by causing the affects, perceptions, emotions, etc. to function like component parts, like the elements in a machine (machinic enslavement). We can all function like the input/output elements in semiotic machines, like simple relays of television or the Internet that facilitate or block the transmission of information, communication or affects. Unlike signifying semiotics, a-signifying semiotics do not recognize persons, roles nor subjects. While subjection concerns the global person, those highly manipulable subjective, molar representations, "machinic enslavement connects infrapersonal, infrasocial elements thanks to a molecular economy of desire". The power of these semiotics resides in the fact that they permeate the systems of representation and signification by which "individuated subjects recognize each other and are alienated from each other". Machinic enslavement is therefore not the same thing as social subjection."

Such overcoding of filters and enclosure of the digital space is deemed "acceptable", and is judged on the basis of a structural logic (itself couched in the mass of performance of the procedures). Semiotic overcoding therefore participates in the evaluation of the "distances", proximity thresholds and the variable processing of content generated by resources extended into the immediate surroundings (subsidiaries, partners, customers, press, share price displayed on the homepage of the intranets of large private groups, etc.). It also defines the integration of a particular entity or professional community, serves as a framework for the discourse of legitimation and imposes a given form of hierarchical ranking by the navigation, entries and menus allotted to each direction, entity or group of actors.

However, the increasing importance of a-signifying semiotics, which is at the very core of the texture of the capitalist world, must be carefully considered. Following on from [GUA 11], regarding mathematical signs and technical and scientific or musical (etc.) complexes, all "these a-signifying semiotics or a-signifying machines certainly 'continue' to be supported by signifying semiotics, but they only use signifying semiotics as a tool, an instrument of semiotic deterritorialization which (thus) enables the semiotic feeds to establish new connections with the most deterritorialized hardware feeds".

We need to achieve an understanding of the various ways in which "signifying semiologies and their linear 'syntagms of power' can be combined with superlinear a-signifying automations. The a-signifying employs the signifying as a 'tool', but they do not work together, either semiologically or symbolically; hence, a-signifying semiotics are not subject to the correct semiological form, although they do still use it as required by the dominant system" [GUA 11]. These are considerable issues to deal with regarding what digital conditions will become, and are therefore closely linked to the *capture regimes*. Capture, as understood by Deleuze and

Guattari, is a process which converges "the terms in two or more heterogeneous series". It qualifies the way in which an assemblage creates a "zone of proximity" between several heterogeneous elements, taken together in a block of becoming, which transforms them without identifying them [DEL 80]. Capture (which, in organizational digital spaces, may pertain to praxes, behaviors or subjectivities, based on traces and documents published by the employees) describes the real processes by which human history is cataloged, and the modes of thought which describe those processes. In that sense, it is becoming a major issue for human and social sciences, whether in terms of the political problem of state training (capture devices) or in terms of the organizational, economic, social, technological (etc.) assemblages. Each time, however, there are at least two possible options presented: one with a stratifying, closed tendency (a completely controlled, hierarchically ordered space), and the other with a transformational tendency, open or deterritorializing (a labile space, from which to open up new connections, explorations and processes). In the two cases, the signifying/a-signifying semiotics has different consequences.

In order to comprehend organizations today, we are obliged to measure the effects of a-signifying semiotics, to determine the nature of their future occurring through these devices which are capable of managing their perceptions by drawing connections between them, attaching them to semiotic feeds, as we shall see when we look at regimes of reflexivity. This impacts not only the time dimensions, the synchronization/diachronization relations, but also what could be called the allures of time in the working process, or the modes of existence at work. Similarly, the automated indexing of feeds and documents substantially alters the working process, opening the way to the process of intellectual work.

This non-representational process is at the heart of what Lazzarato dubs the phenomenon of *machinic enslavement*. It should also be noted that a-signifying semiotics, once integrated into their target milieu, can only partially be "rationally" controlled.[14] Software solutions "embed their

---

14 We find a (relative) echo with Galloway's proposal of the concept of an intraface. The term describes "this imaginary dialogue between the workable and the unworkable: the intraface, that is, an interface internal to the interface. The intraface is within the aesthetic. It is not a window or doorway separating the space that spans from here to there. Gerard Genette, in his book *Thresholds*, calls it a 'zone of indecision' between the inside and outside.

programs with them" and, using various "vehicles" (including the publishers/sellers of software applications), travel from one organization to the next, imposing their semiotics as they go. Using greater or lesser modes of updating, this phenomenon, which is a key process in sociotechnical innovation, constitutes one of the facets of hardware performation and of the dissemination of the "memes" attached to it. Thus, from a certain standpoint, the effects of a-signifying semiotics escape the overcoded and signifying reflexivity of the device's target users, of the *semiotic piloting decision-makers (i.e. the management), opening up a world of possibilities, innovation, processes of alteration and creation.*

These two semiotics are relatively autonomous from one another, but in many cases, are greatly interlinked.

Thus, LDAP directories, which determine the management of the various user rights (access rights to a given section or application, rights to contribute or edit, administration of a space, etc.), are privileged actants of overcoding and formatting of praxes: user-profiling is simply a projection–prescription of the "situation" of the ideal/typical predetermined user (roughly predetermined, that is) by the signifying semiotics (stemming from managerial policies classifying the employees into groups of roughly homogeneous statuses and levels of responsibility) and "activated" from a-signifying semiotics (access codes). Both form part of a regime of interfaces. The forms of government linked to the algorithms used by search engines are obviously based on the articulation of that twofold register, and we also see it at work in the context of corporate social networks. When we analyze the modes of existence at work and wish to redefine social praxes, it appears crucial to take account of what F. Guattari expresses thus:

> "Signifying semiologies and their linear 'syntagms of power' may be combined with superlinear a-signifying automations. The a-signifying makes use of the signifying as a 'tool', though they do not work together, be it semiologically or symbolically; thus, a-signifying semiotics are not subject to correct

---

'It is no longer a question of choice, as it was with Dagognet. It is now a question of nonchoice. The intraface is indecisive for it must always juggle two things (the edge and the center) at the same time' (p. 40). We might return to our mantra, that the interface is a medium that does not mediate. It is unworkable" [GAL 12, p.52]

semiological form, but they can always use correct semiological form in communicating as the dominant system prescribes."

In this fabric which weaves together these two types of semiotics, the modes of existence at work forge a path for themselves between consent and resistance, between repetition and creativity. Taking account of the hybridization of signifying and a-signifying semiotics in the interfaces thus enables us to critically assess the political economies which are at play here, without overlooking the complete positivity of these interfaces – that is, the powers of otherness and creativity which they hold.

In organizations, interfacing politics are strategically important, and therefore shape the working activities; they influence the regimes of subjectivity from the point of view of the workers and the management. These politics are based on the definition of databanks and information reservoirs; they come into conflict with the capacity for action, and the standards which define the distribution of relations of production between the employees and the managers (of which the organigrams, rules of behavior, computer training, etc., are the regulatory and symbolic expressions). The reformulation of social praxes is at the heart of these semiotic politics.

Therefore, we need to adopt an investigative approach which allows us to monitor the development of these politics as closely as possible, the negotiation and evolution of *these new methods of semiotic guidance*, in the current sociotechnical conditions [GUA 83]. Compiling the history, constructing the memory of the interfaces, determining their ability to open up avenues within the organization and understanding the way(s) in which it affects the metastability of these collectives, is no trifling task.

### 3.1.3.2. *A regime of reflexivity*

Digital territorialization involves new modes of orientation and projection of the various relations established, of the "relational views". They are continuously renewed by the decentralized enrichment of the spaces and documents, dynamically produced by the applications (the function of the a-signifying semiotics). Hence, here, the organization has only relative control over the relational territories which can be seen. Firstly, the digital interfaces redistribute the feeds under the conditions of the relations of production, the modes of power. Secondly, they continuously restart the processes of alteration – creation, they produce becomings. On the basis of that, other possible associations can be formed: new heuristics, new interpretative capabilities, methods of enrichment of the "collective intelligences". This does not take away from the conflictive dimensions.

From the work, among others, of the group led by G. Bowker, S.L. Star, W. Turner and L. Gasser [BOW 97], we know that the new praxes of mapping the feeds and interactions within organizations are a key element in reflexive praxes, and a condition for the evolution of sociocognitive dynamics. The well-known praxis of *mapping in the making* resonating with the need for *simplexity* [BER 09] or, put differently, with the need for complex systems and organizations to develop self-simplifying procedures (here, the real-time maps of everything circulating), enable these organizations to use themselves as a model for their own operations [LUH 99, NOY 10b][15]. Mapping praxes therefore occur in the context of that need, and they are all the more necessary when faced with complex, interleaving (crosslinked) processes: those with a centralized tendency and those with an acentered tendency (i.e. networks operating independently of central control systems). The interfaces and software applications (the *design* of the workstation, in the broadest sense of the word) are, incontrovertibly, essential actants for these transformations.

However, it sometimes happens that this recursive loop conflicts with the organization's decisional rationales. Once again, therefore, let us look at the example of search engines. They are, *de facto*, in charge of regulating the degree of visibility and opacity of the available information resources. When the possibility of increased visibility and orientation is perceived as a risk by the project managers, the logics of collective efficiency may be re-examined. This dimension is particularly sensitive for territorial collectives (but any kind of business may find itself facing them). For example, in favor of a reflection on the acquisition of an evolved search engine, the Intranet manager of a large territorial collective told us his worries:

> "Are we going to see what every head of department comes up with, and what is put in place for each commune? Are we not

---

15 "Complexity constrains the selection, and this also holds true in attempts to thematize complexity itself. Each self-observation and each self-description therefore needs to be based on self-simplification" [LUH 99].

> risking exposing the lack of equity between actions carried out on a territory? How can we preserve an informational edge over the representatives of the competition, who can also use the intranet? Should we risk losing a competitive advantage in terms of information?"

Indexing power and classifying algorithms here open up unprecedented potentials, in the face of which the definition of a visibility perimeter (which is also a connectivity perimeter), and the definition of consultation rights (attached to each user and, ideally, taken into account in displaying the search engine's results), arise as solutions to the ever-present desire for control.

From that standpoint, one could think of the issues raised by interfaces (and the proliferation of applications that come with them) as the foundation of a kind of "noonomadology" that pushes to the foreground the diversity of perspectives and the way in which they evolve [NOY 17]. The coupling and integration of digital networks need to be viewed in the light of the worlds with which they are associated.

The reflexive dynamic carried by digital spaces therefore varies from one organization to another. The graphs thus constructed from the traces, micro-assemblages (or, better still, "events"), those traces of trajectories, process traces, behavioral traces, etc., increase our levels of description of the relations.

One of the challenges facing the politics of interfaces is finding applications capable of exhibiting increasingly rich, complex datasets and graphs. On the one hand, today, the goal of simplification (certain people would speak of "solving cognitive overload") is rightly the task of overcoding, programming and algorithms. It is here that we see the creation of rhizomatic maps, maps at different scaling levels, sophisticated "diatopes"[16] superposing different maps on one another, and maps which

---

16 This term comes from the Greek *topos*, meaning "place", and *dia*, which represents "separation/distinction" and "across/through". The diatope is a representation formed by the schematic superposition of different maps. Diatopes in geography are comparable to diachronies in history, constituting an approach which brings together short-, medium- and long-term changes in a single analysis. [LAC 06] presents a geopolitical analysis based on diatopic representations, constructed to illuminate the evolution of influence zones, conflicts and worldwide interdependencies, available at: http://www.cafe-geo.net/article.php3?id_article=1015.

always contribute to the updating of the territories, and their singularization. On the other hand, that goal is set by project managers and management personnel. They can decide on the data to be associated (or dissociated), on the lists of information objects which will or will not form part of the territory to be exploited, on the frames of reference to be built into an application, on the "list zones" present in the forms (lists of companies, places, jobs, skills, training levels, qualifications, etc.). When this reflexive exercise involves the participation of different directions, it is not always easy to settle on a common script (a usage model for the interface).

### 3.1.3.3. *A regime of connectivity*

Each mode of digital territorialization supports one or more regimes of connectivity, meaning that it defines the processes of creation of the relations and the capacities for associations between individuals, between data points, and between data and individuals. As we saw earlier, a regime of connectivity is based on the politics of interfaces and semiotic systems (combining the signifying and a-signifying dimensions to a greater or lesser degree).

Regimes of connectivity apply both to employees (individually and collectively) and to the vast informational and documentary resources of the organizational digital space. In the latter case, the modes of assemblages and processing of relations between the resources are determined: hypertext links, indexing, automated extraction, selection of which databanks to use, connections between different applications, etc. In these conditions, we see the emergence of a politics of information and of knowledge, a political economy of the semantic system. The goal is to define the modes of filtering, updating the information, indexing (including collective indexing through the tools of tags and folksonomies). In addition, we need to define the data-processing algorithms, to define the cartographic modes of orientation in data feeds. The aim is less to create "meaning" than it is to define the political conditions of circulation of information and data, to set up a genuine political economy of the feeds and knowledge immanent to the relations of production in the company. Notably, we find ourselves facing the issue of search engines, with solution publishers acting as intermediaries here, carrying models and sociotechnical scripts. Service providers sometimes constitute a key resource, a lever of learning for project managers who are inexperienced in the area, but it must be noted that, beyond a pseudo-expert discussion about algorithms, there are few profound debates on the proposed functional specifications, of which there as many incarnate micropolitics.

The regime of connectivity is also defined in the company by a political economy of access. It is a set of conditions and apparatuses to determine the possibilities of use of digital spaces at work (applications and resources integrated into the intranet), the Internet and a messaging service. Among these conditions and devices, we find the granting of means of access and the situations of consultation: via an accredited workstation or an open-access workstation, and via nomadic interfaces and/or "beyond the walls" interfaces (such as extranet and mobile phones). Playing a major role in this device, the internal norms (charts, internal regulations, recommendations) determine and frame praxes and are associated with filtering and control mechanisms (technological or human). Further enriched by rights management and user profiling, the regimes of connectivity regulate the range of possibilities for exploration/usage of the immense resources contained on intranets and on the Internet. These regimes define, for example, the consultation/contribution rights which are more or less restricted depending on the employees' profiles, the forms and limits of association/connection with other colleagues (e.g. freedom, or lack thereof, to participate in collective exchange spaces, workspaces). Finally, the role of legal constraints and regulatory prescriptions[17] is fundamentally important, though the business does have a certain margin of autonomy.[18]

The political economy of Internet access constitutes a source of tension which is undeniably more visible than struggles on other fronts (e.g. those surrounding search engines) and is the subject of conflicts between opposing positions and claims. Over the period of 2011–2013, only 54% of the active workforce in France had Internet access at work.[19]

---

17 For example, see ISO 27001/02 on information security management, available at: https://www.iso.org/fr/isoiec-27001-information-security.html.

18 For example, a business is not subject to the obligation to provide all of its employees with a professional messaging service.

19 Internet access at work in Europe (source: Eurostat/Insee; outside of the financial sector, in % of employment). Europewide in 2011, France was in the middle of the table.

What are the barriers to the display of such access? Very commonly, businesses categorize their employees on the basis of their Internet access rights, adopting a principle of authorization based on hierarchical level: the higher you are in the organigram (executive status), the more right you have to extensive usage of the Web – that is, use subject to few filters. However, a certain access prohibition remains in place, not only to illegal sites (viewing such websites will expose the employer to legal liability), but also sites which cause technico-economic problems (e.g. which are particularly hungry in terms of bandwidth); those assessed as not belonging to the "behavioral framework" at work (online betting sites, social networks, etc.); or sites linked to countries presenting a high security risk and geopolitical danger. For a certain number of employees, the inequalities as regards Internet access have significant professional consequences, but above all, they can be viewed as a kind of social discrimination. A critical assessment of digital rights at work shows how professional identity is constructed through an evaluation of the differences between potentials for Internet connectivity, as well as connection to the intranet or messaging service (see Table 3.2). For all these situations, it is also the potential for social connectivity (interactions with colleagues or with outside professionals) which is affected. The formal demand for a private (albeit legal) right of Internet use at work is not necessarily expressed in political and ideological forms, but related more specifically to "management of trust/defiance", with the "double constraints"

---

In the European Union (27 countries), 43% of employees had Internet access at work, so France is part of this trend (in comparison, at the time, 52% of German employees had access, and 66% of Norwegians). In 2016, 69% of European businesses provided employees with mobile access (EU 28/27). Denmark and the Northern European countries are pioneers in the area (between 85 and 94% of businesses). In France, 72% of businesses had equipped their employees with such technology. See: http://ec.europa.eu/eurostat/statistics-explained/index.php/Digital_economy_ and_society_statistics_-_enterprises and http://ec.europa.eu/eurostat/web/digital-economy-and-society/data/main-tables.

According to CRÉDOC, amongst the active population in France, there is very great dispersion in terms of the degree of Internet access: in 2013, only 54% of active French people had Internet access at work, 91% of executives were connected (+ 14% since 2010/2011), as opposed to 71% of intermediary professions, 44% of employees and only a quarter of laborers. The logical correlation is that in many cases, the worker's level of education accounts for their Internet access at work: 78% of the best-educated workers had a connection, which is twice as many as the active population having only a BEPC (national diploma). It should be noted that, in June 2016, 55% of the population used a mobile phone to connect to the Internet (including 39% of the whole population using 4G). Source: CRÉDOC survey, inquiries on living conditions and aspirations, 2016.

and contradictions which are inherent to the politics of businesses described as "hyper-connective" and who claim that "belonging", "participation" and "raising awareness" are at the heart of their business model.

In relation with the regimes of connectivity and reflexivity, Table 3.2 summarizes two positions in the most antagonistic of forms: a managerial "object of value" which would be *immunization*, and for the stance of the employees, that of *amplification*.

| Managers' stance: *immunization* | Employees' stance: *amplification* |
|---|---|
| Main justifications for guidance/restriction of digital access at work:<br>– risk of a loss of productivity<br>– legal risk (in case of an illegal act by an employee on the Internet: visiting an illegal site or making diffamatory comments on a blog, for example)<br>– security risk in the business' information system (propagation of malware: viruses, phishing, spyware etc.)<br>– risk of decreasing the performance of the company's network (in terms of availability of bandwidth)<br>– risk of an information leak<br>– the financial investment (servers, filters, etc.)<br>– pathological digital behavior ("deviant" behavior, addiction) | Justifications and main arguments in favor of increased digital access and perceptions associated with restrictions:<br>– Internet at work: having control over the business' digital territorializations, legitimate right<br>– a professional requirement<br>– inadequate predetermination of the requirements<br>– a waste of time<br>– the induced obligation to work from home or use their personal mobile phones for work purposes<br>– the need for information/customer equality<br>– a legitimate private praxis<br>– an increasing feeling of cybersurveillance<br>– re-examination of the trust/autonomy relationship |

**Table 3.2.** *Semiotic regimes and positions regarding the Internet at work*

Immunization is a policy of defending against supposed risks, whether those risks come from inside or outside of the organizations.[20] Amplification consists of a projection of the employee into a larger digital space, with greater possibilities for connectivity and exploration.

20 One of the reports that exemplifies this stance on the part of the management of information systems (IS) is that of CIGREF 2011 (association of IS managers in large French organizations), in which the major sources of danger include "collaborators", available at: http://www.cigref.fr/les-risques-numeriques-pour-lentreprise.

However, the claim for amplification of the connective resources and praxes available to employees needs to be considered in light of the problems relating to the hyperconnectivity of certain populations.

In a sort of pendular motion, extended connectivity, characterized by an extension of the workspace and working times, is one of the major actants in this process is a messaging system, of which in a certain number of cases assimilated to distance working, which may be perceived as being endured. Three inquiries which we conducted in large French State organizations between 2009 and 2012 show that 75% of executives (the same trend is seen in all three cases) regularly signed into the messaging service over the weekend and during leave period. The right to disconnect has gradually been asserted, in response to the movement of general acceleration examined by [ROS 10][21]. In the case of organizations, the feeling of a shortage of time would be exacerbated by a constant flow of messages, data and documents to look over, information to be produced, etc. – a perception which is also crossed by the need to adapt and the constant change which necessitates constant vigilance.

This phenomenon was also described in the "project-network" model of the organization, formulated by [BOL 99]. The recent measures and legislation on the right to disconnect[22] are therefore presented as a response to a desire for "desynchronization" and as a possible regulation of the included behaviors and hierarchical pressures

---

21 The concept of social acceleration includes three dimensions: technical innovation, social change (essentially, the two institutions of production and reproduction which are work and family) and the "rhythm of life" (a concept borrowed from Simmel) [HAR 10].

22 In France, as of January 1, 2017, businesses must negotiate as to their employees' right to disconnect. That prescription was introduced by article 55 of the Labor Law of August 8, 2016 and integrated into annual negotiation on job equality between men and women, and quality of life at work. The labor code does not provide any legally binding instrument that must be put in place by the employer; it is merely an obligation to discuss the matter. Disconnecting can be viewed as the possibility, for the employee, to enjoy rest periods without any contact with their professional activity. These changes confirm a precedent set by the Court of Cassation, whereby an employee cannot be fired for serious misconduct when s/he does not respond to work-related demands during his/her rest periods. In practice, this may result in the shutdown of messaging servers at the weekend, limitation of the use of work-related messaging and mobile phones outside of working hours, delayed receipt of messages during those times, etc. Available at: https://www.service-public.fr/particuliers/actualites/A11297.

(presuppositions of constant availability), involved in work-related illnesses and psychosocial problems.

### 3.1.4. *A digital and organizational spatium*

The digital milieu enriches the data, relations and praxes of which we are woven and, by that token, today constitutes an associated milieu, from which stems a multitude of individuation processes [SIM 89, STI 08][23]. This continuous and simultaneous weaving together of beings, collectives, subjectivities, writings, feeds, places, roving objects and technologies, characterizes new modes of spatialization or fabrication of a territory. It is the assemblage of connections which creates the territory: it is hypertextual, cross-linked, topological and rhizomatic.

From that point of view, the digital inherits, in a way, from Hume's associationism, according to which we are dealing with "three principles of connection between ideas: namely, the relation of resemblance, the relation of temporal and spatial contiguity and the relation of cause to effect" [HUM 48]. More accurately and correctly, though, it fits in with the Leibnizian school of thought, which is closer to our own position in any case – to the philosophies of relation, put simply. Indeed, the digital folding currently under way complicates the vast system of internal relations which are our worlds, forcing us to live and think within a vast, general ecology.

Any individual (or a country, a business, a web space) is made up of links originating with him/her and leading away, and converging links coming inward. We are a product of the networks, we are traversed by networks and in that sense, we are dealing with continuous processes of coproduction and codetermination.

---

23 "Individuation is not individualization – it is the formation of the individual, always incomplete, always linked to other individuals, always social (as well as mental). Individualization is, rather, a de-individuation." "Anthropological individuation is threefold – it is individuation on three fronts: mental, collective and technical. Human individuation is always simultaneously *mental* ("I"), *collective* ("we") and *technical* (that milieu which links the "I" to the "we" – a concrete and effective milieu, supported by memory techniques). That "*simultaneously*", in no small part, constitutes its definition and the crux of its philosophy" [STI 08].

These spaces are made up of relations, relations of proximity between multiple actants, variable relations of distance and as an assemblage of flows, they are recomposed of the relations of speed and slowness. In the context of the extension and complication of digital milieus, therefore, we are not dealing with a loss of substances, with the "dematerialization" (of the social, of exchanges, of documents), the weakening of the "real", but indeed with a hypermaterialization linked to the extension of ichnology, with a milieu marked by hyperconnectivity and increased synchronicity [VIR 98, ROS 10][24]. At the same time, we need to consider the very fertility of territorial assemblages and open up the potentials of becomings, the constant tension between smooth and striated[25], the productivity of interstices and, more specifically, alteration/creation under way within (more or less) metastable states.

The construction of the social, of collectives, originates from that associated digital medium. As Sloterdijk points out, generally, "life is expressed on simultaneous and interleaved stages; it is produced and consumed in networked workshops; it integrates itself into the space in which it is, and which is within it, always specifically. Yet what is essential from our point of view is this: each time, it produces that space" [SLO 06].

The fabric of the organization, therefore, is found in these vast processes.

Continuous production of multiple territories by a multitude of individuals, creativity relaunched from infinitesimal levels of scale, immanence of anthropological, social, cognitive, political, economic, religious, etc. territories: here are the various vertigoes of the incessant

---

24 "Speed is not a phenomenon, but rather the relationship between phenomena [...] Time is no longer an absolute, space is no longer an absolute, as it was in Newton's time: it is speed which has become the new absolute" [VIR 91].

25 "A space of proximity, with intense emotion and affect, non-polarized and open, unmeasurable, anorganic and populated with events or haecceities, smooth space stands in opposition to striated space – that is a metric, extensive and hierarchical space. The former is associated with nomadism, becoming and the haptic art; the latter with sedentarism, the metaphysics of subjectivity and the optical art [...] Smooth space is a space without depth – an arena of immediacy and contact – which enables the observer to touch the object, to become invested by it and lose himself in it. [...] Smooth space, hinged on the idea of proximity, is also an aformal space. It contains neither shapes nor subjects, but is populated with forces and feeds, making up a fluid, moving space, without anchorage or polarization, without any more than an ephemeral imprint" [BUY 03].

movement of digital topoi. Thus, they exhibit a fundamentally rheological[26] accentuated nature – that is, capacity for particular and numerous transformations and deformations, over differential relations between feeds and variable, increasing viscosities of those feeds. In other words, we are dealing with modes of individuations of the most varied networking modes.

Digital technology, in addition to hypermedia networks and research interfaces associated with numerous software applications, opens up modes of connections (including via the Internet of Things – IoT)[27], toward what could be called the outside world – other territories and actants. It is a complication of spaces, territories, their networks, and an unprecedented and powerful weaving.

As proposed by P. Sloterdjik, B. Latour and later D. Boulier, who each in their own way put forward new avenues for the analysis of digital milieus, a new form of thinking about spaces, territories, worlds, proves necessary and can be applied to organizations themselves. Thus, in his trilogy[28], Sloterdjik develops the idea of a "vital spherical geometry" where one of the key issues becomes the instauration and extension of "indoor becomings" [SLO 06], of spaces to protect against the continuous interaction and interpenetration of "neighbors" (with varying degrees of closeness, because the breakthrough that is globalization is at issue here).

We shall continue this tangential examination of the associated milieu in digital conditions, in order to deepen our approach to the fabric of organizations, discussing both the levels of scaling and the translations/transformations which create that fabric.

Thus, in the eyes of B. Latour, "a territory is, first and foremost, the list of entities on which we depend. Each term is important: it is a list, rather

---

26 Rheology examines the deformation and flow of material under the influence of an applied stress.

27 The Internet of Things represente the extension of the Internet to items and places in the physical world. The IoT is an integral part of our "associated milieu", associated with our cerebralities, and is constantly expanding. "This is an emerging anthropological stratum embroidered of an additional synaptic world that seeps in everywhere, weaving into the texture of the world, weaving against it, tightly adhering to the global fabric. This ever-expanding weaving of links and data are therefore complicated by the interweaving of being[s] and things and beings and objects" [NOY 17].

28 [SLO 02, SLO 05, SLO 10].

than, strictly speaking, a place which can be found on a map; then it is a list of entities which are necessarily highly heterogeneous; finally, and this is the most important point, it is the entities on which we depend – that is, which must be maintained or stay accessible for our very survival (in the broadest sense of the term, rather than simply the alimentary or elementary sense)" [LAT 10b].

As regards the urban environment or public territorial politics, D. Boulier leads readers in carrying on the work of the geographer and urbanist J. Lévy, considering the disturbance of two inherited models by the digital revolution: the first is marked by the constant presence of centrally administered, massively topographic territories; the second by a media and model and clusters whose focus is on attractivity, influence and opinion.

The sociologist proposes substituting (or at least adding, in coexistence) a territory with a chronological assemblage, where communications become polycentric, with interactions distributed in different feeds at the speed of Twitter, urban phenomena and the praxes of the residents ("vibrations"), sensed in real time by *Big Data* [BOU 15]. Similarly, for B. Beaude, in the wake of the synchronization of the world, the process of synchorization, "praxes employed both locally and globally", is the defining characteristic of our digital milieus, meaning that we need to re-examine our ideas of spaces: synchorization is the phenomenon of "developing not only a shared time but also a shared space for humanity. The circulation and control of digital information are now so fast that it is possible to be in contact, interact, collaborate and share with the whole human race" [BEA 12, 15][29]. This question of distances, of the transformation of perceptions of distance in view of the relations of speed/slowness and of feeds, is at the heart of all of anthropology and the political economy of spaces and territories [VIR 97], which digital technology brings to the forefront. Thus, as is pointed out by J.-M Noyer: "machinic interfaces play an active role in the transformation of work temporalities as well as in the transformation of the relationship between speed and slowness, which in turn may "deteriorate our experience

---

29 "It is absolutely crucial to spatially re-examine that space, which is supposedly a-spatial. To deal with this necessity, it is crucial to explicitly define the space in question, in order to better characterize one of its main properties: its capacity to be the arena for practices deployed locally and globally. In this respect, the Internet is not so much a space of synchronisation, but above all a space of synchorisation – that is a space which facilitates a shared action: interaction", in [BEA 12].

of time" in digital network environments. From Koselleck to Virilio and Luhman, these transformations have been considered as issues rising from the compression of the present and the acceleration of sociotechnical change" [NOY 17]. Once again, this echoes the work of Rosa, where this change is perceived as "a quickening of the pace of experiences and expectations which drive action, and a shortening of the periods that may be defined as belonging to the present, for the various spheres of functions, values and actions" [ROS 10]. Following in the footsteps of B. Beaude, who describes new configurations of visibility, marked by "panoptic, catoptic and oligoptic" tendencies, J.-M. Noyer stresses the new relations of power in the process of constitution, notably based on the exploitation of traces and sociodigital networks:

"Someone who can extract and exploit the corresponding graphs from digital traces (singular and/or collective) occupies a position of superiority in the political, libidinal and strategic economies. Someone who can exploit the variations in the relations of speed and slowness between writing systems, the variations of combinatories between 'memes'… operating in the heart of the socio-political question of modes of intelligibility and the processes of subjectivation, acquires a dominant position in the production, circulation and consumption of knowledge." [NOY 13]

The digitization of urban worlds introduces more or less complex topologies between the peak lines, but also the troughs of attraction of overlapping times and spaces, hybridizations of the extensive and intensive spaces, but also within organizations, social and cognitive territories, collective praxes and our modes of residence within these milieus, forcing us to consider them *simultaneously* from a topographic, cross-linked, topologic, chronological, semiotic and political viewpoint. In that sense, we can consider that the proliferation of interfaces, data and networks, affects the modes of existence at work in the same way as our experiences of inhabiting a territory, a town, a "smart city", and cannot reduce the political issue, the establishment of these movements in societies in which control is spatially distributed [DEL 90], and there is surveillance [GAN 09]:

"These new milieus are inhabited at the intersection, increasingly strongly, in the context of performative societies, of an enormously widespread digitization of signs, plants, etc., by deeper study of the vast system of relations which constitutes the world and its territories. [...] If we continue to take the measure of new habitats, the strategico-political question – democratic interrogation for the powers and actors involved in this vast ecological process – is therefore to attain a profound understanding of the nature of the relationship existing between the dissemination/dispersion of intellectual technologies and the creation, in urban and social formations, of new relations of power, founded at the intersection of digital puckering, of devices of "knowledge-power", emerging and associated with the smartness of cities" [CAR 14a].

From this point of view, the instauration of a digital organizational spatium means:

– creation of an assemblage in which each individual, each document, each Web page, each piece of data, each node, each link, each activation, each praxis, each application and its lines of code, etc., constitutes a dimension, an actant;

– creation of a vast topological territory, made up of highly heterogeneous actants including, essentially: documents and sets of documents, links and nodes, memories, databases of varying complexity, software, traces left by the actors in that territory – that is those who interact through it, and who are the expression and the expressed of it;

– creation of a set of interfaces which facilitate paths onto and between different places in the spatium (sites, databases, social networks, etc.), from which we see the packagings, associations, navigations in this vast anthropological stratum, or issuing from it;

– constant creation of traces, hybrid graphs-maps mixing objects and spaces, substances and their displacements, dates and rhythms, individuals and their behaviors, tales and opinions, experiences and knowledge;

– creation of relations of strength between the entities involved, between processes of performation, for commanding and restarting of other possible territorializations in the context of a general politics of interfaces.

By becoming a digital spatium, the "territory" as described on the basis of these modes of instauration must inspire us to drop that term in favor of another, ridding ourselves of its inherited referents (identity, topographic, physical and administrative)[30]. Territorialization is not the same as "redrawing the boundaries" or starting again on the basis of functions on a territory (administrative purpose) and equipping technical infrastructures[31], but composing it from the different networks which pass through us, from what is circulating in those networks and interfaces, mediations, which filter in a defined regime of connectivity, a particular ecology of feeds and relations. The digital spatium, therefore, is closer to the rhizome[32] put forward by Deleuze than to the "dashboard" of the responsibilities of a public actor and attributions of competences for a territorial collectivity.

However, this vision will not necessarily be realized on its own merits. A business, which continually calls itself a "network", is constantly working to reify its boundaries, to define where it stands: to define a collective (a "we", an "indoor") in contrast to its outside, a space of belonging and an "organic solidarity", external resources in contrast to internal resources, a private sphere as opposed to a professional sphere, etc, it mobilizes a set of markers, rules, narrations and inscriptions, designed to carry the weight of the process of identification and integration, to define the coordinates of the *digital spatium* which is acceptable (to the whole business and to all its employees) and its peripheries. Thus, we need to consider the tension between the

30 To describe multiple interconnections and fuzzy topologies, to approximate reality as closely as possible, Deleuze abandons simple geometric figures and posits a new species of diagram which has no beginning or end and does not predispose the organization of the feeds.
31 We shall reiterate D. Boullier's criticism on the use which is made of the expression "digital territories" [BOU 09].
32 In the introduction to *A Thousand Plateaus*: "the approximate natures" of the rhizome are listed in the form of six principles: 1) the principle of connection states that any point in the rhizome can be connected to any other given point, and indeed must be: entropy is greatest in the rhizome; 2) the principle of heterogeneity guarantees that a rhizome – unlike a tree – does not set a specific order, "each trait does not necessarily refer to a linguistic trait"; 3) the principle of multiplicity states that any multiplicity is rhizomatic. "A multiplicity has no subject nor object, but only determinations, values, dimensions which cannot grow without changing in nature"; 4) the principle of a-signifying breakthrough conforms to the rhizome's biological self-regulation. When it is interrupted at any given point, the rhizome begins again in the same direction, but also proliferates in other directions; 5) the principle of cartography makes the rhizome into a map. It is far removed from the linguistic models: "a rhizome is not answerable to any structural or generative model. It is alien to any idea of a genetic axis, or of a profound structure"; 6) finally, the principle of decalcomania holds that the rhizome is not a copy, but a map. "A map has multiple entries, unlike a copy, which is always equivalent to 'the same thing'" [DEL 80].

constitution between "smooth space" and "striated space" – the first, from Deleuze's perspective, corresponds to an open space which we occupy without counting it (without data, for example); the second is presented as a metric, hierarchical space, which we count in order to occupy it (as with the whole rights management apparatus).

Striating the space. The debates surrounding the extension of Internet access rights at work, the elaboration of individual rights defining the possibilities of usage of organizational digital spaces (diverse applications and spaces of infocommunication such as Web portals), the need to process increasing quantities of digital data feeds, politics managing the security (integrity) of systems against "DdoS" (Distributed Denial of Service) attacks and a "threatening" outside world[33], the invocation of urgently required "deperimeterization", the necessary creation of third-spaces (built upon extranets, on authentication and "trust" protocols), dedicated to interactions with partners, customers, etc. – all this contributes to the striation of the territory, to its desire for control, to proving the stability of the territories, and weakens the coordinates and frameworks associated with cloistering semiotics. This proof is, in many ways, full of promise and openness, but it also brings a disorientation which, in certain aspects, is sometimes close to the "spatial sufferance" produced by globalization. For B. Latour, it is not so much the distance separating the production of the product from its consumer, or the directors of a company from its thousands of employees worldwide, which gives rise to concern, but the impossibility of, *a priori*, establishing the list of feeds and of the human, informational and technical entities upon which we depend [LAT 09][34].

---

33 The initiative of a thinktank made up of professionals in information security (large private businesses for the most part) and known as the "Jericho forum" has the task of comparing ideas of the large company directors and defining technical standards, directives "to withstand the dangers linked to security and vulnerabilities". Its position has the original aspect of calling for the demolishing of the "ramparts" which enclose organizations (switch from the model of a fortress to that of a "hub" or an airport), but including in its first "commandments": to "survive in a hostile world", "the security mechanisms must be omnipresent, simple, evolutive and easy to manage". Protocols to authenticate the parties interacting play a significant role here: they become "trusted" devices. Consulted on March 9, 2013, available at: http://www.opengroup.org/jericho/commandments_v1.2.pdf.

34 "That which is so vaguely dubbed 'globalization' is merely the recording and amalgamation of a whole series of tests by which we learn, the easy or the hard way, and more or less quickly, to draw up the heterogeneous list of far and near beings, human or

Within the organization, this "list of entities on which we depend" and whose dependency is discovered through the discussions of a project team, technical failures, reorganization of the working processes, the formulation of digital rights, the establishment of collective workspaces online, etc., therefore includes the diverse range of actants mentioned above. While this cannot possibly be an exhaustive list, we discover the extended computational resources of the Internet, data associated with each document and each participant in the digital space, the learning and skills of the employees, teams and working communities, legal executives, hosting servers in the United States, the load limits of the available bandwidth, access codes, lines of code in the applications, fixed or mobile terminals, technical infrastructures, Russian or Chinese hackers (and even animals)[35].

Thus, continuing to follow in B. Latour's footsteps, "as soon as we set out to distinguish the needs of subjects and objects, in any case, we lose sight of the very concept of a territory, because the list of beings on which we depend is necessarily heterogeneous and, also, symmetrical: starting from humans, you will find objects/items; starting from items, you will inevitably encounter humans. Whilst this point of method may yet seem unusual, ecological crises (responsible for a large portion of the territorial sufferance we wish to study) would surely remind us of it" [LAT 09].

In view of the established list, the territory of an organization will find it difficult to subsist on a one-dimensional map! Indeed, how can we represent such a combination of the "local" and the "global", and the complex connections which are woven amongst this multitude of things? For an Internet user or an employee sitting at their workstation, the interfaces are in charge of filtering the associations, translating the relations and dependencies, to produce usable cognitive representations: this mediation is based on increasingly rich diatopes – that is, it produces visualizations by aggregating pieces of information from varying origins and of diverse

---

others, animate or inanimate, upon which we depend. [...] A territory, first and foremost, is the list of entities on which we depend. Each term is important: it is a list, rather than, strictly speaking, a place which can be found on a map; then it is a list of entities which are necessarily highly heterogeneous; finally, and this is the most important point, it is the entities on which we depend – i.e. which must be maintained or stay accessible for our very survival (in the broadest sense of the term, rather than simply the alimentary or elementary sense)" [LAT 10b].

35 Rats, who gnaw on fiber-optic cables, represent a constant threat to the underground networks used by the RATP (Paris public transport operator).

formats, multilevel combinations (for instance, think of an airplane cockpit, of an immersive space or – to keep it relatively simple – of the applications used for vigilance/intelligence activities, search engines indexing heterogeneous databases, "contextualization" of the results of a search). Therefore, we are dealing with different orders of "values": time periods, feeds, individuals and multiple places, info-documentary descriptors, texts, sounds and still or animated images, usage behaviors, etc.

The instauration of a digital spatium, therefore, is not a "spatial projection" or "a calque" (copy/reproduction)[36], but the process whereby new connections are established between a whole clutch of entities, actants, a diatopic construction, never disconnected, of other milieus with which it is associated, with which it is in relations of coproduction. This has important implications as regards the signifying performation of the architectures of digital spaces: even the most gifted manager of digital politics could never manage to fit an employee's entire world on a "single interface" (the homepage, for example).

### 3.1.5. *Case study: digital discrimination at work*

For the advisors and spokespersons of a "digital organization", business and the economy as a whole appear to be marked by "virtual integration at an intra-business, interbusiness and intercommunity level"[37]. This extensive connection has been manifest since the earliest attempts to build intranets in the mid-1990s, as the new *leitmotif* of communication engineering in an organization and, by exploiting the potential of networks, it appears to have

---

36 Once again, we are approaching the discussion from a rhizomatic perspective, as described by Deleuze: "a rhizome is not amenable to any structural or generative model. It is a stranger to any idea of genetic axis or deep structure. [...] The tree articulates and hierarchizes tracings; tracings are like the leaves of a tree. [...] The rhizome is altogether different, a map and not a tracing. Make a map, not a tracing. The orchid does not reproduce the tracing of the wasp; it forms a map with the wasp, in a rhizome. What distinguishes the map from the tracing is that it is entirely oriented toward an experimentation in contact with the real. The map does not reproduce an unconscious closed in upon itself; it constructs the unconscious. It fosters connections between fields, the removal of blockages on bodies without organs, the maximum opening of bodies without organs onto a plane of consistency. It is itself a part of the rhizome. The map is open and connectable in all of its dimensions; it is detachable, reversible, susceptible to constant modification".

37 Sales document from the computer company SAP, 1999.

found a second wind. With the so-called digital "revolution", which has been helped since the late 1990s by discourse based on raising "computer literacy" and generalized, widespread interconnectivity, organizations are becoming "extended", and therefore nomadic. At the same time, increasing availability of interactive terminals or open-access computer workstations became a priority for the ICT managers[38]. The initiatives taken in the area were widely lauded in the professional press. Today, it is mobile extranet access options (smartphones and multimedia tablets) which are finding favor, along with the politics of regulation of BYOD (*Bring Your Own Device*)[39]. However, it is worth skipping over the first reason for this approach, which is obvious (such as providing all employees direct access to information and to the various professional applications that can be hosted on an intranet), and reflecting more deeply on the performative and political issues at play here: extended connectivity (at work and at home) is a condition for employees' integration, their cooperation and synchronization and formatting of the working praxes we wish to make more efficient.

The digital spatium therefore must handle the construction/exposition of the "identifying link" between a business and its employees, support their mutual commitment and be an arena for the building of a "community spirit" (however temporary), far from the utilitarianism intrinsic to rational action for one's own benefit in the world of work. The goal is to achieve the ideal

---

38 This was a central theme at a Net 2000 conference organized in Paris. The Human Resources director for the Dassault Group posed the burning question: "How do we provide intranet accessibility for posted employees?" In 2000, Delta and Ford provided their employees with computers; in France, that example was followed by France Télécom and Vivendi Universal.

39 BYOD refers to the practice of using one's personal devices for work purposes, in a professional context. In view of the dangers this poses to the computer security of a business' information systems, alternative approaches have developed, such as CYOD (Choose Your Own Device), whereby employees are offered the choice of work machines from a catalog approved by the business. Another example is COPE – Corporate Owned, Personally Enabled – professional hardware purchased by the business, which users can configure ("enable") as they see fit. In the former case, the terminal remains company property, and is strictly for professional use; in the latter, it is still bought and owned by the company, but can be used for personal purposes. A final possibility is virtualization of the workstation: the data are no longer stored in house at the company, but on a Cloud server, and can be accessed from any terminal in the world. See: https://fr.wikipedia.org/wiki/Bring_your_own_device#CYOD and http://www.itespresso.fr/securite-it-parle-byod-rocher-79749.html#wvKsUgPY24B2CRuo.99.

of a digital "community" based on giving of oneself freely for the collective, in a constant and transparent dialog between employees and between them and the management, facilitated by hyperconnectionism. For these professionals, the organizational information system and political access management redefine the boundaries of the organization, its exterior, and act as a vast device for organizational rationalization.

In the following example, we set out to examine how an individual and collective signification is established in a plane at various scaling levels, with interlinked prescriptions and constraints (ideological and material), interfaces and programs, subjectivities and affects, normative referential frameworks and personal histories. This "symbolic capital" (I am, or am not, part of the whole) thus results, in part, from a process of narrative performance deployed in the register of revisited belonging, the connection, the "virtual managerial community", but also from a process of performation which is not exclusively linguistic, because it involves a number of technical actants ("material performation") and also "experiential performation" as the updating/testing of significations of the individual uses and skills acquired by the employees, be it within or outside the organization.

The company we shall use as a case study [CAR 12] has over 140,000 employees, and is characterized by a structure widely spread across the whole of France[40]. It presents as a service provider, also having expertise in the fields of logistics, engineering and maintenance. Its digital space is made up of hundreds of intranets (evaluated as around 400, but the organization was unable to give an exact figure), secure professional sites which can be accessed, for example, from home (extranets), with which we can also associate a set of Internet resources assessed as being useful in a professional context, and messaging services. The technopolitics of access implemented by the organization, which, today, operates widely elsewhere on the basis of the same model, uses meta-directories to manage, at once, the access rights

40 The results used here are taken from an investigation carried out within a large public-sector organization over the course of six months, done in three phases: an exploratory phase based on interviews with several categories of actors (from the ICT project team to ordinary employees), an online survey and finally, a second series of interviews and targeted observations of employees identified as occasional or non-users of ICT at work. These "prevented and excluded" people, made up of constrained non-users and occasional users with restricted usage rights, form a group which is (unsurprisingly) made up of a considerable majority of employees in the "Operations" department (field technicians, salespeople and public advisors, itinerant personnel, etc.), who account for 55% of the group.

(and codes) to the intranets and the usage rights to the resources (read, publish, approve, administration); a "white list" of a hundred or so websites authorized for consultation (external company sites, practical sites, etc.); extended consultation rights for the Internet at work, offered mainly to executives, using a highly regulated procedure which forbids the use of any sites deemed illegal, dangerous for network security or too bandwidth hungry. Thus, in our case study in 2009, only 40% of the organization's executives had Internet connection at work, and that degree of penetration also decreases with decreasing hierarchical level. All of this is part of a vast apparatus of filtering and cloistering, which is not condemned by the existing labor law[41], further reinforced by behavioral standards written into the internal computer use charters. It should be stressed, at this point, that for an employee, this normative territory of information and professional communication is by no means limited to the boundaries imposed by the organization. Digital socialization between the employees of that company is increasing and is independent, using relational technologies based online (through social networks and discussion forums). Furthermore, we are dealing here with a high population of employees occupying technical jobs, "roaming" or customer relations, for whom access to the intranets and professional messaging services is still far from perfect and often criticized. The number of workstations connected to the intranet was evaluated at between 90 and 100 thousand units (the exact figure could not be found), but this includes a certain number of open-access workstations, which are not attached to a particular employee. Indeed, a variety of solutions have been implemented by the management in an attempt to serve the imperative for connectivity which it has, itself, encouraged for years: the creation of an extranet, giving access to a reduced version of the intranet on a connection from home, for example; the offering of open-access terminals and workstations in offices, in break rooms or on screens not visible to the customers (for agents in contact with the clientele); the installation of digital screens displaying information published by the central or local management. It is also as a result of the often-chaotic use of these access devices that the employees' technical profiles are constructed. "Degraded" use, characterized by restricted rights or complete exclusion from the

---

41 French labor law does not require all employees to have access to professional messaging services, nor obligate employers to provide Internet and intranet access. In addition, authorization of access to ICT must never hamper a business' operations, nor endanger the security of its network. That being the case, the business is able to draw up a computer usage charter.

company's digital territory, results in the formation of a particular organization, bringing together a community which we call the "prevented and excluded", with a population who have privileged access.

This investigation helps refine our understanding of the data, through the analysis of the reasons for non-use and the perceptions of the employees, but also through *in situ* observation of the working conditions and the methods of connection used by employees without a dedicated workstation. Thirty interviews were conducted between January and May 2009, primarily with agents working in what we shall call the "operations" category. Thus, we are looking at a specific population of "prevented and excluded" people, prioritizing extracts from reports expressing the tensions between the desire for connectivity, presented as an absolute imperative, and the frustration employees feel when faced with an inaccessible device, or even one perceived as alienating. On this basis, we can distinguish five forms of tension, accompanied by various demands, at the heart of which is the coupling between a connective identity and a professional identity.

### 3.1.5.1. *A critical ideological tension*

Within that population, the intranet arouses very strongly held positions, jealously defended. While those positions often demonstrate an only nascent appropriation for a large portion of employees, much more than a technophobic viewpoint, they cannot be dissociated from a turbulent social climate and employees' concern for their future. Thus, the "prevented and excluded" are aware of the imperative for connectivity, certainly, as a pressing need for access in order to exist socially in the organization, but also as a sudden demand to use the intranet. It is this managerial pressure which gives rise to this feeling of ideological discrimination, because it is denounced by a critical tradition which places emphasis on the two-fold alienating power of the sociotechnical device and the management. To begin with, the intranet may be perceived as a factor in job losses, as highlighted by the experience related to us by an agent.

The establishment put in place a partnership with Armor Lux to order the outfits worn by agents in contact with the public. The agents can only choose the clothes they want to wear on the intranet. That service was not used, because the employees believed it would put their colleague, who had traditionally been in charge of ordering clothing, out of a job.

Next, the intranet is often seen as a tool devoted exclusively to propaganda from the management. Hence, the communications director of an establishment told us: "there is a kind of reciprocal dislike – a defiance. People deliberately do not take the time to read notices put up by the management. The same holds true for computers. For the chats with the managers, I've tried to reflect on what kind of communication we can put out to persuade people to take part. It's not an easy task. If I'd drawn up a great big poster, I might very well be facing a strike notice (!)".

Finally, the intranet can also be perceived as a local surveillance tool. Its usage, or non-use, becomes a differentiating criterion. For example, the implementation and use of interactive terminals represent a large part of the issue surrounding access to the intranet on an open-access workstation. All the terminals we were able to observe are located in places where the consultation cannot be private. As a terminal dedicated solely to intranet consultation, the terminal attaches a stigma to its user, labeling them as an "intranaut employee", not just for the hierarchical authorities, but also for their coworkers (a reference group). In certain cases, trade unions exploit the intranet to their own ends, and therefore shift away from the usage script initially intended by the company. Agents of an establishment attested to the fact that the first page visible on the screen was the website of the *Confédération générale du travail* (CGT – French General Workers' Union): an employee who was a member of the union came in every evening to use the terminal, and deliberately left the CGT's page open so that any user would have a priority view of the union's information the next day.

### 3.1.5.2. *Chronocratic tension*

Itinerant employees and "mechanical technicians" are the workers who are least favored in terms of access to the internal network. For a number of these "prevented and excluded", the consultation process is not particularly easy. Itinerant staff, who benefit from open-access machines in break rooms or service rooms, point out the limitation of their usage time. They need to be quick in order to leave time for their coworkers, which makes it impossible to go beyond looking at the service of the day. This chronocratic discrimination is exacerbated by the need to share the connection with hierarchical superiors. Of course, for maintenance agents, it is not natural to borrow a superior's computer. As is indicated by this mechanical engineer, "the lambda colleague in terms of production only has intranet connection via the computer of their nearest manager. However, as she is in her office with her Outlook inbox open, the manager will not be happy to have someone coming in and looking". Finally, the limited confidentiality is a not-insignificant hindrance, as the experience of this other maintenance agent reflects:

> "We have a break between 08:00 and 08:20, so I try to get online then, using the machine shared by the whole team. But I've always got every Tom, Dick and Harry looking over my shoulder to see what I'm up to".

Time has proved to be one of the major constraints connected to the profession. Many of the 262 "prevented and excluded" employees to whom we were able to put our online questionnaire said that they think the intranet is an interesting idea, but they themselves do not have the time to look at it. However, even though privileged periods of use did emerge (e.g. very late evening for receptionist agents, break times or others) and the enrichment of the extranet opened up new prospects (notably for itinerant employees with intranet access in foyers equipped with connected computers, in wifi-equipped hotels, for any others by home Internet connection and via 3G mobile networks), it is difficult for the near management to view intranet usage time as productive activity. As a maintenance agent points out, "we are not paid to go on the intranet".

### 3.1.5.3. *A cognitive discrimination*

It is also important to gauge the forms of discrimination operating on the basis of cognitive resources and skills: they are instrumental (technical abilities, command of the functions and operation), procedural (capabilities employed in realizing a plan of actions, in an activity course), reflexive (contextualization and analytical capability), integrated into a collective working process which needs to be accepted, and the capacity to evaluate the informational resources available and mobilizable for action (strategic skills). From the digital milieu we see the development and negotiation of the creation of distributed infocommunicational skills, abilities put to use at all levels of the company, rather than remaining the preserve of experts or executives. In our case, the managers of the organization have recently been focusing on the dangers of this "counterproductive" discrimination in connection with issues linked to the optimization of "intellectual capital" management and organizational processes. Similarly, on the employees' side, the need for training is often clearly expressed: numerous non-users of the intranet declare themselves "not at ease in using computers in general, and Internet/intranet sites". Interviews have revealed an explicit need for ICT training, even for local managers; consider, for example, the words of this branch manager who feels himself less capable in computing than those beneath him hierarchically: "I would like to have a better idea of what services the intranet can provide, so that our teams can benefit from them. In addition, around young people who have a far better command of technology than I do, I feel I'm lagging behind".

The same phenomenon is observed in situations of usage by other supervisors, who suffer from a lack of technical skills, which has a *de facto* impact on their other capabilities, including their attempts to use search engines or home pages. The cognitive effort required then becomes considerable. The need for contextualization and meta-information is also strenuously highlighted. All the interviewees spoke of an almost total lack of information and help understanding the digital resources from the executives and directors. It should also be noted that certain maintenance agents are completely unaware of the consultation terminal installed in their workshop. This may be indicative of manifest disinterest, on the part of the management, in the intranet, or also of the keeping of logics of control over sources of information. To counter this problem, self-organized regulation processes may be put in place. For example, it sometimes happens that employees with a good command of the intranet (in particular, young non-executives) show others how to use it. Thus, the intranet is learnt through links of solidarity, by more techno-happy coworkers, who play the role of advisers. Such is the case with the following employee, who explains:

"The terminal was installed three weeks ago in our building. I don't know about the other buildings. The terminal is in the workshop, locked in a block. I went there once, and then a second time to show my colleagues. There was no information. Initially, the terminal was in the offices. Then, on my way into the workshop, I came across it by accident. A lot of my coworkers don't even know it exists".

### 3.1.5.4. *Tension over socialization capabilities*

The possibilities for use of collaborative spaces, open to contribution and potentially offering opportunities for exchanges between coworkers, also discriminate between employees. Access to these spaces often requires a specific account, which numerous employees in the field do not have. In addition, if the employee does have those access rights, the dynamics linked to knowledge- or experience-sharing devices which could lead to the constitution of a community connection built around the exchange of operational information, are hampered by the cumbersome administrative processes of hierarchical validation of information. The contribution on an online innovation device exists, even for "prevented and excluded" employees; however, the absence of quick, clear feedback on the proposals put by head office, and the complexity of the device, can affect the initial motivation. Thus, in the eyes of this maintenance operative:

> "The technicians have loads of ideas, but they do not fit into the 'innovation' database. People have innovative ideas, but they are reticent to the use of the base, which they feel is restrictive in form".

Generally speaking, what we see is mistrust of the professional communities on the intranet. Some of the "prevented and excluded" employees whom we interviewed speak of deficiencies in terms of knowledge-sharing within the same team, the same establishment or the same directorate, and the advantage of developing such services, in order to discover the skills developed in other regions. Online "professional" communities can then be viewed as dynamic databases focused on technical problems or procedures. These exchange devices could also prove valuable in creating a connection, sharing and getting past certain traumatic experiences. This is manifested by the following statement by a receptionist:

> "I would be happy to give my opinion on forums for "receptionists" or other people. I'm not concerned whether it's read by my boss or anybody else – everyone has the right to express their own opinions. It's not necessary to give a negative opinion. I'd like to have an exchange with other receptionists in other establishments, in other regions. We might talk about the pace of work, share stories about customers we've dealt with. You see, having walked in one another's shoes, we would

understand each other. It would help us to vent a little bit, so we can take things less seriously".

In the meantime, very numerous agents are deprived of an exchange which would help them to become more familiar with the praxes of coworkers in other regions. The online experience-sharing which the managers want to implement, and which is part of the reason for the necessity of connectivity today, is lacking here. The absence of digital exchange devices therefore prevents the excluded employees from enjoying a certain form of organic solidarity, from participating in "networks" of praxes, values and shared interests, establishing the peculiarity of a group and reinforcing their professional identity.

The situation we have just examined cannot be generalized, but the observations to which it opens the door confirm considerable tendencies as to the ambivalent role of digital apparatuses in an organization: simultaneously devices for the employees' emancipation and socialization, but also instruments of social control, surveillance and discrimination against the employees. Those same issues were found in two other public-sector organizations (inquiries in 2011–2012), where it is, for example, the lack of generalized access to messaging and Internet access which constitute one of the major points of criticism. As we have just seen, the paradox of the necessity for connectivity is that the consensus it seems to bring about jeopardizes the social contract in the organization. Indeed, given the necessity which is ultimately shared by managers and certain "prevented and excluded" employees, to become intranet users, the often genuine obstacles to connectivity are perceived as a demotion. Although for a very few of them, refusal to use the Internet is an act of militant resistance, most employees are painfully aware of the lack of recognition, which they feel demonstrates their exclusion from the apparatus. In addition, the technopolitics of organizations tends today to be doubly destabilized: firstly by the digital praxes and cultures of *digital natives*, which appear here as a driving force and a new ideal-type justifying non-investment in the support of many businesses (though we know the idea is highly contested); and secondly, by the creation of spontaneous professional communities on the Internet (with relative autonomy in relation to the constraints of digital apparatuses at work).

## 3.2. Corporate sociodigital economy

By examining the sociodigital praxes emerging in organizations, we can reveal a number of phenomena inherent in a pragmatism of interfaces, signifying and a-signifying semiotics which are devised within organizational digital spatiums. With this in mind, we want to emphasize the need to look at the digital stratum in its micropolitical dimensions, and fully comprehend the debates surrounding the devising of new semiopolitics.

The recent rollout of "social network" platforms in organizations offers the opportunity to examine (and question) the instauration of certain digital organizational spatia using a potent semiotic overcoding apparatus: overcoding of users, collectives, praxes, documents, subjectivities, relations between documents and between users. These apparatuses bring together multiple signifying and a-signifying semiotics, drawn from computer programs in charge (notably) of activation of relations (social and documentary). All of this contributes to the intensive striation of the organizations, and the development (as we saw earlier) of the regimes of connectivity and reflexivity.

### 3.2.1. *Data management and social engineering*

In the beginning, there were databases. Some of them contain a set of entries already pre-identified and pre-filled: tables listing places, languages, functions, possible actions (accepting or refusing a connection with a co-worker, for example) – a veritable organization thesaurus. In addition, we have blank tables devoid of all content: tables which will list the employees enrolled in the application (they will receive member status), groups set up over the course of time (often given community status), etc. The relational database management system is made up of programs which serve as intermediaries between the databases and users. It, therefore, performs the function of mediation (as the activation is largely transparent, the user does not have "access" to all the operations). The programs have a grammar of their own: they are distinguished on the basis of their manipulation of the data; the return to the user by activation of a function; the capacity to associate tables with others; and so on.

| Business directory properties | Enriched properties (enriched by the employee) |
|---|---|
| – Marital status<br>– Surname<br>– First name<br>– Group ID<br>– Telephone number(s)<br>– Mobile<br>– Office<br>– Address<br>– E-mail | – Manager<br>– Primary assignment<br>– Secondary assignment<br>– Functional manager<br>– Language used<br>– Function<br>– Skills<br>– Goals |
| System properties | Notification parameters |
| – ID/Password<br>– Signed charter (general usage conditions); joining date<br>– Directory account statement<br>– Profile last updated<br>– Blog URL (personal Website, if there is one)<br>– Social activation function[42] | – Language preferred for e-mails<br>– Frequency of notifications about contact activity; frequency of notifications about community activity<br>– Be alerted (about my communities): new announcements, new discussions, filing of new documents, new members, new events |

**Table 3.3.** *Data associated with "PROFILE": "profile page" root*

On this point, a firm of consultants on "social networking" apparatuses in businesses states:

> "When using corporate social networks, users are required to publish information and content, be it personal or otherwise. This ranges from declarative data such as content, rich profiles, tags or 'likes', to more dynamic data such as relational proximity or audit data, such as the list of pages visited and documents downloaded. These data are present in the system and can potentially be used to suggest people and content to the

---

42 Publisher presentation: "Within the social network, this function provides an environment in which the actors can make use of their relations to accomplish tasks together. Every individual can exploit their relations by creating a private or public conversation on their personal page, can take part in communities or create their own communities. Conversations can start in the social network itself and be continued in the messaging service, allowing users to adopt new conversational uses at their own pace, without adversely affecting their adoption by the whole of the group. It also encourages voluntary sharing or automatic propagation of information and interactions within the social network".

users, but also to analyze user behavior and understand the way in which the network operates".

Below are a few tables of data (or objects) used in a platform of a large business: they relate to the "Profiles" and "Communities" sections. This example shows the extent of the traces used, the modes of qualification of documents, individuals and their praxes: the apparatus is based on different semiotic components attached to the programs and their interfaces – components about which we shall detail certain aspects.

| Contacts | Community belongings |
|---|---|
| Name, group, link to profile page | Community name, URL |
| Tags and notes | Connect request |
| – URL of tagged page, tag title<br>– Content of note | – Request date, issuer, recipient<br>– Message |

**Table 3.4.** *Data associated with "PROFILE": "social base" root*

| Public documents | Private documents |
|---|---|
| Name, title, description, file type, upload date, date last modified, uploaded by | Name, title, description, file type, upload date, date last modified, uploaded by |
| Blog | Microblogging |
| – Blog entries: title, body, category, author, creation date, publication date<br>– Categories: title, author, creation date<br>– Entry comments: entry content, entry ID | – Wall: content, date<br>– Private conversations: content, date, participants, parent conversation element<br>– Public conversations: content, date, participants, parent conversation element |
| Images | Daily humor |

**Table 3.5.** *Data associated with "PROFILE": "personal site"/"microblogging" root*

| Community directory criteria |
| --- |
| Name, secret, private, public, description, leaders, number of members, default language, creation date, date of last contribution |

| Members of a community |
| --- |
| Marital status, surname, first name, coordinates, link to complete profile page |

| Article pages |
| --- |
| Title, body, author, creation date, date modified, creator |

| Documents |
| --- |
| Name, title, description, file type, upload date, date last modified, uploaded by, creator |

| Announcements |
| --- |
| Title, body, expires on, rating, number of ratings, creation date, modification date, author, creator |

| Calendars |
| --- |
| Location, start and finish times, full day?, periodicity, attachment, associated workspace (URL) |

| Forum | Blog |
| --- | --- |
| Object/subject, body, rating, number of ratings, creation date, modification date, author, creator | – Blog entries: title, body, category, author, creator, creation date, publication date, modification date<br>– Categories: title, author, creation date<br>– Comments on entries: content of entry, entry ID |

| WIKI |
| --- |
| – Pages: name, title, comment, contact, e-mail, contact name, contact image, page content, rating, number of ratings, wiki category<br>– Categories<br>– Documents: name, title, description, file type, upload date, modification date, author<br>– Images: name, title, description, file type, image date, upload date, date last modified, uploaded by |

| Inquiries |
| --- |
| Inquiry name, description, creation date, number of responses |

**Table 3.6.** *Data associated with "communities"*

This platform collects an initial dataset which is used, in conjunction with a specific referential framework, to construct profiles of the users and groups formed (e.g. a group of people united around a particular professional issue). We associate this first category of data with the class of *"identifying features"*: for an individual, their identity, details, skills, position, role and rights on the platform[43], etc.; for a community: its title, creation date, number of contributors, number of subscribers or visitors, and so on. These data may be produced by the users themselves or be mined from other databases (for example, the formal description of an individual may come from a rights-management meta-directory, or from an HR database which automatically fills in certain fields in the "profile"). A second dataset pertains to the content written by each member, such as "conversations" and "posts" (in long form, or abbreviated as a tag, for example), the documents produced in various formats and within the various associated spaces (blogs, wikis, forums, etc.). This constitutes the class of *"narrative components"*, in addition to which we have *"indexing components"* for the members and texts/documents (qualification and rating by tags[44], or by scores used in the scoring/rating of individual or pieces of information). A fourth set relates to the recording of actions linked to the pragmatism of the interfaces and their different functions. This is the class of *"experiential components"*: they are essentially traces of a user's praxes, often described by events ("Mr. X tagged this member of the network, updated that document, joined that particular group, etc."; public information on a profile's updates, with indication of a date; information on the activity of a community, such as the last document published, etc.) or based on activated features ("receive alerts about the group's latest activities"; "follow the activities of a particular member"; "activate my wall"; "connect request", etc.). Many events are quantified, such as the number of ratings received by a document, number of times it has been viewed, etc.

---

43 Example of hierarchical ranking of statuses on the basis of users' involvement in a group: *Creator* = point of reference for published content and primary administrator of the group for its subscribers; *administrator* = organizer and co-leader of the group; *poster* = person to whom the founder and/or other administrators have granted rights to post contributions, comments, etc.; *member* = a subscriber who can view the content of the group, and receive notifications about the information published there, but who does not have the right to comment or post items in a group; *visitor* = not subscribed to the public group, and can only read the content, not post.

44 In an application, the rating is presented under the umbrella term "social action", and includes descriptors such as "I like/I do not like", "I recommend", etc.

*All of this can be extended.* Third-party applications can be linked to the apparatus: document libraries (link with certain functions of the electronic document management system), messaging users (in certain cases, authorizing the importing of a discussion with an external interlocutor into the "internal social network" space[45], human resources applications[46], professional applications, the search engine used for the general intranet, etc. This interfacing occurs by means of "connectors": thus, synchronization may be formed between a document on a database and a "conversation", or thread, on the social network. The document is contextualized, "augmented" by the comments from the social network. These data and the components to which they are attached (here categorized into four groups for simplicity's sake) are exploited by the system, its programs and its functions.

This is indicative of the integration, into the corporate world, of usage scripts adopted by the well-known social networks on the Web, and of the reproductive power of the processes of "technical performances"[47].

Yet this transition is open, giving rise to debate and to differences. The construction of the "authorities", for example, holding the same kinds of roles as they do on the Internet, is the result of a managerial choice which has considerable socio-political implications: what are the aims and the consequences of certain procedures such as rating a document[48], rating a member, forming a hierarchy between experts and novices in a subject? In addition, the different classes of components (identifying, narrative,

---

45 What happens here is that the employees who are members of the platform are "connected" to the external actors who do not have access to the corporate social network (e.g. in the case of a project involving service providers).

46 Many feel that this interconnection with HR data is crucial, notably to automatically manage entries (recruitment) and exits (leaving) of employees (the issue of what to do when an employee leaves, though, is still very much open: what is to be done with the contributions, documents, etc., produced by that employee? If keeping those contributions, ought we to keep the employee in the directory?).

47 See Chapter 2 and the heteropoietic dimension of the narratique.

48 A common postulate in businesses (echoing certain principles of websites) is to display the documents which are scored most highly, or have been downloaded most often, first on the interface. On the latter point, the self-learning functions of corporate search engines appear to be built on a specific "popularity" indicator: they are based not necessarily on an internal *page rank*, but rather on the *click stream* (for instance, "if 80% of employees click on the fifth link on the first page of results, that document is relevant").

indexing, experiential), which can be associated with many other pieces of information gleaned from applications and various information systems, show the incessant proliferation of descriptors and data within corporations. Granted, the purpose of such an apparatus might be to enrich internal interactions and support new dynamics of participation and socialization (to this end, it can contribute). However, despite what certain commentators have said, the organizational information system is always (and more than ever) an assemblage of the processes of data creation/sampling/capture. From our point of view, we are not seeing the transition from a "data-centered IS" to a "social IS", but rather the expansion of relational technologies (writing of relations between documents, praxes, individuals) to an "overdetermining grammaticalization" of these relations.[49] It is also in this respect that we are dealing with a regime of capture, as defined by Deleuze and Guattari – that is capture seen as "a process which brings the terms of two or more heterogeneous series to convergence". It defines the way in which an assemblage creates a "zone of proximity" between several heterogeneous elements, taken together in a "block of becoming", which transforms them without identifying them [DEL 80].

### 3.2.2. *Views of the network*

Echoing the regimes of reflexivity and connectivity, the capacities of association thus become a central aspect in the modes of existence at work. The "social" argument of these new interaction platforms leads us to think of the employees as a "nexus", and to think of the organization in terms of relational and behavioral ethologies. The focus on the members' "profiles", and on the semiotic apparatus used on those profiles, is a striking illustration of this point. Here, signifying semiotics are dominant: they feed into a performative economy of the "identities", authorities, social and symbolic capital, for which the presupposition is that "value creation" can be achieved by the number of contacts attached to a member, or their position in the

---

49 "Grammatization (the process of describing and formalizing human behavior into letters, words, writing, and code so that it can be reproduced; compared to Weber's concept of "rationalization" and Agre's concept of "capture"; adapted from Derrida) facilates the discretization and reproduction of feeds (flux or flows) by which individuals and human groups are distinguished (become what they are) by expressing themselves. [...] It is merely a new political technology, in the sense of Foucault's technologies of power. Here, though, what is at stake is not just biopower, but also psychopower" [STI 10b].

ranking of most active contributors. The necessity to take care of one's internal "e-reputation" is never far away (certain companies, such as IBM, already offer "real-time" information feeds on the so-called *buzz around you*, which can be seen by anyone in the company).[50] However, this is indubitably not the most essential thing.

Connectivity is the differentiating element of organizations, and the capability of collective reflexivity is a majorly important cognitive and political issue. In order to examine these different organizational regimes, we must analyze the choices made and their processes of development, the ways in which praxes are framed, and the action taken by automated programs.

### 3.2.3. *Opacity/transparency*

What is it that governs the development of the modes of presentation of the links, and in which conditions is the decision made to connect all members to one another? Settings (such as *connect all*) can enable all the members of a platform to enter into contact with one another, make all users members of all groups, make all users of the platform posters, etc. In reality, though, the majority of large organizations seem to adopt the view that the collective cannot function without the maintenance of certain filters and cutoffs necessary for the co-existence of micro-worlds.

Which are the most commonly selected settings to define the degree of visibility of profiles and communities? There are multiple options, which tend to be determined by managerial decision (more rarely a local decision – i.e. by the users themselves): selection of the data fields and components of

---

50 This issue of maintaining one's visibility is connected to M. Crawford's scathing criticism of the world of business, whereby most managers are usually in a situation in which "the art of talking but saying nothing" is cultivated. Are the key skills and the elements of strategic decoding (comprehension of "reality") really put to use in corporate social networks? Are these apparatuses merely an addition to other apparatuses and practices which sustain what certain authors describe as a "functional stupidity" characteristic of organizational inertia? Functional stupidity is induced by today's economy of persuasion, which places more emphasis on the symbolic rather than the "substantive" aspects of organization life [CRA 16].

an employee's profile which will be publicly visible; selection of the descriptors attached to communities; selection of a privacy level for a group (*public*, open to all, *private*, accessible only by approval of the founder; *secret*, not referenced in the directory of groups or the search engine, etc.). The level of visibility is evaluated in light of the social connections, the power/knowledge relations, the zones of transparency and opacity, and the surveillance reports, which characterize the organization. Thus, while certain managers bemoan the frequency of requests to set up "secret" groups (whose subject the general administrator may not deem worthy of such a degree of confidentiality), there are many employees who condition their uses of the platforms to maintain complete control over the degree of visibility of the data concerning them, or concerning the groups to which they belong. Open publicization of one's network of colleagues may be perceived as weakening the strategic position of the informal networks which have arisen over several years; as possibly revealing the user's position as an intercessor (known as a *broker* or a *bridge*) between separate working groups. Indeed, it is important to take account of all the subjectivities which may be linked to the occupation of "structural holes" and the activation of "weak links"[51].

Reflexive hyperconnectivity as a dominant managerial paradigm, therefore, does pose some problems; in that case, the apparatuses upon which the vast process of filtering of the feeds and associations (what to let through and what to filter out) are based play a strategic role in the methods of semiotic piloting. Referring to a text by M. Foucault, G. Deleuze [DEL 86] reminds us that power is "a set of actions upon other actions": "inciting, inducing, diverting, facilitating or hampering, expanding or limiting, making

---

51 In the view of M. Granovetter (1973, 1983), a bridge is "a line in a network which constitutes the only possible path to link two points" [GRA 83]. The "strength of weak links" refers to the situation where the social distance between two individuals offers a higher likelihood of access to non-redundant information and to opportunities than is the case with close, strong links. Bridges are always weak links. The strength of a link is "a (probably linear) combination of length of time, emotional intensity, intimacy (mutual trust) and reciprocal services which characterize that link". Similarly, the sociologist R. Burt [BUR 92] put forward the concept of a structural hole, describing the "holes" between non-redundant contacts, a redundant contact being a link which provides the same information as another. The greater the cohesion of a group, the more redundant the information. The *broker* is the intermediary, positioned in a structural hole, which she can use to her advantage (strategic, commercial, etc.).

more or less likely... There is a list of categories of power", and the motors, applications and interfaces are at the very heart of it.

### 3.2.4. *Recommendations*

We have seen a number of presuppositions relating to the dynamics of "voluntary aggregations" to form what we call "communities". They may – and most often do – take the form of "cliques" made up of "strong links" and marked by an economy of trust (states of trust and their equipment). This approach is further enriched by software programs.

In the case of a corporate sociodigital network, what are the automatic associations formed between the identifying/narrative/indexing/experiential components? For a manager, or rather for a collective of managers, it is worth defining the data fields to be processed here, and a mode of connectivity between the different descriptors, to determine the means of restitution of the relations (lists, facets, maps, etc.). This definition is partly based on the algorithms of the search engine for the social network and recommendations[52]. On this point, the principle is to suggest a "connection" to the employee (consult the profiles of these coworkers, send a request for reciprocal integration into one another's contact lists, etc.)[53]. Replicating the associative models offered by Web-based social networks, suggestions can be made on the basis of a structural proximity within the network of relations (suggestion of intermediaries – of bridges – that can reduce the "distance" between two individuals), of a predisposition for homophily[54] and/or on the

---

52 Extract from an editor presentation: "the driver of social recommendation is an extension module whose functions are directly integrated. No installation or configuration is required on the part of the user".

53 Much like the network of "friends" on Facebook, certain solutions enable users to select the means of approach (direct, on recommendation, by mutual agreement, etc.).

54 It would be helpful to examine the updating of these processes of homophily in the organizational context, their evolutions, and the expressions associated with individuals' practices: in creating my network, I shall choose to associate primarily with "similar" people (whom I am more likely to be able to trust) and associated with the performative prescriptions of the driving ideas. In addition, it is wise to study the organizational implications of aggregation of identical profiles into a list of contacts or into the various groups (but a profile defined using which data?), the consequences of the automatic recommendations as to documents (or sources of intelligence, for example) consulted by the user's immediate network. From the standpoint of innovation and informational value creation, "the strength of weak links" (Granovetter's idea) is not given much credence.

basis of shared "keywords". The community "action theory" is still that of social mimesis or "common ground" (shared values or a shared project), as proposed by F. Tönnies in his day[55], all based on powerful management of the possible interconnections, on rules designed to "safeguard" the whole community.

Hence, it is complex to automatically determine the relevance of the data fields to be exploited. To design the recommendation system, which criteria should be taken into account? The user's self-declared skills (though not always filled in, and formulated quite randomly)? Their centers of interest? Their profession (but in a large company, there may be various denominations)? The department to which they are attached? Their hierarchical superior (who would simply assemble the team already constituted around himself)? The geographic location, the documents and contributions (if any) produced by the user? The title and topics of the communities? The communities only consulted by the different users? The ratings (the score field) associated with the members? The list goes on. Must we put all or only some of these descriptors into use?

The "socialization" model chosen thus applies the filter of what could be called organizational indexing (attached to a pertinence model), a social and cognitive algorithmic strategy[56]. This can potentially affect the managerial strategies and the human resources politics, the dynamics of cooperation (of "transversality"), the enrichment of praxes and experiences, and capitalization on knowledge and innovation. We can see the advantage of

---

55 Negotiation and management of the regimes of connectivity and reflexivity may engage communities from another perspective. According to R. Esposito, the community is not founded on the sharing (gifting) of something of one's own (a common project or shared values). It should be reconsidered on the basis of the "modern immunity project", characteristic of a risk-obsessed society, insecurity being linked to the existence of other people [ESP 10].

56 Example of a publisher's presentation of their application: "using the social recommendation engine, (the application) finds and identifies those people you should know in your network, based on your shared interests, what those people do and whom they collaborate with. The social recommendation engine detects and suggests, in your communities, the conversations and content which you might find helpful. Thus, you have an overarching view in your corporate social networks, and can easily access certain information you would surely have overlooked. In having the right information at the right time, your tasks become easier and your productivity is improved".

recommending documents or communities dealing with topics similar to one's own interests, a suggestion of contact with other employees working on the same subjects as you. However, social and cognitive similarity, as the dominant principle in calculating the "relevance" of the recommendations, as an incitative and performative model, raises some questions.[57] Indeed, the proposed combinations (*matching* between data) ignore all the sociocognitive processes which are based on the differentiation of beings, the singularity of a theme, the emergence of relations between "worlds" which, *a priori*, seem discontiguous. *In fine*, the crystallization of pre-existing networks (designed as such) appears to be the rule chosen, and the effects of "reinforcement" appear, at least, to conflict with the transformational dynamics sought.

### 3.2.5. *Graphs*

Graphs are lists established by a recommendation engine and the platform's search engine, presenting as relational maps of varying degrees of richness, as dynamic ontologies. In view of the limitations described above for the former, the performance of the latter is founded on a capacity to offer open-ended explorations, fortuitous relations and a restitution of heterogeneous (multi-scale) views of the network: not just individuals, time periods, places, but above all, varied discussions and documents attached to them. Search interfaces must be able to facilitate access to different points of view on a topic, to relevant debates, to the "associated worlds" of a query. These interfaces could contribute to the production of successive loops of updating of sociosemantic relations, open to new processes of "reflexive individuations" [STI 12]. However, this prospect seems, as yet, not to be very widely implemented by organizations. The managerial reflexivity of "Enterprise 2.0" is obsessed with the "social graph" as a condition of regulation and stimulation of collectives. Thus, questions emerge here and there regarding the importing, into the enterprise, of a *social graph* and a

---

57 It is important to distinguish the use of similarity made in these social networks from the similarity as the basis upon which search engines work. In the latter case, documents are found by comparing the similarities of the request and the indexed documents. Similar documents can be extracted in a number of ways: lexical, lemmatic, etc. or by recognition of forms with regard to images, computation of book purchases and proximity of topics (such as Amazon), etc.

*graph search*[58] such as Facebook's, the visualization of cross-linked structures which define each employee member, the means of access to behavioral information or experiential traces ("followers" and "followed", expertise calculated on the basis of the contributions, degree of interaction with others, the employee's "timeline", etc.)[59]. The becoming-graph of any business, any collective, is constantly under construction. It can be fed by any type of data, but it is not the graphs inherent to reflexive exploration of decision-making and knowledge-construction in an organization which are privileged (see the still current richness of "Mapping socio-technical networks in the making")[60]. What is currently envisaged is a representation of an employee's portfolio of skills (a return to the "skills/knowledge trees" of the 1990s?), gaping holes in the network of knowledge and cooperation, or – more simply – a representation of the geographic distribution (these maps give geolocations and indicate the distances in kilometers between members of a network), but above all, the issue seems to be the objectivation of an "informal" social network: "revealing the invisible through *analytics*" according to professional commentators).

---

58 Facebook's *graph search* function, launched in January 2013, based on information harvested from the social network's users, allowed searchers to find friends, places, photos and centers of interest among the vast quantity of available data, using a natural-language keyword search.

59 Numerous technological solutions are already available to facilitate these treatments. With regard to Facebook's "timeline" feature, launched in April 2012, it presents in the form of a "diary", showing all of your actions since joining the network. Applied to the world of business, everyone could (if they have the right) access the employee's history on the networks. Similarly, we can imagine this projection of a "memory" of all groups, or the whole of the organization.

60 The authors propose: "A modeling system to capture" and "represent the varied perspectives to the evolving design." "Moreover, it could aid in keeping track of how decision are reached and how information strutters are built in an ongoing design project. In others words, such a computational environment could support the creation and the maintenance of shared memory that can be used to inform future negotiations within and across design project. It would be an environment for creation and reflection where the process of artefact construction could be at the same time a process for theory construction both in design and of design and where theory and practice could be integrated both in design and research about design" [IRA 97].

### 3.2.6. *Organizational network analysis*

The different components of the semiopolitics of sociodigital networks are based on engines, as we have seen. Such engines act by a generative process to create graphs/maps, based on Web crawling, indexing and algorithms. Datamining, applied to the world of business, can have multiple purposes. These include the possible development of enriched organizational intelligence (ranging from an "inherited panopticon" to a redistribution of the networks of knowledge) or indeed, a better understanding of its social dynamics, of the morphogenesis of the networks, so always coupled with a technogenesis, and multiple processes of technical performance. For the time being, in terms of network analyses, the organization thus "formulated" remains focused on simple – if not trivial – indicators. Firstly, we see the establishment of what certain people call a social "ROI" (Return On Investment) or a "ROSL" (Return On Social Link): the criteria chosen are the level of adoption (number of employees registered on the platform and in the communities)[61], the mean number of individuals on the contact list of a member, the volume of documents published. The aim here is to identify the most active member(s). Secondly, a more organizational perspective would seek to study the modes of interaction between entities (to measure the exchanges between services or countries), the evolution of the flow of interactions over time. Thirdly, a functional layer devoted to the (more "qualitative") analysis of a platform would aim to exploit the mass of information left as the trace of "social activities": we need to "have a better understanding of a user's centers of interest, their recognized expertise and the relations between the individuals, by providing services of relation". Finally, the interest may pertain to the identification of the employees/attractors, to the construction of microlocal authorities, the zones of influence and the "informal" networks. Amongst the profusion of "network analysis" services on offer, we find this recent recommendation from a prescriptor: "relationships between people are invisible"; "by making them visible you can make them controllable. You can illuminate gaps in collaboration, you can build them and you can strengthen them"[62]. This is a

---

61 One company sets out its planned goals for the platform thus: "Over a pilot program of 90 days, 'success' would be to achieve 500 active users and the creation of at least 50 groups, with each member belonging to at least 5 groups and publishing at least 5 posts per month."
62 See: http://edition.cnn.com/2012/01/06/business/map-influence/index.html, CNN, 6 January 2012 and http://www.innovisor.com/services/collaboration-management/, consulted on December 15, 2015.

clear expression of the political choice of some people and their fantasy of control.

It is clear that in terms of network analysis and "metrics", the managers are feeling around, and that sociosemantic approaches are by no means that simple to implement (unlike what the most audacious professional "experts" state, and it is perhaps better that way!). To engage that movement, we also need to get rid of all the rhetoric which tends to depoliticize the organization and the world of work. Some people advocate bringing out slogans on "2.0", but at the same time, they can proclaim themselves to be the end of formal hierarchies ("the sociogram has replaced the organigram"). Rare are those who risk opening the "black box" of their organization. Should they open that black box, they could find that, in spite of what they set out to do, fundamentally the distribution of power remains the same: thus, certain corporate applications link the profile of the employee belonging to the social network with a visualization of their place in the official organigram, and within this space we witness the construction of new authorities, and potentially the emergence of new relations of strength. After all, remember that, depending on the assemblages which make them up (the milieu in which they are deployed), cross-linked forms are heterogeneous. At the level of the whole organization, or at the level of microcollectives, we see the coexistence of centralized, hierarchical and a-centered, distributed modes; with varying forms of hybridization, there may be the joint development of a *rogue swarm* (the ephemeral swarm of a group of employees) and a *mainframe grid* (a highly structured, relatively stable network). The programs carried by the applications are constantly working on this hybridization between polycentric, a-centered and centralized becomings.

This complication between different modes, its very productive potential, lies precisely in the possibilities offered by dynamic mapping of the networks of knowledge (sociosemantic networks) which, if redistributed widely and opened up to multiple forms of updating (bottom-up), could constitute a major lever for innovation. This sharing of reflexivity is, to our minds, one of the preconditions for organizational transformations and their socio-political ecologies.

## 3.3. Prospects for the analysis of sociodigital assemblages

### 3.3.1. *A polemology of networks?*

We know, and it is constantly being proven, that everywhere in today's world is the network as the principle of intelligibility and organization, but also as a central black box [NOY 11]. We see the proliferation of the idea of a network, of the network as a concept, of networks as devices, as territories, as organizational modes, and as politico-strategic actants. This applies for all possible substrates, including "gray matter". There are networks everywhere, at all levels of scale, and within those networks, there is the constant generation of maps and graphs. There are nodes and edges. We measure links, we study connectivity, stability, the strength or – conversely – the fragility/plasticity of those links. They are distributed within a complex geological system. Underground networks or surface networks are evaluated through the lens of the "infinity of mob networks". They are again infinitely differentiated on the basis of the number of actors and actants they contain. They are venerated or detested – in many cases it is tantamount to the same thing. The organizational world, as we have seen, is a battlefield, with people fighting for control of a cross-linked milieu, modes of capture (of traces), connectivity and reflexivity. This is observed, for example, with the phenomenon of cohabitation of autonomous and free spaces of praxis and expression on the Internet (union websites, forums or social Web apparatuses used by employees)[63], and the use of managerial apparatuses such as a "corporate social network" as described above. At the very heart of each of these different spaces, we can observe internal processes of striation, hierarchization, control or self-regulation, creation of new connections outside of the platform (via reference to various external sources)[64], but also from within it. It is in the latter case that we observe the rhizomatic potential of digital spaces (of the Web as a whole or of certain spaces self-regulated by the actual employees). "The rhizome has no beginning or end, but always a milieu, which it pushes past and from which it spills over". It is in constant motion, and each of its points "can, and must, be connected to any other point" [DEL 80].

Thus, we are dealing with highly varied, hybrid forms of networks: centralized, a-centered, distributed, fragmented, of greater or lesser density,

---

63 Some people are creating spaces which do away with union mediation and institutionalization.

64 See later on, for an analysis of numerous online communities of employees.

with internal or external conflictuality, etc. These forms, not just from a structural standpoint (a criterion which is far from sufficient for description), are a function of the types of actants which make them up, of the specific assemblages in which they are based, notably associating digital apparatuses. From the point of view of our political economies in general and organizational politics in particular, one of the major questions and points of tension is finding out whether or not we are seeing the relative weakening of centralized, localized control systems and, at the same time, the strengthening of systems where control is immanent to (infused into) the (physical) system of production of the distributed networks. [GAL 07] examines different configurations, within which computer protocols occupy a crucial position, and describe a *networked power* based on a dialectic between two opposing processes: one distributes control through autonomous spaces; the other attempts to put hierarchical control systems in place. Also echoing a number of publications in political economy, in "philosophy of networks" or indeed in strategy, the authors put forward a grid which can help identify the types of networks as a function of different criteria, which we shall adapt slightly here: type of formation of power or of social formations (centralized, territorialized or distributed in nature), reasons/values, weapons employed, digital praxes, and areas of weakness. Multitude, for example, is characterized by the action of crowds of people which are more or less fragmented (a sort of rogue swarm, ephemeral aggregations, impossible to localize, and open territory), not "institutionalized", used the "social" Web, collective intelligence or any other action typical of collective hacking. In keeping with modern analyses of "multitude" (notably those conducted by Negri and Hardt), we believe that the "One" of the multitude is a transcendental "One", which unifies a collective, an immanent "One" (we could speak of "univocality") which is like the precondition of possibility for collective organization.

Thus, we witness a proteiform investment of digital spaces and networks. This has at least two consequences:

1) organizational digital fabrics can only be examined from within the managerial information systems, and it is worthwhile moving out into the factory workshops and onto the Internet;

2) without wishing to be derogatory towards believers in "neomanagement", "social software" and other mouthpieces of "enterprise 2.0" (or that which is likely to come next in the never-ending dance which is constantly fed by new slogans), to draw a comparison between the "network

form" and the organizational form is, at best, a rhetorical effect for performative purposes, and at worst an oversimplification which stops us from fully appreciating the complexity of the transformations which are under way (or both at once).

### 3.3.2. Conflicts in networks: employees on the Web

In many organizations which we have studied, the intensity of the sociodigital praxes can be observed directly on the Internet. Thus, the online presence of the employees of large public-sector organizations, including La Poste (France's postal service) and the RATP[65] (Paris public transport network), enabled us to examine the development of interactions between coworkers, notably on forums (one of which had 10,000 members) and networks such as Facebook. In the case of the different organizations studied, we are dealing with the use of Internet as territories of professional socialization and expression. Using ethnodigital approaches, we observed the networks and groups bringing together numerous employees of this organization, taking account of the spaces with different functions and technical constraints: forums, collective blogs and digital social networks.

In this "perspective", technological coconstruction of social aspects is at the heart of the analysis. It is all the processes which human beings use to associate with one another, to form collectives which have their own identities and can last for a certain amount of time. This stance, therefore, doubly resonates with the subject of interest to us here: the apparatuses of the "social Web" and the new assemblages of professional socialization designed independently by the employees, which are evaluated in regard to organizational politics and issues. Based on an ethnographic approach, using infometric methods analyzing the content of websites, we studied the formation of self-organized spaces (not piloted by the management of La Poste), envisaging them as socialization apparatuses and potential spaces for the updating of a professional community. The hypothesis of crystallization of the pre-existing sociabilities, already observed in numerous publications, is therefore adopted. The use of the term "community" here

---

65 Between 2008 and 2012, we carried out several ethnographic research projects within La Poste, RATP and SNCF.

refs to *shared* ideas, values and signs which establish the identity of the group – its collective individuation[66].

The degree of reciprocity and therefore of interactions is taken into account. On interfaces, this degree of reciprocity may be explicit (number of answers to a discussion subject, for example) or implicit, linked to non-contributor members (number of visits). Thus, the spaces exhibit various functions and information, which enable us to assess the collective and community character: counters regarding the number of members, message counters, visit counters, counters of users online, ratings of a comment (by a score, the number of people who "like this", for example), etc. All of this has the aim of expressing the sensation of mutual, collective copresence (*awareness*).

To begin with, then, we set out to select a set of sites where the collective nature of the interactions was strongly expressed. Such is the case of the *forum des Postiers* (Postal Workers Forum) and the *forum des Facteurs*[67] (Mailmen's Forum), where the use of pseudonyms encourages interactions. Secondly, we studied apparatuses representative of the "social Web" or "Web 2.0" – that is, digital social networks. They constitute a different type of corpus, marked by very great heterogeneity of usage: for example, the same person may use Facebook for personal purposes (family, friends, "egology", etc.) and for professional ones too (communication/marketing; business exchanges; searching for job opportunities; and so on). Subject to the specific technical constraints of each network, and respecting the confidentiality of the information (privacy settings which the users have set to varying levels of stringency), the analysis pertained to:

– Facebook, where we see the cohabitation, or collision, of "official" institutional accounts; accounts set up by collectives of agents (microcommunities) sharing the same centers of interest; accounts based on the encouragement of a single person; accounts created by customers or

66 In Simmel's view, a community exists if there is reciprocity (sociology is the science of reciprocal forms). Also see Esposito's viewpoint [ESP 10]. He points out that the etymological root of both "community" and "immunity" is *munus*: offering, giving to others. The community is not founded on the sharing (gifting) of something of one's own (a common project or shared values). It should be reconsidered on the basis of the "modern immunity project", characteristic of a risk-obsessed society, insecurity being linked to the existence of other people.

67 See: http://www.leforumdesfacteurs.com/portal and http://www.postiers.net/.

associations of users (either defending or criticizing public services)[68]. In this regard, Twitter is becoming increasingly important in the media arena inhabited by the management of the organization, the agents and users, with all three possibly interacting. Keeping control of time periods, here, becomes crucially important, and "viral" phenomena are a key factor. Thus, in the case of the RATP, for instance, there are Twitter feeds relating to delays, breakdowns or incidents on the metro or the bus[69];

– purportedly "professional" digital social networks (LinkedIn, Viadeo), but on which few La Poste groups or discussion groups were found[70]. Here, it is the tendency of the profiles present which is studied. The "community" aspect is only evaluated in relation to the "associating" of members based on the criterion of belonging to the same enterprise. It is the career paths and positions held which constitute the heart of the informational data. Members' real identities are used, and it is the capacity of the spaces for "networking" which is sought.

On the basis of the data available on each network, analyses were performed: of the density of the collective and its points of view; of the degree of exposure: perimeter/degree of exposure and of use of the functions offered by the forum (e.g. personal description criteria used or not); of the profile of the participants: based on the available public data; of the content and interactions.

---

68 Examples: Facebook group "facteur/factrice" – Facebook group "La Poste" (not run by the management of La Poste) – Facebook group "Pour que la Poste reste un service public" (Keep Post Public) (Belgian in origin) – Facebook group "La Poste officiel" (the Official Post Office) (run by the management of La Poste).

69 Similarly, the SNCF constantly exploits tweets for *datamining*, in order to identify train incidents based on information direct from passengers (the efficiency of the social network makes up for the slowness of the internal procedures).

70 Example of a group attached to La Poste on LinkedIn: "ESCP Europe – La Poste group" (with only one member); a group for the Belgian postal service (501 members): "bpost"; "UPU – Electronic Postal Services": Universal Postal Union (Switzerland), looking at evolutions of customer relations and electronic services (76 members). On Viadeo, searching for communities with the terms "La Poste", "Postiers", "Facteur", "Courrier" and "Banque Postale" produces no results; the "hub" search gives three relevant results including "Dématérialisation – Externalisation Processus : Les Experts GD La Poste", 49 members, led by a sales support director, La Poste, Communauté de commerciaux (Ged, Internet, TIC).

| Activity and density of the community | – Number of members, messages, associated resources (links to other spaces, etc.)<br>– Age and endurance of the collective, interactions |
|---|---|
| Points of view expressed | – Projects and points of view expressed in the community; profiles of the founders and administrators |
| Interfaces | – Semiotic approach; functions available, logics of interfaces, constraints, etc.; management of users' endogenous reputation and rating of messages… |
| Identifying regime | – The data attached to the individual (their profile, messages, actions and network) and degree of personal exposure |
| Governances | – Access regimes: filtering, positioning, recommendation, etc.<br>– Editorial regimes: moderation present or absent, styles and forms of writing, individual/collective, interaction rules (charters, ethics of discussion); forms of expressions of a distributed authority, etc.<br>– Collective visibility regimes: expression of copresence; ratings of leading figures and messages; construction of leadership of a unique entity or an association of individuals |

**Table 3.7.** *Series 1 descriptors of a sociodigital space*

| Analysis of participants' profiles | Based on the description of the participants for example, whether or not pseudonyms are used, age, level of education: profession, etc.; perimeter/degree of exposure and use of the functions offered by the space (example: whether or not personal description criteria are used) |
|---|---|
| Quantitative topical analysis | Volume of messages per section |
| Analysis of attendance and interest in the subjects | Intensity of the consultations on the subjects under discussion |
| Structural and relational analysis | Density of the network of relations; phenomena of structural leadership (centrality of a node); forming of "hard cores"; phenomenon of cliques (the majority of links lead to only a few peaks) |
| Semantic and sociosemantic analyses | Topics discussed; analysis of what is attached to the active members/messages; etc. |

**Table 3.8.** *Structural and semantic descriptors (series 2)*[71]

---

71 As a function of the density of exchanges and individual data available.

The regime of visibility, identifying regime, counting of the number of messages attached to a person, etc., contribute to the construction/expression of popularity by the interfaces. This also stems from what, in the case of cooperative spaces, is called *awareness* – a semiotechnical expression of copresence or "mutual awareness"[72]: the perception that each person has of the presence, location, identity or availability of another person at a given time, when they sign in. Furthermore, the concept of awareness can be extended to the perception of what has occurred between two successive entries into the network, the history of the group's activity.

In addition, we need to carry out thematic analyses and interaction analyses (semantic and sociosemantic treatment).

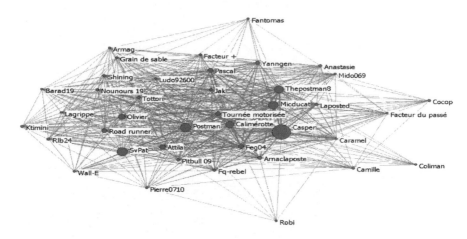

**Figure 3.1.** *Example of structural analysis models of a network of interactions between the members of a forum*

For this representation of the interactions between the members of a forum, a corpus of messages between the 40 most active users on a forum was constructed. It included messages exchanged over the past three months. On the basis of that corpus, a graph can be generated, with each point

---

72 Publications in the *Computer Supported Cooperative Work* journal in the 1980s [CAR 97]. In the case of coordination and cooperation systems, we also work with the concept of "distributed attention"; these aspects are discussed in the context of the approaches of situated action and distributed cognition. See [GRO 05].

representing a user, and the interactions being modeled by lines linking those points to one another (see Figure 3.1).

The structure appears to confirm the hypothesis that the forum's activity is driven by a hard core of polyvalent actors who weigh in on a great many subjects, beyond the bounds of the topical sub-spaces or sections. Here, we see a very dense network – a quasi-clique, where each of thirteen nodes has strong links with at least ten neighboring nodes.

This approach, though, proves insufficient in fully understanding the dynamics at play here. It is also less useful in knowing these spaces (the most active users are very easily identifiable by the post counters on the sites). With regard to the structural analysis of a network and its limits, we consider that it does not cover the analysis used in ANT (actor-network theory) or in general, the complexity of the dynamics of networks and their morphogenesis of digital collectives.[73] From our point of view, it essentializes and functions as an objectifying lure and difficulty to unveil, recursive loops, multi-positioning and trajectories. In addition, sociosemantic analysis, founded on the co-occurrence of heterogeneous aspects and the overlapping of topologies (their relative individuation, or once again, rhizome) and of the scales does not enrich the structural analysis. We could consider that it places it in context.

For this reason, we enriched the methodology with non-automated topical analyses, but also with the initialization of automated semantic and sociosemantic processing. Table 3.9 shows an initial set of descriptors for the analysis of the messages produced in these spaces. In addition, simultaneously with these approaches, an ethnographic analysis was conducted, spanning several months over numerous workplaces, and nearly a hundred interviews were carried out with people in various professions (a portion of that fertile ground was exploited in this book).

---

73 See [CAL 06]. Also, for example, see Ronald Burt's analyses of organizational networks which, based on his concept of a structural hole, indicates that: "the question: to know whether, in an organization, an actor whose network has a lot of 'structural holes' produces more good ideas than others". Burt's conclusion: "there is recognition of an idea (*An idea is as valuable as an audience is willing to credit it with being*) to the detriment of the process of invention: *the brokerage value of an idea resides in a situation, in the transaction through which an idea is delivered to an audience; not in the source of the idea, nor in the idea itself. It is the organizational recognition of the idea which makes it a good idea*, and that validation is more important than the content and is more important than the conditions of the invention" [BUR 04].

| Dimensions and characteristics to be examined |
|---|
| Stances (see Table 3.10 on communities): political, critical, in solidarity, intelligence, identity-based, professional, learning |
| "Strategic"[74] polemology |
| "Tactical" polemology |
| Narrations/discourse with conceptual content (political, economic, social, strategic analysis) |
| Narrations/discourse with event-based content (dysfunction, resistance, symptoms of various states of ill-being and sufferance) |
| Rhetoric and linguistic mastery |
| Passionate narrations |
| Distance (strong or weak codetermination) between the narrations/discourse in the forums and the managerial narrations, from the general direction[75] |
| Internal reflexive capability[76] |
| External reflexive capability |
| The Internet, digital and social networks and Web 2.0 as topics for discussion |
| Critical analysis of the transformations of the world of work linked to digital technology; organizational, cooperative dimensions, etc. |

**Table 3.9.** *The (series 3) descriptors of narrative and sociosemantic types*

---

74. Polemological dimensions: strategic conflictive stances (conflict between two political, social, economic concepts) and tactical stances (confrontations, resistance expressed in working practices, for example).

75 Distance: we must stress the importance of codetermination of the discourse in the forums with the general management of La Poste. Thus, in conflictive relations, the critical discourse on the postal workers forum is strongly codetermined with the managerial discourse: the general management of La Poste is highly present in the content. This holds true right up to the reproduction of internal documents and notes. It is not the case, it seems, in the postmen's forum, where the expression, critical and reclamatory, is less coupled with the discourse of the company (numerous internal documents are quoted, but in a different form: a library of documents on the homepage).

76 Internal reflexivity: capacity to analyze and debate one's own positions, but also one's own uses of new technologies. External reflexivity: capacity to analyze one's position in relation to a complex environment.

| Stances | Explicit and practical goals |
|---|---|
| *Critical politics* | Criticism of the organization's politics; expression of concerns regarding its projects, its HR policies, etc.; communication media in the context of a conflict; strike-monitoring tool (union sites and blogs have this stance, but collectives claiming to be autonomous also inhabit this field) |
| *Solidarity politics* | Defense of the organization and its professions (counter-attack in response to customers' criticisms, for example) |
| *Intelligence/vigil* | Search for sources of general information between co-workers (on competition, the HR aspects, labor law, etc.); transmission of general documents about the company; press vigil, etc. |
| *Identity* | Publication and updating of "semiotic markers" (jargon, photos, videos of equipment, of a workspace), a desire to preserve the "memory" of the profession or the organization, its history and its cultural norms |
| *Profession/Praxes* | Exchange of savoir-faire and knowledge relating to a professional problem, exchange which may carry mimetic learning and may lead to an epistemic community (creation of new knowledge); helping one another on very operational subjects (information about a new piece of equipment, etc.) or psychological mutual support (in case of sufferance at work) |
| *Learning/Integration* | Putting across a professional vision with an educational purpose, information about the recruiting process, advice to candidates, to new recruits, etc. |

**Table 3.10.** *Position of communities of employees on the Internet*

## 3.3.2.1. *Elements of comparison of the positions and narrative types*

Finally, we extracted six main stances characterizing community collectives[77].

---

77 Term taken in the sense meant by Tonnies (1922), drawing a distinction between *Gemeinschaft* (community), an association of human beings where the group takes priority over the individual, and *Gesellschaft* (society), where private interest wins out over common interest. The use of the term "community" here refers to a *common*: shared ideas, values and signs which establish the identity of the group – its collective individuation; the identity of the members of the group is fed by that collective identity.

Identity as a metastable process – or unstable, in certain conditions – requires a set of boundary connectors ensuring the co-existence of the "organizational/social" dimension and the "professional" dimension. This also ensures the living codetermination of the scales – "local" and "global". Thus, it enables us to think about the "redistributions", displacements and tensions which may be expressed between an identity characterizing a community of praxis and the transformations of strategic identities in an organization. It is embodied by "semiotic markers" (jargon, photos, videos of equipment, of a workspace), the will to preserve the "memory" of the profession or of the organization, its history and its cultural norms.

Within these communities, each of these dimensions may be present to varying degrees. We are dealing with hybrid spaces. For example, a discussion forum with nearly 3,200 members and 50,000 messages, on its very home page, indicates its critical political stance, and offers a list of links to various union sites (in this instance, it acts as a sort of portal). It also provides information on environmental vigilance, societal intelligence, human resources and finally, a number of exchanges pertain to a set of problems relating to professional procedures. Yet another forum (2,100 members and over 55,000 messages), which is more in line with the company politics, is oriented around "HR information" for candidates wishing to work for the company. It also plays host to numerous interactions expressing solidarity between colleagues, a defense of the professionals and sometimes even of the organization and of certain "values". Finally, Facebook groups (most with only a few hundred members), with free-to-access content, can be used as supplementary media to the Websites (case of trade-union-type organizations) or as a space for the aggregation/ dissemination of a professional memory (photos of equipment, videos of employees carrying out their work, old adverts or prior communications by the company). The position of these communities and the richness of the interactions between the two types of platforms are explicitly conditioned by the degree of exposure the participants want, or constrained by the tool used (for example, Facebook does not appear to encourage frequent exchanges and lengthy discussions). Thus, whilst on critical-political forums, it is common to use a pseudonym, the use of a real identity (surname/first name and photo, usually of oneself or one's family), on Facebook, is typical: the fact that the network is anchored in a "private life" stance, and the use of typically only one account, favors the overlapping of private and professional territories. We are also aware of the debates surrounding the complex subtleties of settings on one's public profile on the network.[78]

We shall not go into detail, here, about all the analyses conducted on these communities, as the results can be discussed at length elsewhere.

For the management teams of the organizations studied here, this collective extimity[79] and the professional worlds on the Web bring converging opinions. For the heads of ICT and HR projects, the risks of "informational intelligence", loss of confidentiality of information, competitive and social intelligence are removed, giving rise to the production of new rules (or "good practice" guidelines) intended to regulate behaviors deemed disruptive by the organization. Having to deal with strong commercial constraints and human resource management constraints, the actors also raise the risk of "headhunters" and facilitated attempts to poach employees. Finally, in the eyes of some managers, the independent professional communities are in competition with the intranet (a controlled, and controllable, spatium) and with the strategies of external communication (the market of "e-reputation" comes into its own here). In this context, the hypothesis of creation of "digital social networks" within the intranet (a corporate version of Facebook) is seen, by the heads of ICT and Human Resources, as an opportunity to compete with the employees' digital territories, expanding beyond the normative boundaries of the organization. Thus, the conflict between devices and semiotic regimes updates the biotechnopolitical dimensions attached to a desire for control over the modes of professional individuations and control of traces. These traces, which collect cascades of increasingly elaborate transformations, are eminently paradoxical, because "the more widely digitization spreads, the more we can track what ties us together" [LAT 98]. Thus, in view of the employees' sociodigital praxes, organizations are obliged to reflect, not only strategically but ethically as well, about freedom of expression, control and exploitation of the data, of an extended organizational digital territory, freely established.

---

78 See, for instance, the *New York Times* article, May 12, 2010, stating that at that date, Facebook offered 50 privacy buttons and 170 options, available at: http://www.nytimes.com/2010/05/13/technology/personaltech/13basics.html?pagewanted=print. It has since been further complexified and enriched.

79 This echos the desire for extimity as the exposure of one's deep self [TIS 02].

On this matter, obviously, we need to monitor the evolution of the legal framework, of which we are aware of the iteration but also the occasional paradoxes. The judgment handed down by the labor court of Boulogne-Billancourt in 2010 established, *de facto*, an absolute need to master the subtle ins-and-outs of Facebook settings and the ways in which they are evolving[80], considering in passing that the sphere of "friends of friends" was a public arena. In 2011, though, the court of appeal of Besançon drew a distinction between Facebook posts available for all to see, and "wall" posts, access to which is limited to direct contacts and which should, therefore, be considered a private space. Finally, the court of cassation appears to have settled the matter in 2013: a Facebook profile is not a public arena if its owner has authorized access only to a *very limited number* of "friends"[81]. If there are few of them, and they are of a similar mind, the authors and readers are linked by a "community of interest", and the employees' posts can therefore not be the subject of legal action for defamation or public libel. These distinctions also are open to various debates regarding professional/private spheres within a company: which regime of visibility and what kind of relational economy should apply to the rollout of internal social networks (which, in certain cases, are not part of the essential tools for working)?

It should be pointed out that while citations of unions or mentions of conflicts are commonplace, the debate can sometimes be very animated. *Thus, these services are not absolutely consensual spaces, unanimously*

---

80 In this case, the court upheld the dismissal of employees who had expressed criticism of their superior, with that superior having access to the exchanges as a "second-level" friend (the friends of friends of the employees in question could see their "wall"). An "open" Facebook profile, therefore, is considered a public arena, whilst a profile reserved strictly for first-level "friends" is a private space. However, there remains the issue of cascading links. Remember that according to article L2281-3 of the labor code, "employees cannot be sanctioned or dismissed for opinions which they express under the terms of their right to freedom of expression, whatever their place in the professional hierarchy". Restrictions relate to defamatory, slanderous statements, or ones which are justified by the nature of the task at hand.

81 On April 10, 2013, the judges of the court of cassation declared that an employee who, on her Facebook page and her MSN account, said that "bosses like [hers] should be killed", as should "bosses [...] who make our lives a living Hell", could not be punished for having expressed these views publicly, because they were visible only to her "friends" or "contacts". The verdict of the Court of Cassation is available at: http://www.courdecassation.fr/jurisprudence_2/premiere_chambre_civile_568/344_10_26000.html.

*subscribing to certain trade-union views.* In addition, a number of people may contribute to the debate in these forums without necessarily being registered as "members".

This multiplication of expressions and digital modes of individuation comes from a desire for new control, or at the very least, an openness of one's modes of existence at work. Our analysis also shows that Facebook cannot be the only arena in which these praxes take place. Numerous types of rival social networks are already in place or are being developed, using emerging and ad hoc approaches to cater for specific needs of assembly associated with the need for privacy, which is not only greater in the short term, but also more long-lasting (conditions which explain the maintenance and dynamics of the discussion forums in the case of the organizations studied here). It is highly likely that we shall see the phenomena of convergence and strengthening of certain types of community, through the sharing of praxes, narrative modes, levels of knowledge, etc. Another trend will combine these phenomena of concentration with fragmented expression phenomena: current becomings appear to indicate the reinforcement of this hybridation where "molar organizations" and "molecular organizations" coexist and, even better, resonate with one another. This will occur even more often in the future, owing to the rollout and the increasing mastery of relational technologies, of new meta-search engines, new modes of indexing and filtering resources, and the collaborative spaces available.

### 3.3.3. *Digital methods at work*

In today's world, *digital methods* (some of them long-established at this stage – see [CAR 14b, LAT 12, ROG 14][82] are employed by researchers, who notably use them for quali-quantitative approaches [VEN 09][83], but may also

---

82 It should be pointed out that – following in the footsteps of Bruno Latour and Tommaso Venturini – "digital technologies (which) are supposedly in the process of revolutionizing social sciences, as they have previously revolutionized the natural sciences (are not necessarily in this situation)".

83 Venturini and Latour [VEN 09]: "in order for new methods to be able to realize their innovative potential, each step in the searching process must be consistently renewed: 1) identification of information silos should give priority to digital archives, the Web, media and online networks, digital documentation and literature and, more generally, all kinds of digital traces; 2) data extraction should be based on aided browsing or on the various data-collection techniques (crawling, querying, scraping, parsing, etc.); 3) the integration of data from various sources (known

become an exploratory tool for decision-making and for enhancing the visibility of organizational and sociodigital dynamics. Note, however, that trade unions have never presented/exploited that aspect. Yet these cartography tools are constantly deepening this question of enhancing visibility. With these approaches, it is possible to take a view from the internal standpoint, for example, of the social, technical (etc.) controversies reigning in the organization. Similarly, and this is indubitably the most important point, employees and communities of employees could find, in digital methods, new means of exploration, or of counterpower, matching intelligence analyses (and quantitative analysis) used by the management.

In Carmès and Noyer [CAR 14b], we set out a number of points regarding the effects of the increasing, rapid production of corpora of traces and of digital empirical data about research praxes in human and social sciences. The rise of algorithmic technology and *datamining* in so-called "performative" societies is increasingly evident. We addressed the epistemological and political debate sparked by Chris Anderson, demonstrating the weaknesses of Anderson's arguments. However, at the same time, we advocated the necessary use of digital methods, and illustrated their importance and the advantage they offer in the context of thinking-action in complex, open societies.

To borrow the words of Bruno Latour, "digital" brings to light a new way of "rematerializing social phenomena by rendering the interactions visible". Similarly, in the crowd, we see the development of social physics which, as Pentland says, "mathematically describes connections between the flow of ideas and information among individuals [...] and the people's behavior" [PEN 14][84]. We know that in Pentland's view, Big Data, when used in

---

as data mashing) should be done with indexing in a relational database; 4) the analysis and modeling of the data should be based on Web- or digital tools and, if possible, open source; 5) research results should be published on the Web, preferably in open-access archives and in a standard format, so they can be easily reused".

84 "Big Data" is increasingly about real behavior, and by analyzing this sort of data, scientists can tell an enormous amount about you. They can tell whether you are the sort of person who will pay back loans. They can tell you if you're likely to get diabetes. As a consequence analysis of Big Data is increasingly about finding connections, connections with the people around you, and connections between people's behavior and outcomes. Big Data shows us the connections that cause these events. Big Data gives us the possibility of understanding how these systems of people and machines work, and whether they're stable. [...] The notion that it is connections between people that is really important is key, because researchers have mostly been trying to understand

combination with a powerful set of algorithms, must help develop "a causal theory of local structure". Many objections and criticisms have been, and continue to be, made of this view; in passing, we could demonstrate the links of the this outlook *with certain branches of transhumanism[85] and, as indicated in the organizational context discussed here, with a data-centric becoming of the internal management, founded on "mastery" and the constant (self-legitimizing) control of an anthropological and political reality, the destiny of which is, for the time being, connected to the dominant neoliberal and entrepreneurial models.*

However, it is important to note (following in Maignien's (2013) footsteps) that for human and social sciences, the digital revolution is at once the object and the instrument of the current major development of the discipline. As the instrument: digital infrastructures, as for all sciences, must equip and instrument the various disciplines of human and social sciences. In actuality, given the semantic and methodological diversity and richness of the disciplines, far from being a monolithic structure, an infrastructure project is, firstly, the complex organization of hefty generic tools (constant archiving, storage, computation, hosting, posting and publishing) leading to a "service grid", from the primary observed data to theorizing on the basis of the operational results. Also, it is "a hierarchy of tools to applications specific to a given discipline, as closely as possible to the semantic issues [...]". These specific tools are more or less closely integrated and are interoperable depending on the disciplines. Regarding this issue with the

---

things like financial bubbles using what is called Complexity Science or Web Science. But these older ways of thinking about Big Data leaves the humans out of the equation. What actually matters is how the people are connected together by the machines and how, as a whole, they create a financial market, a government, a company, and other social structures".

85 To briefly indicate a few noteworthy criticisms, see Nicolas Carr's article in the *MIT Technology Review*: "The Limits of Social Engineering, Tapping into Big Data, researchers and planners are building mathematical models of personal and civic behavior. [...] But the models may hide rather than reveal the deepest sources of social ill". This raises some important points. In particular, Carr notes that Pentland's idea of a *data-driven society* poses a number of problems. In this strategic option, he sees encouragement to preserve the status quo on the basis of established relations of political and anthropological force, without the possibility to favor alternatives, constraining the changes and becomings in a sort of strategic chreodes and evolutive politics, meaning that actors wishing to introduce change are left only with a simple calculation of maximization of the becomings within stable models. In passing, this is one of the major dangers of "performative societies", of a "constructal" vision. On this subject, see Noyer [NOY 17].

semantic Web – or the sociosemantic Web for human and social sciences – digital technology cannot be viewed solely as an instrument. It must, at the same time, be the subject of in-depth analysis and theorization about the transformations of what the digital produces in society, work, culture, knowledge, education, information, organization of territories, biopower, communication, creation, the global economy and politics. It is for this reason that we wish to demonstrate that the rise of algorithmic technology and sociosemantic treatments must be given a closer, more complex analysis than that formulated by Anderson (and more recently by Pentland), and more consistently, by [HEY 09][86].

The spaces for expression and socializing on the Internet constitute new empirical digital resources, which are pertinent for followers of marketing and Big Data, but also for examining organizational fabrics (here, on the basis of employees' autonomous praxes), but we must nevertheless consider the goal of linking those empirical data to the larger milieus from which they are constituted. The pairing of situated ethnographies (observations in the field, interviews, etc.) with digital ethnographies is a condition of the pertinence of the scientific method. These digital ethnographies mean we must look at not only the forces that are constituted and recomposed generally within a professional assemblage, the semiotics of those devices and praxes, the sociological natures of the participating agents and the dynamics, but also the semantic worlds associated with the participants. In the context of this research, effort is invested in understanding the sociotechnical assemblage of the interactions, analyzing the participants and "what is discussed": functional descriptions, formatting of interactions by technique and by network structure, typology of contributors and construction of "digital identities", discussion topics, relations between individuals, relations between topics and individuals, relations of strength within the space, regulation of exchanges, etc.

Notably, here, we are pursuing the line of the "*actor-network theory*" advanced by Callon and Latour, taking into account the associations and distributions which emerge. "[There are] two fundamental processes: localization (i.e. the isolation of an exchange or an activity from the other members of the society) and globalization (quite the opposite, the transport

---

86 See Hey [HEY 09]: "The collection of essays expands on the vision of pioneering computer scientist Jim Gray for a new, fourth paradigm of discovery based on data-intensive science and offers insights into how it can be fully realized".

of small modules from the world which, as representatives, can be brought together in one place and associated). From this point of view, technologies are the heart of the social phenomenon and are considered to be a constant process of "association" [CAL 86]. The goal is to gainfully exploit *datamining* methods to explore enormous corpora of exchanges (hundreds of thousands, in our case) and make use of means of exploration and modeling in addition to the aforementioned analyses. The tools of *datamining* and *social network analysis* are, in this sense, assistance for sociological analysis.

The aim here is not to get bogged down in statistical positivism, the limitations of which were very clearly demonstrated by Levy[87]. Remember that before Chris Anderson's provocative claim, ethnographic approaches and a whole set of works on the anthropology of science and technology set out to study the "social" phenomenon as it is currently manifesting itself (not as it is thought to be), discarding the *ante* categories, the magma of collective representations, structures, psycho-sociologisms and symbols.

In the context of the development of the sociology of translation and the research program as announced in 1984 in the book *Irréductions* (1984),

---

87 "How do we transform data torrents into 'knowledge rivers'? How this problem is solved will determine the next step in the evolution of the algorithmic medium. Certain observers enthusiastic about the statistical processing of Big Data – such as Chris Anderson, the Editor-in-Chief of Wired – have rushed to declare that scientific theories (in general!) are now obsolete. No longer will we need massive data streams and statistical algorithms. [...] The figures appear to speak for themselves. However, what is clearly overlooked here is that, before any computations can be done, we first need to determine the relevant data, to know exactly what we want to count and to label (i.e. categorize), the patterns which emerge. In addition, no statistical correlation can directly show us causal relations. Those causal relations must inevitably be determined through hypotheses which explain the correlations demonstrated by powerful statistical computations, occurring on "cloud" platforms on the Internet. In the views of these commentators, theories – and therefore the hypotheses they propose and the thinking from which they stem – are part of a bygone age in the scientific method. [...] Chris Anderson and his disciples are reviving the positivist and empiricist vigil method which was in fashion in the 19th Century, according to which only inductive reasoning (i.e. reasoning based solely on data) is scientific and valid. [...] This position involves rejecting or silencing the theories – and therefore the hypotheses put forward on the basis of one's own thinking – which are necessarily at work in any kind of data analysis process, and which are manifested by decisions of selection, identification and categorization. We cannot initiate a statistical treatment and interpret its results in the absence of a theory" [LEV 13].

Bruno Latour and Geneviève Teil set out the conditions for working on new bases, the relations between methods and problems, concepts and constructions of empirical corpora. Their article "The Hume Machine: Can association networks do more than formal rules?" [TEI 95] lays out the fundamentals of their approach and their need for new (statistical) tools to deal with the problems of description and modeling posed by the sociology of translation and the *actor-network theory*[88]. The following issues are outlined, and the authors ask how they should be overcome:

> "Despite contemporary progress in statistics, the social sciences are still too divided between quantitative and qualitative methods."

The ground gained by ethnomethodology is recognized:

> "This step forward, conjointly made by ethnomethodology, the new sociology of science and semiotics has not yet been operationalized by specially designed methods of data analysis. In the absence of methods adapted to it, those who are developing the network ideas are forced to hesitate between statistical groups that are too large-scale and detailed analyses that are too fine-grained – or to despair of ever finding suitable quantitative methods. It then becomes easy to accuse those using the idea of networks of making a slogan of it (the network is 'a seamless web') which does not enable one to differentiate as effectively as traditional notions using groups of acceptable size, and which does not enable one to carry out a relativist program."

They continue:

> "Thus we need to give qualitative workers a Computer Aided Sociology (CAS) tool that has the same degree of finesse as

---

88 "The study of science and technology by social scientists has led some of us to develop a theory of the growth of socio-technical imbroglios in terms of associations. 1) The word "social" in the expression "social science" would no longer refer to "society" but to the "associations" established between humans and non-humans. The problem encountered by such a theory is to decide whether or not one should qualify the associations beforehand".

traditional qualitative studies but also has the same mobility, the same capacities of aggregation and synthesis as the quantitative methods employed by other social sciences."

Elsewhere, Gloria Orrigi's (2008) statement echoes this sentiment:

"A new science may emerge in the petabyte age – a branch of science which tries to answer the question of how collective intelligence processes are possible, thanks to the vast quantities of data now available which can be easily exploited and combined by powerful algorithms. It is perhaps a 'gentler' new form a science, not burdened by the rigor of the 'quantitative methods' which make scientific articles such heavy going to read, leaving that burden up to the algorithms and allowing the free mind to 'dance' around the data in a more creative way."[89]

This also resonates with the position of Michel Serres who, in his exchanges with Bernard Stiegler [SER 12][90] points out that algorithms which automate a number of intellectual tasks offer greater creative conceptual freedom, both upstream and down of scientific processes and cognitive processes in general. Based on the work in sociology of sciences in the 1960s, the Centre de sociologie de l'innovation de l'École des Mines de Paris (Center for Sociology of Innovation, École des Mines Engineering School), in the early 1980s, began working with what were then known as large documentary corpora, and then designed the analytical tools for research communities, proposing to expand the description of search dynamics and the identification of networks of actants, using the method of *co-word analysis* [CAL 83]. For a description of the evolutions of those methods, see Noyer [NOY 95].

In this context, it is interesting to briefly examine how the importing of quantitative-qualitative methods to extract knowledge from collective assemblages of utterance as expressed on the intranets or on the blogs

---

89 For the debate "On Chris Anderson's the end of theory", see [ORR 08].
90 Dialog between Michel Serres and Bernard Stiegler, organized by *Philosophie magazine*, available at: https://www.youtube.com/watch?v=iREkxNVetbQ, 2012.

associated with a given organization, has complex effects which work on two levels.

Firstly, these effects occur in a representational way – for example in our work on employee forums, where we use info-metric tools with a view to revealing the "collective micro-assemblages of utterance" expression and expressed communicational pragmatism of the agents (here La Poste employees).

These micro-assemblages (which partially express), the perceptions, processes of subjectivation, the argumentative strategies and the various ways of behaving in the debates and controversies surrounding organizational and corporate life from the employees' point of view, are assemblages constructed using methods drawn from co-word analysis. The aim is to identify the networks constituting the agoras and their topics, collectives, their density and consistency and their respective degrees of importance in the general collective, which is expressed by the utterances. Again, the aim is to find new means of exploring the system of internal relations making up the organization, through the concrete expression of the actants themselves.

### 3.3.3.1. *From Leximappe to Calliope: the exemplarity of co-word analysis*

Before going any further, we need to linger a moment to look at the co-word analysis method, which co-emerged in the early 1980s at the Centre de sociologie de l'innovation de l'École des Mines and which is, in a way, a "capture of the heart of another stratum (statistical data analysis) of the other becoming (that of irreductions and of sociology of translation)" [NOY 95].

This method emerges at the intersection between two becomings: the "statistical becoming of the philosophy of Entelechies" [LAT 84] and the "associationist-neoconnectionist becoming of data analysis" within one another, interconnected unequally by way of alliances, for example, struck with other actors and in other conditions; the rise of digital empirical corpora (digital traces left by the actors in the course of their praxes) being one the of the major intermediary "actants" (Data and Big Data).

Thus, this method, coming in the wake of the work done on processing quotes, develops the idea that we can reveal, first in the scientific and technical domain (*and then very soon afterwards in other sectors*) the actor-networks, entelechies, chains of translation which go with them, based on the keywords used to index the documents in the databases. More specifically, by calculating the frequencies of the co-occurrence of these words across the whole of a corpus, we can try to reveal aggregates, assemblages, devices more or less convergent/stabilized, more or less strongly interlinked. The method enables us to express areas of common interest between actors, actants (in the broadest sense of both terms), to reveal assemblies and assemblages, and rank them depending on the nature and size of the corpus on which we are working – a corpus which, remember, must be validated and closed. The question of the traces and their pertinence is essential here more than ever – the word, as the expression and the expressed of any given actant involved in the domain, as the domain in turn is expressed by the corpus of documents analyzed, here being the minimum trace which can be considered pertinent. This approach, therefore, will very quickly expand to a great many fields.

Briefly, then, this method is based on the co-occurrence of the indexed terms. The association of two keywords (i, j) – whose occurrence (Ci, Cj) is greater than or equal to 2 – is measured as a function of the number of times they both appear (co-occurrence) in the documents which they index (Cij).

The statistical indicator which measures the value of the association between the keywords is the coefficient of equivalence. If Cij represents the co-occurrence between i and j, and Ci and Cj are their occurrence, the indicator can be written as follows:

$$E_{ij} = (C_{ij} / C_i) \times (C_{ij} / C_j) = C_{ij}^2 / C_i \times C_j.$$

Thus, the associations are assigned a value. All the pairs of terms obtained are sorted by decreasing values. Next, we go through the classified list of pairs, in sequence, to construct clusters. All of the elements are to be clustered initially form a single vast network of associations. This is a valued network – that is, a system of relations in which the words are connected by links of varying strength.

The network of associations is broken up into clusters on the basis of a criterion of readability – specifically, their size: setting the minimum and maximum number of components and the number of links. If a pair of terms belongs to the same cluster, the link between those terms is considered to be an internal link within that cluster. If the terms in a pair belong to two different clusters, their link is considered an external link – that is, a link between clusters. Thus, we express the respective position of the assemblages in relation to one another, the degree of stability of those assemblages and their capacity "to assign or to be assigned". The clusters are located in a two-dimensional space and are situated in a plane defined by a coefficient of internal coherence of the topic and by a coefficient of centrality.

The "internal coherence" of an assemblage, here, is the mean of the values of the "internal" associations. This value is represented on the vertical $y$ axis of the map. The higher that mean, the more it is considered to be a well-structured, recognized assemblage. The "centrality" of an assemblage (cluster) in the network is measured by the mean of the total number of external associations existing between the given cluster and the others. That value is represented on the horizontal $x$ axis of the map. The higher the value of the mean, the more the cluster in question is considered to be a point of reference (centrality) for the whole. Other nuggets of information are produced, pertaining to, for example, the profile of association for each actant in the whole network, the mean values of centrality and density for each cluster, the number of documents used to construct the cluster, and so on.

We cannot focus at length, here, on the development of the data resulting from in-depth methods of analysis, writing, navigation and the interconnection of the different strata of documents, texts and fragments involved in one domain or another, or in such and such a set of problems. However, it is important to take a closer look at the process of reduction which takes place, from the constitution of the documentary corpus representing the field under study to the unveiling of the actants and their assemblages.

Remember that this new type of instrumental tool comes into its own with the processing of linguistic entities, and for the time being (with the exception of too rare exceptions), does not cater for the potentials of probabilistics or other types of analysis which could, using the current process of digitization of sounds and images, have a major impact on the approach of "morphogenesis", the problem of meaning and expression, the foundation of a "phenomenal topology" [PET 94] taking account of the vast domain of the emergence of forms (visual, audio, plastic), and giving rise to approaches that are not exclusively linguistic, unprecedented explorations from the point of view, for example the energy mobilized in the set of forms, come to upset the traditional modes of narration in terms of images (from the most ancient cave paintings to virtual images, and so on), and sounds.

Thus, let us look anew at the process of reduction. This process involves a number of steps. First, we have:

1) reduction to the actors associated by the texts;

2) reduction of writing to the written text;

3) reduction of the associated actors to the associated words.

Put differently, the approach is:

1) reduction of the text to the co-words (constitution of the corpus);

2) reduction of the texts to their words;

3) reduction to associations of words.

Based on this process of reduction, co-occurrence analyses enable us, by characterizing lexical praxes, to focus solely on the knowledge present in the corpus – lexical fragments which actually tell us something. From this point of view, we are continuously shifting from the order of words to the order of things, in a renewed interpretative praxis regarding the emergence of the phenomena, interactions, problems, and their interleaving [TEI 91].

Returning to the subject of the importation of algorithmic methods, text-mining tools derived from the sociology of translation and co-word analysis are of particular interest. For our analysis, we used Calliope – the direct descendant of the seminal software Leximappe. This can enable us to: *describe the socio-semantic universes of "what" interacts, and their relative positions in the whole of the network (in the form of a set of micro-networks – clusters – corresponding to assemblages of actants that are more or less heterogeneous); add a dynamic dimension to the traditional topical maps, helping users to interpret what is being exchanged and discussed, presented in a cartographical manner; directly access messages in the forum by clicking on the group of associated terms (clusters), which might be called descriptors, or on specific expressions/words; to sort the most significant terms in the documents into three categories, reflecting their changing levels of importance within the text: emerging, stable or declining terms; to conduct comparative analyses between corpora, etc.*

Between Carta and Mappa, this dynamic analysis is no substitute for the user's reasoned assessment and judgement, but it can help illuminate their thinking process and their intelligence operations.

To begin with, Calliope assists the user in their quest for answers through the interactivity of its maps, trend graphs and document search.

We have the "essentialist" and molar map of the actants, marked on the axes of density and centrality (Carta), and the maps of the internal networks and dynamics, etc., which represent the possible connections (Mappa) and constitute those same actants. As we shall see, the difficulty in using these mappas in the day-to-day life of the organization, to openly redistribute the relations of power/knowledge and to share what the organization "knows", stems from the disruptive power of that possible dissemination.

The transformation of the collaborative and open dimensions of the organization can only be truly effective if done on the basis of the sharing – always negotiable, in law and in fact – of the deployment of counterpower and renewed spaces for discussion. It affects the possibility of a greater relative autonomy of the actants and third spaces for the emergence of genuine compromises.

Simply put, the use of the *datamining* tools described here is intended to extend the possibilities of access to the actants, to support interpretation and decision-making – that is to increase their reflexive capabilities, but also, to facilitate possible reconfigurations of the relations of strength between collective intelligences in the organization.

Returning to the subject of our work with Calliope, based on an initial semantic analysis of the messages, we established a list of criteria acting as major elements of differentiation between the different interaction sites[91]. In particular, we look at the critical, political and polemological aspects (lively debates, conflicts), at the internal reflexivity (the capacity to analyze and debate about one's own positions, but also one's own uses of new

---

91 See sections 3.3.2 and 3.3.2.1.

technologies) and the external reflexivity (capacity to analyze one's position in relation to a complex environment). Finally, the forums can be distinguished in terms of the "passionate" dimensions (a sort of economy of emotions) carried by each of them. In addition, huge corpora of messages have been compiled, enriched with metadata and processed with the software Calliope[92].

### 3.3.3.2. *The fabric of sociosemantic analyses*

In studying a corpus, we can distinguish between two phases of work: data acquisition, and analyses of those data. Data acquisition is frequently done with various software tools and techniques (search engines, smart agents, push, etc.), either systematically or on demand.

The next step is to sort, classify and archive the information, to be used either immediately or later on. All that remains is the analysis.

The results of automated analyses obviously depend on the relevance of the information sources, but also on the quality of the linguistic, semantic and statistical preprocessing. Data acquisition is frequently done with various software tools and techniques (search engines, smart agents, push, etc.), either systematically or on demand.

Then, we need to sort, classify and archive the information, to be used either immediately or later on. All that remains is the analysis.

The results of automated analyses obviously depend on the relevance of the information sources, but also on the quality of the linguistic, semantic and statistical preprocessing.

The critical, political and polemological aspects (lively debates, conflicts) of the forums are thus put in perspective on the basis of the content and the relational device that expresses them. Similarly, the level of abstraction associated with the types of narrations used and the choice of events told enable us to better measure the reflexive dimensions of the forums:

– internal reflexivity: the capacity to analyze and debate about one's own positions, but also one's own uses of new technologies;

92 For examples of the use of Calliope, see [DES 14].

– external reflexivity: capacity to analyze one's position in relation to a complex environment. It goes without saying that this distinction is "forced".

Last but by no means least, the relational and semantic morphologies open the way for a comparison between the "passionate" dimensions (a sort of economy of emotions) carried by each forum: the results of the conventional lexicometric automated analyses demonstrate at least – and at best – the validity and quality of the underlying methods and algorithms. However, it is not easy – indeed it is sometimes impossible – to detect new avenues, weak signals, "constructive noise", changing power relations: in brief, anything which is essential for monitoring and decision-making in changing contexts, for perceiving new projects, ideas, factors, objectives, actors, etc.; and the fact that they emerge, decline or remain stable.

### 3.3.3.3. *Example of automated processing on employee forums*[93]

Calliope enables us to display the relations between topics on two axes. Firstly, we have the axis of centrality, which indicates the hierarchical relations between the different topics (clusters). *The more a topical cluster is linked to others, the greater is its importance in the discussions (its centrality). Thus, we can assign a rating* of the effect of entrainment of a topic on others, the modes of influence of one topic over another. Then we have the axis of density, which expresses the internal consistency of a topic – that is *the number of actants/terms (expressed in words) which make it up, and the strength of association of these terms (degree of co-occurrence).*

In Calliope, the results are presented on these two axes in what is known as the "strategic diagram", divided into four quadrants. Thus, we obtain an overall view of the whole corpus (the messages) and the position of the most popular topics in terms of the two axes described above.

The strategic diagram shows the main clusters in the whole of the forum: a cluster is a collection of descriptors which constitute a topic represented by a word.

The distribution of the clusters (with a word representing an association of linked words/topics) is organized into four quadrants, along the axes of density and centrality. *Clicking on a cluster shows the details of the actants/terms making it up, down to the messages themselves.* It thus enables

---

93 Work by Mathilde de Saint Léger, Maryse Carmès and Jean-Max Noyer.

us to navigate around the word graph (representing the actants – ideas, concepts, people, order words etc., as expressed in the messages).

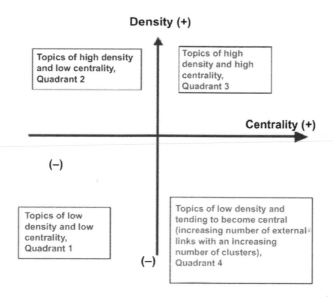

**Figure 3.2.** *Calliope analysis matrix: the strategic diagram*

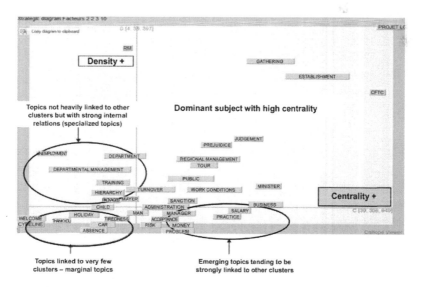

**Figure 3.3.** *Strategic diagram of Calliope: datamining applied to discussion forums*

The co-occurrence expression (x) – the threshold beyond which it is considered pertinent to take account of a pair of words which is associated at least twice – indicates the level of finesse of the analysis. 2 corresponds to a fine analysis and 5 to a cruder analysis.

In this example, the clusters are calculated with a co-occurrence of 2.

### 3.3.3.3.1. How to read the diagram

– *Quadrant 1 (bottom left)* = here, the clusters are not very dense or central. "fatigue", for example, is a cluster of low density, which is not very present in the discussions and therefore refers to few clusters. Marginal topics or "passing zone" or emerging.

– *Quadrant 2 (top left)* = the clusters here are very dense but not very central, such as that of "unemployment", are made up of strongly associated terms (high internal density), but its low index of centrality shows that it is a cluster that is relatively isolated from the other discussion topics.

– *Quadrant 3 (top right)* = both the most central and the densest clusters are found here. Mailman's "round" is a cluster composed of numerous associated terms, and its topic is heavily linked to other discussions.

– *Quadrant 4 (bottom right)* = these clusters are not very dense but are very central. The topics "danger" and "safety" have relatively low density (few associated terms) but high centrality – that is, they are linked to numerous other discussions. This can also constitute a set of emerging topics.

In an in-depth analysis on dominant or emerging topics, particular attention is paid to Quadrants 3 and 4.

For an analysis of subjects which are not much discussed, we focus more on Quadrant 1, and we see how it may move (extension or lack of centrality).

For an analysis of topics, that are not closely linked to other discussions and are in which specialized exchanges take place, we concentrate on Quadrant 2.

In the forums, customers are associated, on the one hand, with operational aspects of the job (problems, complaints, loss of parcels, for example), with services provided (schedule or others) or, on the other hand, with more political topics such as defense of the public service (the expression "user" or "citizen" is then positioned as being the term to defend), as opposed to privatization (in the latter case, the perspective of profitability and objectives of turnover also draw upon the figure of the customer). We have isolated discussions illustrating the "professional" stance and the services rendered to La Poste's clients/users. The topical clusters are shown in Figure 3.5.

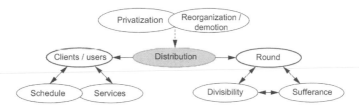

**Figure 3.4.** *Example of central topics in the discussions about the organization of work at La Poste. The distribution is a transverse axis linked to multiple sub-topics. However, automated analysis shows its relation with two major dimensions: "round" and "clients/users"*

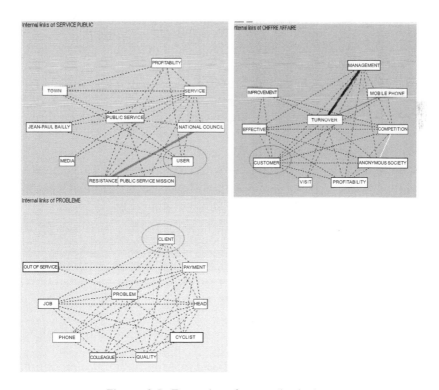

**Figure 3.5.** *Examples of semantic clusters*

The interpretation of the automated processing algorithms cannot be relevant without having multilevel, on-the-ground knowledge of the crises that the public organization has had to face. The general context of the transformation of La Poste strongly determines the perceptions associated with the distribution. What is considered privatization and reorganization are associated with a general worsening of working conditions. This is expressed directly at the organizational level (rounds) and also, with a view to defending the public service, in terms of relations with the users (expressed in the forums in connection with the notion of service). The schedule, for its part, constitutes a particular point of analysis of such customer relations, in which we find a contrast between the "public service" spirit and the commercial goal.

This example is, of course, too limited in terms of the needs of analysis of traces, which should be amply discussed. These traces are present in increasing quantities and are increasingly heterogeneous: behavioral traces, semantic traces, trajectories of the actants and spatio-temporal coordinates, geo-location, formation and de-formation of the aggregates, series of translation (in the sense of sociology of translation), etc. However, it illustrates the perennity of the issues raised by the École des Mines CSI in the 1980s. They resonate again with the work of Deleuze and Guattari, who combined a set of concepts which opened up the possibility of developing a sort of hyperpragmatism that is not exclusively linguistic [DEL 80, GUA 80, NOY 05].

Concerning these traces, the digitization of the sign gives us an ever larger and increasingly heterogeneous quantity: behavioral traces, semantic traces, trajectories of the actants and spatio-temporal coordinates, anthropo-geolocation, formation and deformation of the aggregates, series of translation (in the sense of sociology of translation), etc.

### 3.3.4. *Inhabiting and describing the assemblages: a program in the service of the analyses of the organization and managerial approaches involving digital humanities*

Inhabiting and describing the assemblages involves several postures, the main ones of which may be as follows: tracking the movement of the relations and thinking about the heterogeneity. Monitoring the connections and their development; tracking the variations and the interleaving of extended assemblages; tracking the formation/formatting of the attractions/repulsions, and achieving a visualization; tracking the monads or the rhizome "by its milieu"; following the processes of transformations and semiotic captures.

How can the Deleuzian view of assemblages transform the work of digital ethnography and its analyses? How does Bruno Latour resonate (reason) on the basis of (with) assemblages?

Before going any further, it should be noted – echoing the observation made by Bruno Latour and Tommaso Venturini – that "digital technologies [which] are supposedly in the process of revolutionizing social sciences, as they have previously revolutionized the natural sciences [are not necessarily in this situation]":

> "The situation in social sciences (as they see it) is more akin to that of natural sciences in the 15th Century, following the introduction of the printing press. As Elizabeth Eisenstein (1979) describes it, the press was one of the main causes of the scientific revolution, but not an immediate cause. Decades after Gutenberg's invention, naturalists were still printing the same mistakes that they had copied by hand. Today, social sciences are in a similar situation. Instead of being rejuvenated by digital technologies, they are still taking great pains to apply the old methods to the new data. Cyberculture, virtual communities, online identities, computer-mediated work, communication – all these concepts have been developed to quarantine the new aspects of the electronic media. Every day, though, this inertia becomes more untenable in view of the speed at which digital technology is infiltrating modern life. Thanks to their capillary diffusion, digital media often offer far more than an application for the existing methods: they offer a chance to re-examine the study of social phenomena." [VEN 09]

### 3.3.4.1. *First posture*

What interests us, in the first instance, is the possibility of describing and inhabiting the transformation currently under way (of collectives, of their narratives, of the debates, the relations of strength, etc.), the movements, the trajectories of the actants, the events, and bearing witness to it. The immense production of digital traces allows us access to these dynamics, enabling us to develop new cartographic praxis and new types of reflexivity, by means of a relatively complex semiopolitics of interfaces. In addition, as noted above, the complexity of the various semiotic regimes and their differential relations and the modes of transformation, translation and hybridation at work through digital translation, are driving forward the development of a general narratique and of its "abstract machines"[94], which have a "leading role [...] which does not operate to represent even something real, but to construct a reality to come, a new type of reality". Thus, they are not "outside of history, but rather 'ahead' of history, at each moment when (they) constitute points of creation or of potential".

While algorithmic work may have a considerable echo in new ethnological and anthropological approaches in particular, and in Deleuze's view and the concept of assemblage, this is because the new formulations are powerful, and go hand in hand with the proliferation (for better or worse) of traces. Even in terms of long translation chains of actors–networks and assemblages (from Deleuze's sense of the term), new intellective technologies have a crucial role to play:

> "The utterance is the product of an assemblage, always a collective one, involving populations, territories, becomings, emotions and events, both inside and outside or ourselves. [...] The assemblage is co-operation, it is empathy, it is symbiosis" [DEL 77].

Similarly, for sociology of translation, the goal is to account for the transformations by way of painstaking and precise observation of the displacements, of any entity, of their associations, the bifurcations, the trials

---

94 "The abstract machine in itself is destratified and deterritorialized; it has no form of its own (much less substance) and makes no distinction within itself between content and expression, even though outside itself it presides over that distinction and distributes it in strata, domains and territories. An abstract machine in itself is not physical or corporeal, any more than it is semiotic; it is diagrammatic (it knows nothing of the distinction between the artificial and the natural either). It operates by matter, not by substance; by function, not by form. Substances and forms are of expression "or" of content. But functions are not yet "semiotically" formed, and matters are not yet "physically" formed. The abstract machine is pure Matter-Function – a diagram independent of the forms and substances, expressions and contents that it will distribute" [DEL 87a].

(as the term is understood by Latour)[95] of which they are both the expression and the expressed.

### 3.3.4.2. *Second posture*

Describing the creation and evolution of the links, listing elements which are clustered in them, all of this runs from graph theory through network science, scientometry, search engine algorithms, etc. The research published in 2012 by Latour *et al.* takes the opportunity to exploit digital traces (a database of scientific articles), and thus suggests an approach based on navigation through the data – an approach which gives us "navigable" empirical corpora, where there is constant reversibility between the entity and the network. Form and content emerge simultaneously.

More broadly now, Latour stresses the fact that "quali-quantitative methods are not the simple juxtaposition of statistical analysis with ethnographic observation. Removing the boundary between micro and macro means preparing to receive and manage an unprecedented quantity of data. (And) focusing on the construction of the social phenomena involves following each of the actors concerned and each of the interactions between them".

Whatever the ethnodigital approaches employed, they therefore must avoid two temptations: firstly, that of a return of structuralism (from which the structural approaches of networks inherit), of its system of points and

---

95 In *Irréductions*, chapter 1, 1984. "There is nothing but proof, because a thing is not, in itself, irreducible to any other, and what is never reductible or irreducible must be proven, reported and measured constantly".

1.1.1 Nothing is, by itself, either reducible or irreducible to anything else. I will call this the "principle of irreducibility", but it is a prince that does not govern since that would be a self-contradiction (2.6.1).

1.1.2 There are only trials of strength, of weakness. Or more simply, there are only trials. This is my point of departure: a verb, "to try."

1.1.3 It is because nothing is, by itself, reducible or irreducible to anything else that there are only trials (of strength, of weakness). What is neither reducible nor irreducible has to be tested, counted, and measured. There is no other way.

1.1.4 Everything may be made to be the measure of everything else.

1.1.5 Whatever resists trials is real. The verb "resist" is not a privileged word. I use it to represent the whole collection of verbs and adjectives, tools and instruments, which together define the ways of being real. We could equally well say "curdle", "fold", "obscure", "sharpen", "slide." There are dozens of alternatives.

1.1.5.1 The real is not one thing among others but rather gradients of resistance".

positions in relation to a structure, always encouraging us to either "reveal the informational structure" that we expect, or to "fix" the behaviors of the social actors in a signifying system; and secondly, that of a totalizing design.

By this token, we always obtain a fragmentary result when establishing the list of associated entities (or the connections, which is tantamount to the same thing), rolling out the network of an individual or a document in order to "identify" it (or rather, using the ANT approach, going into their processes of identification, and in line with Simondon's approach, in the processes of individuation). Because we need to go through the whole extent and complexity of the relations developed and transformed therein, because it is, in itself, connected to other assemblages, an assemblage can only be partially described. This has brought great joy to many detractors of ANT, and Latour himself points out the "bizarreness" of their empirical ontology, which could not process new objects, quite complex to trace: "machines and facts – that is innovations" [LAT 10a]. The Internet and the range of digital data offer it the opportunity of a new milieu of application, with the ANT then being "like a fish in water" [LAT 10a].

### 3.3.4.3. *Third posture*

We need to monitor the formation/formatting of attraction/repulsions and obtain a view of them. The assemblage, made up of actors/networks is the milieu where, in various modes, the production of relations between utterances, artefacts, brain/body, the relations of proximity and the boundaries are defined and stabilized, where the connections, associations, disseminations and percolations are updated and deployed. From this standpoint, it is helpful to remember that one of the major problems of any organization, institution or collective, is creating zones of proximity between multiple heterogeneous devices, taken together in a block of becomings (more or less subject to control) and where, playing a crucial role in their metastabilization, the anaphoric work, that is the work of recovery and renewal, the interpretative work and the selection of micro stories and big ones too, the transformation of those stories, are rooted in the battle field of entelechies.

For Deleuze, the assemblage is characterized by "alliances", "alloys", "attraction and repulsion", "sympathy and antipathy", etc., that it facilitates or censors. The algorithmic approaches based on the definition of forces of "repulsion" between the nodes and a force of "attraction" between the links enable us to understand the phenomenon increasingly clearly. This power of attraction/repulsion is given neither by an overarching structure (culture, habitus or any other explanatory "supra-organism"), nor by the aggregation of "simplified", atomized agents, on which we then impose "rules of interaction" to reveal a potentially lasting structure:

> "Both approaches are founded on quasi-identical data collection techniques. The main difference between them lies in the chronological order in which they list the two concepts: from micro to macro for the first, and from macro to micro for the second. What the second treats as its starting point, the first treats as its end goal" [DEL 77].

### 3.3.4.4. *Fourth posture*

We need to explore a world of monads and take rhizomes by the "milieu". Whilst he recognizes the relevance of some of these approaches (in the case of collective phenomena with relatively simple rules and parameters such as traffic jams, crowd movements, etc.), Latour takes the digital milieu and the opening up of new analytical possibilities as revealing impasses (already widely described and criticized), where we place holistic theorists and "atomistic" theorists to study complex social processes. Faithful to the ANT approach, he proposes an alternative which enables the observer to get around a passage from the micro to the macro level, or vice versa: the coming together of Gabriel Tarde's monadology with tools for processing and viewing vast sets of data and relations on the Web, which can be navigated and quantified. However, researchers remain highly dependent on the quality and quantity of information, and the viewing techniques available to them.

For Bruno Latour, digital data today are able to do justice to Tarde's position. In the article, "Le tout est toujours plus petit que ses parties. Une expérimentation digital des monades de Gabriel Tarde" (The whole is always smaller than its parts. A digital experiment with Gabriel Tarde's monads), the authors "revisit" Tarde's thinking, "which completely passes over concepts such as the individual or society" [LAT 12].

"Our argument is that when it was impossible, cumbersome or simply slow to assemble and to navigate through the masses of information on particular items, it made sense to treat data about social connections by defining two levels: one for the element, the other for the aggregates. But once we have the experience of following individuals through their connections (which is often the case with profiles) it might be more rewarding to begin navigating datasets without making the distinction between the level of individual component and that of aggregated structure. It becomes possible to give some credibility to Tarde's strange notion of 'monads'. We claim that it is just this sort of navigational practice that is now made possible by digitally available databases and that such a practice could modify social theory if we could visualize this new type of exploration in a coherent way [...] In the strictest sense of the term, we should no longer speak of collective phenomena as opposed to individual phenomena; simply a variety of different ways of *collecting* phenomena" [LAT 12][96].

However, each time, the writings, praxes, various entities, etc., must be viewed in relation to desiring machines, dealt with in the milieu of the largest assemblages, within which they are included:

"In an assemblage, it is as though there are at least two faces or two heads of the state of affairs, the state of the bodies (bodies

---

96 Also see Venturini and Latour [VEN 09]: "It is in this possibility of openness that the promise of digital lies. However, in order for that promise to be kept, the whole of the research chain must be digitized. As long as digital methods are confined to only one part of the chain, the full innovative potential of navigation in the digital landscapes of data cannot be realized. The mixed chains which characterize most current research are unable to fully exploit the potentials of digital technology, and generate all sorts of incompatibility effects. [...] The digital data are representative if each link of their processing chain (identification, extraction, integration, analysis and publication) is consistent with the work of the construction of the social actors. This is why it is so important to digitize the whole research chain in social sciences. A completely digitized chain would enable us to describe the social fabric by describing the interweaving of each of its threads." The two authors go on to explain: "We are not saying that quali-quantitative methods will be able to deal with the full complexity of collective life. On the other hand, the advantage they hold is that they are sufficiently flexible to monitor certain social phenomena in every aspect. There is no research method which provides a panoptic view of collective existence, and quali-quantitative methods are no exception. Digital methods can only provide an oligoptic view of society (Latour, Hermant, 1988), no more or less partial than that of traditional methods; yet for the first time in the history of social sciences, this view will at least be contiguous."

interpenetrate, mix with one another, transmit emotions to one another); but also utterances, regimes of utterances..." [DEL 77].

We can then, with a hybrid expression between "Deleuze, Guattari and Latour", say that the translation chains are chains of transformation produced within an actor-network and between actor-networks, within an assemblage or between assemblages. This is the reason why we must describe and think about all pragmatism, including communicational pragmatism as a complex relation between internal pragmatism (expressed in and by internal heterogeneses within the assemblage or the actor-network) and external pragmatism (expressed in and by external heterogeneses between assemblages and between actor-networks).

An actor-network is not simply a graph of links and nodes, but an evolving assembly of evolving forces; "the network, in the technological sense, is the result of the establishment of an actor-network (either by the researcher, or by those whose trajectory he/she is following)".

> "An actor is the list of their relations *plus* the transformation that each of the items on the list has undergone in proximity to, or by virtue of, that relation."

More radically, for Latour, the actor-network constitutes more a "theory on research in social science":

> "The research *begins* with a mediation, *follows* or threads together the translations and *comes across* a series of *surprises* (for the researcher) or trials, where the very question of the actors and their network is unraveled" [LAT 10a, VEN 09].

### 3.3.4.5. *Fifth posture*

We need to track the processes of semiotic transformations and captures, but taking account of the need to rethink the pragmatism based on a view of the semiotic issue and Tarde-esque regimes of imitation or dissemination – a view which is still overly simplistic. These processes of transformations and captures, indeed, qualify the way in which an assemblage creates a "zone of proximity" between several heterogeneous elements, taken together in a block of becomings, which transforms that without systematically identifying them. Deleuze repeatedly makes the point that the capture he is talking about expresses a becoming with resemblance or imitation:

"Becoming is never the same as imitating, acting like, or conforming to a model of fairness or truth. Becomings are not phenomena of imitation, or of assimilation, but of twofold capture, of non-parallel evolution, of a marriage between two realms" [DEL 77].

For Félix Guattari:

"Thus, pragmatism would be divided into two components rather than two regions, because these components will be constantly recomposed – generative pragmatism corresponding to the *modes of "linguistization" of semiotics and a transformational non-linguistic and a-signifying pragmatism*".

He writes:

"We divide pragmatism into two series of components: firstly, interpretative transformational components (which are also known as generative components), which imply the priority of semiologies of signification on non-interpretative semiotics. They too will be divided into two general types of transformations: analog transformations stemming from, say, semiotic semiologies; and signifying transformations, stemming from linguistic semiologies. There are two corresponding types of "sources of power over content", by reterritorialization and subjectivation, which are based either on territorialized assemblages of the utterance, or on an individuation of the utterance.

Then, we have

"non-interpretative transformational components, which can reverse the power of the above two transformations. They are divided into two general types of transformations parallel to the previous two: symbolic transformations, stemming from intensive semiotics (for example at the perceptive, gestural, mimic level, etc.), and then diagrammatic transformations, stemming from a-signifying semiotics, which carry out a deterritorialization pertaining jointly to the formalism of the content and that of expression, and involving abstract machines manifested by a system of signs/particles" [GUA 11].

These postures open up the possibility of a sort of radical bifurcation in the way of being a "new milieu of research" in the milieu of continuous creation of organizations, their instauration which always comes before them, at the heart of the interlinked, more or less complex anaphora, which both ensure their metastability and guarantee the becomings. This guarantee of becomings, alone, offers permanence of the futures and lends virtue to the inevitable disagreements against, completely against, the organization.

# Bibliography

[AKR 87] AKRICH M., "Comment décrire les objets techniques ?", *Techniques et Culture*, no. 9, pp. 49–64, 1987.

[AKR 88] AKRICH M., CALLON M., LATOUR B., "À quoi tient le succès des innovations ? 1 : L'art de l'intéressement ; 2 : Le choix des porte-parole", *Les Annales des Mines*, pp. 4–29, 1988.

[AKR 91] AKRICH M., "L'analyse socio-technique", in VINCK D. (ed.), "La gestion de la recherche", De Boeck, Brussels, pp. 339–353, 1991.

[AKR 98] AKRICH M., "Les utilisateurs, acteurs de l'innovation", *Éducation permanente*, no. 134, pp. 78–89, 1998.

[AKR 06] AKRICH M., CALLON M., LATOUR B., *Sociologie de la traduction : textes fondateurs*, Presses des Mines, Paris, 2006.

[AKR 10] AKRICH M., BARTHE Y., MUNIESA F. *et al.* (eds), *Débordements, mélanges offerts à Michel Callon*, Presses des Mines, Paris, 2010.

[ALL 93] ALLIEZ E., *La signature du monde ou qu'est-ce que la philosophie de Deleuze-Guattari*, Éditions du Cerf, Paris, 1993.

[ALT 10] ALTER N., *L'innovation ordinaire*, Presses universitaires de France, Paris, 2010.

[ALV 09] ALVESSON M., BRIDGMAN T., WILLMOTT H., *The Oxford Handbook of Critical Management Studies*, Oxford University Press, New York, 2009.

[ALV 11] ALVESSON M. (ed.), *Classics in Critical Management Studies*, Edward Elgar, Cheltenham, 2011.

[AUS 62] AUSTIN J.L., *How to Do Things with Words: The William James Lectures Delivered at Harvard University in 1955*, Clarendon Press, Oxford, 1962.

[BAR 07] BARBIER R., TREPOS J.-Y., "Humains et non-humains : un bilan d'étape de la sociologie des collectifs", *Revue d'anthropologie des connaissances,* vol. 1, no. 1, pp. 35–58, available at: http://www.cairn.info/revue-anthropologie-des-connaissances-2007-1-page-35.htm, January 2007.

[BAR 09] BARTOLI A., *Le management dans les organisations publiques*, 3rd edition, Dunod, Paris, 2009.

[BAR 13] BARTHE Y. *et al.*, "Sociologie pragmatique : mode d'emploi", *Politix*, no. 103, March 2013.

[BEA 12] BEAUDE B., *Internet, changer l'espace, changer la société*, FYP, Limoges, 2012.

[BEA 15] BEAUDE B., "Spatialités algorithmiques", in SEVERO M., ROMELE A. (eds), *Traces numériques et territoires*, Presses des Mines, Paris, 2015.

[BER 97] BERNARD R., *L'intranet dans l'entreprise*, Sybex, San Francisco, CA, 1997.

[BER 09] BERTHOZ A., *La simplexité*, Odile Jacob, Paris, 2009.

[BOL 91] BOLTANSKI L., THÉVENOT L., *De la justification*, Gallimard, Paris, 1991.

[BOL 99] BOLTANSKI L., CHIAPELLO E., *Le nouvel esprit du capitalisme*, Gallimard, Paris, 1999.

[BOO 13] BOOTZ J.P., "L'évolution du manager : un pilote de communauté de pratique entre l'expert et l'intrapreneur", *Management & Avenir*, no. 63, May 2013.

[BOU 09] BOULLIER D., "Au-delà des territoires numériques en dix thèses", in ROWE F. (ed.), *Sociétés de la connaissance et prospective : hommes, organisations et territoires*, University of Nantes, pp. 1–15, 2009.

[BOU 13] BOURCIER D., DE FILIPPI P., "L'*Open Data* : universalité du principe et diversité des expériences ?", *La semaine juridique*, pp. 1–9, 2013.

[BOU 15] BOULLIER D., "L'écume numérique des territoires", in SEVERO M., ROMELE A. (eds), *Traces numériques et territoires*, Presses des Mines, Paris, 2015.

[BOW 97] BOWKER G., STAR S.L., TURNER W. *et al.* (eds), *Social Science, Information Systems and Cooperative Work: Beyond the Great Divide*, Lawrence Erlbaum, Hillsdale, 1997.

[BOZ 16] BOZZO-REY M., "Influencer les comportements en organisation : fictions et discours managérial", *Le Portique*, Document 3, accessed on March 09, 2017, available at: http://leportique.revues.org/2816, March 2016.

[BRA 07] BRASSAC C., "Une vision praxéologique des architectures de connaissances dans les organisations", *Revue d'anthropologie des connaissances*, no. 1, pp. 121–135, January 2007.

[BRI 08] BRIATTE F., "Interview with David Bloor", *Tracés. Revue de Sciences Humaines*, accessed 26 December 2016, available at: http://traces.revues.org/227, May 2008.

[BRI 14] BRISSET N., "Performer par le dispositif ? Un retour critique sur la théorie de la performativité", *L'année sociologique*, vol. 64, 2014.

[BUR 92] BURT R., *Structural Holes: The Social Structure of Competition*, Harvard University Press, Cambridge, 1992.

[BUR 04] BURT R., "Structural holes and good ideas", *American Journal of Sociology*, vol. 110, no. 2, pp. 349–399, 2004.

[BUY 03] BUYDENS M., "Espace lisse/Espace strié", in SASSO R., VILLANI A. (eds), "Le vocabulaire de Gilles Deleuze", *Les Cahiers de Noesis*, no. 3, p. 130 and 132–134, 2003.

[CAB 05] CABIN P., CHOC B., *Les organisations. États des savoirs*, Éditions Sciences Humaines, Auxerre, 2005.

[CAH 16] CAHUC P., ZYLBERBERG A., *Le négationnisme économique, et comment s'en débarrasser*, Flammarion, Paris, 2016.

[CAL 83] CALLON M., COURTIAL J.-P., TURNER W. et al., "From translations to problematic networks: An introduction to co-word analysis", *Social Science Information*, March 1983.

[CAL 86] CALLON M., "Éléments pour une sociologie de la traduction : La domestication des coquilles Saint-Jacques et des marins-pêcheurs dans la baie de Saint-Brieuc", *L'année sociologique*, no. 36, pp. 170–208, 1986.

[CAL 90] CALLON M., LATOUR B., *La science telle qu'elle se fait, une anthologie de la sociologie des sciences de langue anglaise*, La Découverte, Paris, 1990.

[CAL 98] CALLON M. (ed.), *The Laws of the Markets*, Blackwell Publishers, Oxford, 1998.

[CAL 01] CALLON M., LASCOUMES M., BARTHE Y., *Agir dans un monde incertain : Essai sur la démocratie technique*, Le Seuil, Paris, 2001.

[CAL 02] CALLON M., MÉADEL C., RABEHARISOA V., "The economy of qualities", *Economy and Society*, vol. 31, no. 2, 2002.

[CAL 06] CALLON M., FERRARY M., "Les réseaux sociaux à l'aune de la théorie de l'acteur-réseau", *Sociologies pratiques*, vol. 2, no. 13, pp. 37–44, February 2006.

[CAL 10] CALLON M., "Performativity, misfires, and politics?", *Journal of Cultural Economy*, vol. 3, pp. 163–169, 2010.

[CAL 13] CALLON M., "Qu'est-ce qu'un agencement marchand ?", in CALLON M. *et al.* (eds), *Sociologie des agencements marchands*, Presses des Mines, Paris, 2013.

[CAR 97] CARDON D., "Les sciences sociales et les machines à coopérer : Une approche bibliographique du Computer Supported Cooperative Work (CSCW)", *Réseaux*, no. 85, pp. 13–51, May 1997.

[CAR 10] CARMÈS M., "L'innovation organisationnelle sous les tensions performatives : Propositions pour l'analyse d'une co-construction conflictuelle des politiques et pratiques numériques", in DEBOS F. (ed.), *Les cahiers du numérique*, no. 4, 2010.

[CAR 12] CARMÈS M., GALIBERT O., "La discrimination numérique en organisation : une analyse des identités connectives et des revendications au sein d'une grande entreprise française", in CORDELIER B., GRAMACCIA G. (eds), *Management par projet : Les identités incertaines*, Presses de l'université du Québec, Quebec, pp. 81–98, 2012.

[CAR 13a] CARMÈS M., ANDONOVA Y., "Les politiques numériques internes à l'heure de l'e-administration", in GUILHAUME G., MONSEIGNE A. (eds), *La mutation du métier de communicant public*, available at: http://www.grico.fr/publications/maryse_carmes/, no. 41, pp. 87–100, 2013.

[CAR 13b] CARMÈS M., "Les collectivités numériques vues par leurs agents", available at: http://www.grico.fr/wp-content/uploads/2013/02/Resume_Collectivit%C3%A9 snum%C3%A9riques_GRICO_Fev2013.pdf, 2013.

[CAR 13c] CARMÈS M., NOYER J.-M. (eds), *Les débats du numérique*, Presses des Mines, Paris, 2013.

[CAR 14a] CARMÈS M., NOYER J.-M. (eds), *Devenirs urbains*, Presses des Mines, Paris, 2014.

[CAR 14b] CARMÈS M., NOYER J.-M., "L'irrésistible montée de l'algorithmique : Méthodes et concepts en SHS", *Les cahiers du numérique*, no. 4, 2014.

[CAR 15] CARMÈS M., NOYER J.-M., "Désirs de data", in SEVERO M., ROMELE A. (eds), *Traces numériques et territoires*, Presses des Mines, Paris, 2015.

[CAR 16] CARMÈS M., "L'Open Data territorial dans ses tensions : L'ouverture des données de marchés publics comme instrument techno-politique", *Revue internationale d'intelligence économique*, vol. 8, pp. 17–36, January 2016.

[CAS 91] CASTEL R., "Savoirs d'expertise et production de normes", in CHAZEL F., COMMAILLE J. (eds), *Normes juridiques et régulation sociale*, LGDJ, Paris, pp. 177–188, 1991.

[CAS 15] CASILLI A., CARDON D., *Qu'est-ce que le digital labor ?*, INA, Bry-sur-Marne, 2015.

[CHA 15] CHATEAURAYNAUD F., "L'emprise comme expérience", *SociologieS*, accessed on 25 July 2015, available at: http://sociologies.revues.org/4931, February 2015.

[CLI 86] CLIFFORD J., MARCUS G. (eds.), *Writing Culture: The Poetics and Politics of Ethnography*, University of California Press, Berkeley, 1986.

[CLE 11] CLEGG STEWART R., DANY F., GREY C., "Introduction to the special issue critical management studies and managerial education: New contexts? New agenda?", *M@n@gement*, vol. 14, pp. 272–279, May 2011.

[COH 10] COHENDET P., HÉRAUD J.-A., LLERENA P., "La dynamique de l'innovation : une interprétation de l'approche de Michel Callon en termes de communautés de connaissance", in AKRICH M., BARTHE Y., MUNIESA F. *et al.* (eds), *Débordements, Mélanges offerts à Michel Callon*, Presses des Mines, Paris, 2010.

[CON 04] CONEIN B., "Cognition distribuée, groupe social et technologie cognitive", *Réseaux*, vol. 124, no. 2, pp. 53–79, 2004.

[COO 10] COOREN F., "Ventriloquie, performativité et communication ou comment fait-on parler les choses", *Réseaux*, vol. 163, no. 5, pp. 33–54, 2010.

[CRA 16] CRAWFORD M.B., *Éloge du carburateur : Essai sur le sens et la valeur du travail*, translated by Marc Saint-Upéry, La Découverte, Paris, 2016.

[CRE 09] CREPLET F., JACOB T., *Réussir un projet intranet 2.0*, Éditions d'Organisation, Paris, 2009.

[DAS 12] DASTON L., GALISON P., *Objectivité*, translated by Sophie Renaut and Hélène Quiniou, Les Presses du Réel, Dijon, 2012.

[DEB 04] DEBANG D., "Le langage de l'individuation", *Multitudes*, no. 18, p. 101–106, available at: http://www.cairn.info/revue-multitudes-2004-4-page-101.htm, April 2004.

[DEG 05] DE GAULEJAC V., *La société malade de la gestion*, Le Seuil, Paris, 2005.

[DEJ 98] DEJOURS C., *Souffrance en France*, Le Seuil, Paris, 1998.

[DEL 72] DELEUZE G., GUATTARI F., *L'anti-Œdipe*, Éditions de Minuit, Paris, 1972.

[DEL 78] DELEUZE G., "Philosophie et minorité", *Critique*, no. 369, February 1978.

[DEL 80] DELEUZE G., GUATTARI F., "Introduction : Rhizome", *Capitalisme et schizophrénie* : *Mille plateaux*, vol. 2, Éditions de Minuit, Paris, 1980.

[DEL 86] DELEUZE G., Le pouvoir 10, Course, available at: http://www2.univ-paris8.fr/deleuze/article.php3? id_article=442, 1986.

[DEL 87a] DELEUZE G., GUATTARI F., *A Thousand Plateaus : Capitalism and Schizophrenia*, University of Minnesota Press, Minneapolis, 1987.

[DEL 87b] DELEUZE G., GUATTARI F., "Postulates of linguistics" in DELEUZE G., GUATTARI F. (eds), A *Thousand Plateaus : Capitalism and Schizophrenia*, translated by Brian Massumi, University of Minnesota Press, pp. 75–110, 1987.

[DEL 90] DELEUZE G., *Pourparlers,* Éditions de Minuit, Paris, 1990.

[DEL 91] DELEUZE G., GUATTARI F., *What Is Philosophy?*, translated by Hugh Tomlinson and Graham Burchell, Columbia University Press, New York, 1991.

[DEL 94] DELEUZE G., GUATTARI F, *What Is Philosophy?,* translated by Tomlinson H. and Burchell G., Columbia University Press, New York, 1994.

[DEL 96] DELEUZE G., PARNET C., *Dialogues*, Flammarion, Paris, 1996.

[DEL 98] DE LA VILLE V.-I., "L'apprentissage organisationnel : perspectives théoriques", *Cahiers français de La Documentation française*, no. 287, pp. 96–103, July–September 1998.

[DEL 04] DELEUZE G., *Foucault*, Éditions de Minuit, Paris, 2004.

[DEL 09] DELANDA M., "Agencements versus totalités", *Multitudes*, no. 39, pp. 137–144, April 2009.

[DEL 16] DELANDA M., *Assemblage Theory*, Edinburgh University Press, Edinburgh, 2016.

[DEN 06] DENIS J., "Performativité : Relectures et usages d'une notion frontière", *Études de communication*, no. 29, 2006.

[DEN 09] DENIS J., "Une autre sociologie des usages ? Pistes et postures pour l'étude des chaînes sociotechniques", *Archive ouverte en sciences de l'Homme et de la Société*, available at: https://halshs.archives-ouvertes.fr/halshs-00641283, 2009.

[DEN 14] DENIS J., GOËTA S., "Exploration, extraction and "rawification": The shaping of transparency in the back rooms of Open Data", *Neil Postman Conference*, New York University, New York, 2014.

[DER 71] DERRIDA J., "Signature, événement, contexte", *Congrès international des sociétés de philosophie de langue française*, Montreal, Canada, 1971.

[DES 04] DE SUTTER L., GUTWIRTH S., "Droit et cosmopolitique : Notes sur la contribution de Bruno Latour à la pensée du droit", *Droit et société*, nos 56–57, January–February 2004.

[DES 14] DE SAINT LÉGER M., JUANALS B., MINEL J.-L., "Linguistique textuelle et textmining appliqués à l'analyse contrastive des médias : le cas de la médiatisation de la protection des données personnelles et des technologies sans contact", *635th symposium of the 82nd Congrès de l'Acfas : Langues naturelles, informatique et sciences cognitives,* Montreal, Canada, available at: https://halshs.archives-ouvertes.fr/halshs-00989309, May 2014.

[DIM 83] DIMAGGIO P.J., POWELL W.W., "The iron cage revisited: Institutional isomorphism and collective rationality in organizational fields", *American Sociological Review*, vol. 48, no. 2, pp. 147–160, 1983.

[DOD 95] DODIER N., *Les hommes et les machines*, Métaillié, Paris, 1995.

[DOU 89] DOUGLAS M., *Ainsi pensent les institutions*, Usher Editions, Paris, 1989.

[DUR 97] DURAND J.P., WEIL R. (eds), *Sociologie contemporaine*, Vigot, Paris, 1997.

[EIS 79] EISENSTEIN E., *The Printing Revolution in Early-Modern Europe*, Cambridge University Press, New York, 1979.

[ERT 15] ERTZSCHEID O., "Usages de l'information numérique : comprendre les nouvelles enclosures algorithmiques pour mieux s'en libérer", *Revue française des sciences de l'information et de la communication*, accessed June 2015, available at: http://rfsic.revues.org/1425, January 2015.

[ESP 10] ESPOSITO R., *Communauté, immunité, biopolitique*, translated by Bernard Chamayou, Les Prairies ordinaires, Paris, 2010.

[FAY 72] FAYE J.-P., *Langages totalitaires : critique de la raison et de l'économie narrative,* Hermann, Paris, 1972.

[FIS 14] FISCHER M.M.J., "The lightness of existence and the origami of "French" anthropology : Latour, Descola, Viveiros de Castro, Meillassoux, and their so-called ontological turn", *Journal of Ethnographic Theory*, vol. 4, no. 1, 2014.

[FON 14] FONDEUR Y., "La professionnalisation du recrutement au prisme des dispositifs de sélection", *Revue française de socio-économie*, no. 14, February 2014.

[FOU 75] FOUCAULT M., *Surveiller et punir*, Gallimard, Paris, 1975.

[FRA 06] FRAENKEL B., "Actes écrits, actes oraux : la performativité à l'épreuve de l'écriture", *Études de communication*, no. 29, pp. 69–93, 2006.

[FUC 14] FUCHS C., *Digital Labour and Karl Marx*, Routledge, New York, 2014.

[GAB 04] GABRIEL Y., *Myths, Stories, and Organizations: Premodern Narratives for Our Times*, Oxford Press University, Oxford, 2004.

[GAN 09] GANASCIA J.G., *Voir et pouvoir : qui nous surveille ?*, Éditions du Pommier, Paris, 2009.

[GAL 07] GALLOWAY A.R., THACKER E., *The Exploit, A Theory of Networks*, available at: http://dss-edit.com/plu/Galloway-Thacker_The_Exploit_2007.pdf, 2007.

[GAL 10] GALINON-MELENEC B., "Réseaux sociaux d'entreprise et DRH", *Communication et organisation*, no. 37, pp. 41–51, 2010.

[GAL 12] GALLOWAY A.R., *The Interface Effect*, Polity Press, Cambridge, 2012.

[GAR 08] GARCIA S., "L'expert et le profane : qui est juge de la qualité universitaire ?", *Genèses*, no. 70, pp. 66–87, January 2008.

[GER 97] GERMAIN M., "D'internet à intranet : L'entreprise et les nouvelles technologies de l'information", *Les cahiers de la communication interne*, no. 1, p. 18, September 1997.

[GIR 05] GIROUX N., MARROQUIN L., "L'approche narrative des organisations", *Revue française de gestion*, vol. 159, no. 6, pp. 15–42, 2005.

[GRA 73] GRANOVETTER M.S., "The strength of weak ties", *American Journal of Sociology*, vol. 78, no. 6, pp. 1360–1380, May 1973.

[GRA 83] GRANOVETTER M.S., "The strength of weak ties: A network theory revisited", *Sociological Theory*, vol. 1, pp. 201–233, 1983.

[GRA 14] GRAY J., "Towards a genealogy of Open Data", *General conference of the European Consortium for Political Research*, University of Glasgow, Glasgow, 2014.

[GRE 86] GREIMAS A.J., *Sémantique structurale*, Presses universitaires de France, Paris, 1986.

[GRO 05] GROSJEAN M., "L'awareness à l'épreuve des activités dans les centres de coordination", *Revue activités*, vol. 2, no. 1, 2005.

[GUA 83] GUATTARI F., ALLIEZ E., "Le capital en fin de compte : systèmes, structures et processus capitalistiques", *Change international 1*, pp. 100–106, 1983.

[GUA 89] GUATTARI F., *Cartographies schizo-analytiques*, Galilée, Paris, 1989.

[GUA 91a] GUATTARI F., "L'hétérogenèse machinique", *Chimères*, no. 11, 1991.

[GUA 91b] GUATTARI F., "Les systèmes d'interface machinique", *Terminal,* no. 52, 1991.

[GUA 92] GUATTARI F., *Chaosmoses*, Galilée, Paris, 1992.

[GUA 07] GUATTARI F., *Micropolitiques*, Les empêcheurs de penser en rond, Paris, 2007.

[GUA 11] GUATTARI F., *Lignes de fuite : Pour un autre monde de possibles*, Éditions de l'Aube, La Tour d'Aigues, 2011.

[GUA 12] GUATTARI F., *La révolution moléculaire*, Les Prairies ordinaires, Paris, 2012.

[HAB 87] HABERMAS J., *Théorie de l'agir communicationnel*, vol. 1, Fayard, Paris, 1987.

[HAM 08] HAMEL G., BREEN B., *La fin du management : inventer les règles de demain*, Éditions Vuibert, Paris, 2008.

[HAR 10] HARTMUT R., *Accélération : Une critique sociale du temps*, La Découverte, Paris, 2010.

[HEN 13] HENNION A., "D'une sociologie de la médiation à une pragmatique des attachements", *SociologieS*, available at: http://sociologies.revues.org/4353, June 2013.

[HEY 09] HEY T., TANSLEY S., TOLLE K., *The fourth Paradigm: Data Intensive Scientific Discovery*, Microsoft Corporation, 2009.

[HUA 11] HUAULT I., PERRET V., "L'enseignement critique du management comme espace d'émancipation · Une réflexion autour de la pensée de Jacques Rancière", *M@n@gement*, vol. 14, pp. 282–309, May 2011.

[HUM 48] HUME D., *A Treatise of Human Nature*, 1748.

[HUT 95] HUTCHINS E., *Cognition in the wild*, MIT Press, Cambridge, 1995.

[HUT 00] HUTCHINS E., Distributed Cognition, Working paper, University of California, San Diego, 2000.

[JAR 09] JARROSSON B., *Vers l'économie 2.0 : Du boulon au photon... !*, Éditions d'Organisation, Paris, 2009.

[KIT 14] KITCHIN R., *The Data Revolution: Big Data, Open Data, Data Infrastructures and their Consequences*, Sage, London, 2014.

[LAC 06] LACOSTE Y., *Géopolitique, la longue histoire d'aujourd'hui*, Larousse, Paris, 2006.

[LAL 15] LALLEMENT M., *L'âge du faire : Hacking, travail, anarchie*, Le Seuil, Paris, 2015.

[LAM 00] LAMONT M., THEVENOT L., available at: https://books.google.fr/books?id=0Po1DgAAQBAJ&pg=PA167&lpg=PA167&dq=sociology+pragmatic+approach+trials&source=bl&ots=JVfeB8SsHL&sig=565fk65rrq2tBijWqdnfmcPf0-c&hl=fr&sa=X&ved=0ahUKEwiNqO-05cHYAhXCI1AKHXIYCDgQ6AEINTAC#v=onepage&q=sociology%20pragmatic%20approach%20trials&f=false, 2000.

[LAR 81] LARUELLE F., "Homo Ex Machina, Comment On Devient Homme-Machine", *Revue Philosophique De La France Et De L'étranger*, no.105, 1981.

[LAS 04] LASCOUMES P., "La gouvernementalité : de la critique de l'État aux technologies du pouvoir", *Le portique*, available at: http://leportique.revues.org/625, pp. 13–14, June 2004.

[LAS 10] LASCOUMES P., "La démocratie électronique et l'Open Government de Barack Obama sous l'œil critique des STS", in AKRICH M., BARTHE Y., MUNIESA F. *et al.* (eds), *Débordements : Mélanges offerts à Michel Callon*, Presses des Mines, Paris, 2010.

[LAT 79] LATOUR B., WOOLGAR S., *Laboratory Life: The Social Construction of Scientific facts*, Sage Publications, Beverly Hills, 1979.

[LAT 84] LATOUR B., *Les microbes: guerre et paix*, Editions Métailié, Paris, 1984.

[LAT 88] LATOUR B., "How to write 'the prince' for machines as well as for machinations" in ELLIOTT B. (ed.), *Technology and Social Change*, Edinburgh University Press, 1988.

[LAT 91] LATOUR B., *Nous n'avons jamais été modernes : Essai d'anthropologie symétrique*, La Découverte, Paris, 1991.

[LAT 93] LATOUR B., *The Pasteurization of France*, translated by Alan Sheridan and John Law, Harvard University Press, Cambridge, Massachusetts and London, England, available at: https://archive.org/stream/BrunoLatourThePasteurizationOfFrance1993/Bruno%20Latour-The%20Pasteurization%20of%20France%20(1993)_djvu.txt, 1993.

[LAT 94] LATOUR B., "Getting beyond the technology/society dichotomy: An overview of the various sociologies of technology", in LATOUR B., LEMONNIER P. (eds) *De la préhistoire aux missiles balistiques : l'intelligence sociale des techniques*, La Découverte, Paris, 1994.

[LAT 95] LATOUR B. "Social theory and the study of computerized work sites", in ORLIKOWSKI W.J. *et al.* (eds), *Information Technology and Changes in Organizational Work*, Chapman Hall, London, 1995.

[LAT 98] LATOUR B., "Petite philosophie de l'énonciation : Pour Paolo à la mémoire de notre amie commune Françoise Bastide", in BASSO P., CORRAIN L. (eds), *Eloqui de senso. Dialoghi semiotici per Paolo FabbriOrizzonti, compiti e dialoghi della semiotica. Saggi per Paolo Fabbri*, Costa & Nolan, Milan, pp. 71–94, available at: http://www.bruno-latour.fr/sites/default/files/75-FABBRI-FR.pdf, 1998.

[LAT 04] LATOUR B., *La fabrique du droit, une ethnographie du Conseil d'État*, La Découverte, Paris, 2004.

[LAT 06a] LATOUR B., "Le prince : machines et machinations", in AKRICH M., CALLON M., LATOUR B. (eds), *Sociologie de la traduction*, Presses des Mines, Paris, 2006.

[LAT 06b] CALLON M., FERRARY M., "Les réseaux sociaux à l'aune de la théorie de l'acteur-réseau", *Sociologies pratiques*, no. 13, pp. 37–44, 2006.

[LAT 06c] LATOUR B., *Changer de société, refaire de la sociologie*, La Découverte, Paris, 2006.

[LAT 07] LATOUR B., "Faits, fétiches, faitiches, la divine surprise de l'action", in LATOUR B. (ed.), *L'espoir de Pandore : Pour une version réaliste de l'activité scientifique*, La Découverte, Paris, 2007.

[LAT 09] LATOUR B., *Sur le culte des dieux faitiches : Suivi de Iconoclash*, Les Empêcheurs de penser en rond, Paris, 2009.

[LAT 10a] LATOUR B., "Avoir ou ne pas avoir de réseau : that is the question", in CALLON M., AKRICH M., BARTHE Y. *et al.* (eds), *Débordements : Mélanges offerts à Michel Callon*, Presses des Mines, Paris, 2010.

[LAT 10b] LATOUR B., "La mondialisation fait-elle un monde habitable ?", *Territoires 2040*, no. 2, 2010.

[LAT 11] LATOUR B., *Pasteur : Guerre et paix des microbes, suivi de Irréductions*, La Découverte, Paris, 2011.

[LAT 12a] LATOUR B., *Enquête sur les modes d'existence : Une anthropologie des Modernes*, La Découverte, Paris, 2012.

[LAT 12b] LATOUR B., JENSEN P., VENTURINI T. *et al.*, "Le tout est toujours plus petit que ses parties : Une expérimentation numérique des monades de Gabriel Tarde," *British Journal of Sociology*, vol. 63, no. 4, 2012.

[LAV 88] LAVE J., *Cognition in Practice*, Cambridge University Press, Cambridge, 1988.

[LAZ 04] LAZZARATO M., *Révolutions capitalistes*, Les Empêcheurs de penser en rond, Paris, 2004.

[LAZ 06] LAZZARATO M., "Le 'pluralisme sémiotique' et le nouveau gouvernement des signes", available at: http://eipcp.net/transversal/0107/lazzarato/fr, 2006.

[LEM 07] LEMIEUX C., "À quoi sert l'analyse des controverses ?", *Mil neuf cent* : *Revue d'histoire intellectuelle*, no. 25, pp. 191–212, January 2007.

[LEM 15] LEMIEUX C. (ed.), "'Société critique' et sociologie des épreuves – Retour sur 'Irréductions'" Online seminar, accessed May 16, 2015, available at: http://www.archivesaudiovisuelles.fr/FR/_video.asp?format=68&id=343&ress=2681&video=95590, 2015.

[LES 15] LES ÉCHOS, accessed January 3, 2016, available at: http://www.lesechos.fr/politique-societe/societe/021552597172-quand-veolia-joue-les-maitres-decole-1183977.php, December 2015.

[LÉV 94] LÉVY P., "Plissé fractal ou comment les machines de Guattari peuvent nous aider à penser le transcendantal aujourd'hui", *Chimères*, no. 14, pp. 167–180, 1994.

[LÉV 13] LÉVY P., "Le médium algorithmique", available at: https://pierrelevyblog.com/2013/02/17/le-medium-algorithmique/, 2013.

[LIC 08] LICOPPE C., "Dans le "carré de l'activité : perspectives internationales sur le travail et l'activité", *Sociologie du travail*, no. 50, pp. 287–302, 2008.

[LIC 10] LICOPPE C. (ed.), "Un tournant performatif ? Retour sur ce que 'font' les mots et les choses", *Réseaux*, 2010.

[LOR 13] LORDON F., *La société des affects : Pour un structuralisme des passions*, Le Seuil, Paris, 2013.

[LUH 90] LUHMANN N., *Essays on Self-reference*, Columbia University Press, New York, 1990.

[LUH 95] LUHMANN N., *Social Systems*, Stanford University Press, Stanford, 1995.

[LYO 79] LYOTARD J.-F., *La condition postmoderne*, Éditions de Minuit, Paris, 1979.

[LYO 83] LYOTARD J.-F., *Le différend*, Éditions de Minuit, Paris, 1983.

[LYO 88] LYOTARD J.-F., *The Differend*, University of Minnesota Press, Minneapolis, 1988.

[MAC 84] MACKENZIE D., "Marx and the machine," *Technology and Culture*, vol. 25, no. 3, pp. 473–502, 1984.

[MAR 68] MARCUSE H., *L'Homme unidimensionnel*, Éditions de Minuit, Paris, p. 77, 1968.

[MAR 15] MARTUCCELLI D., "Les deux voies de la notion d'épreuve en sociologie", *Sociologie*, vol. 6, no. 1, accessed August 17, 2016, available at: http://sociologie.revues.org/2435, May 2015.

[MAL 04] MALABOU C., *Que faire de notre cerveau ?*, Bayard, Montrouge, 2004.

[MAT 80] MATURANA H.R., VARELA F., "Autopoiesis and cognition: The realization of the living", *Boston Studies in the Philosophy of Science Series*, no. 42, 1980.

[MAU 73] MAUSS M., *Essai sur le don : Forme et raison de l'échange dans les sociétés archaïques*, Presses universitaires de France, Paris, 1973.

[MER 09] MERZEAU L., "De la surveillance à la veille", *Cités*, no. 39, March 2009.

[MER 12] MERCIER A., "Dérives des universités, périls des universitaires", *Questions de communication*, no. 22, pp. 197–234, 2012.

[MER 42] MERTON R.K., *Social theory and social structure*, Macmillan Publishers, London, 1942.

[MIN 75] MINSKY, M., *The Psychology of Computer Vision*, McGraw Hill, New York, 1975.

[MIN 82] MINTZBERG H., *Structure et dynamique de l'organisation*, Éditions d'Organisation, Paris, 1982.

[MOR 14] MOROZOV E., *Pour tout résoudre cliquez ici : L'aberration du solutionnisme technologique*, FYP, Limoges, 2014.

[MOU 07] MOULIER-BOUTANG Y. (ed.), *Le capitalisme cognitif : La nouvelle grande transformation*, Éditions Amsterdam, Paris, 2007.

[MUN 08] MUNIESA F., CALLON M., "La performativité des sciences économiques", *Papiers de recherche du CSI*, no. 10, 2008.

[NEG 00] NEGRI A., HARDT M., *Empire*, Exils, Paris, 2000.

[NEL 82] NELSON R.R., WINTER S.G., *An Evolutionary Theory of Economic Change*, Harvard University Press, Massachusetts, 1982.

[NEW 09] NEWFIELD C., "Structure et silence du cognitariat, *Multitudes*, vol. 39, no. 4, pp. 68–78, 2009.

[NON 95] NONAKA I., TAKEUCHI H., *The Knowledge-creating Company*, Oxford University Press, New York, 1995.

[NON 06] NONNENMACHER F., *Business Blogger*, Éditions d'Organisation, Paris, 2006.

[NOY 95] NOYER J.-M., "Scientométrie, infométrie : pourquoi nous intéressent-elles ?", *Solaris*, 1995.

[NOY 10a] NOYER J.-M., "Les hétérogenèses de l'agencement science fiction/speculative fiction (SpF)", in WILLMANN F. (ed.), *La science-fiction entre Cassandre et Prométhée*, Presses universitaires de Nancy, Nancy, 2010.

[NOY 10b] NOYER J.-M., "Connaissance, pensée, réseaux à l'heure numérique : Pour une nouvelle Renaissance", *Les cahiers du numérique*, vol. 6, pp. 187–209, available at: http://www.cairn.info/revue-les-cahiers-du-numerique-2010-3-page-187.htm, March 2010.

[NOY 10c] NOYER J.-M., CARMÈS M., "Les interfaces machiniques comme problème sémio-politique", in BROUDOUX E., CHARTRON G. (eds), *Enjeux politiques du document numérique*, Éditions ADBS, Paris, 2010.

[NOY 12] NOYER J.-M., CARMÈS M., "Le mouvement Open Data dans la grande transformation des intelligences collectives et face à la question des écritures, du web sémantique et des ontologies", *Colloque ISKO*, Hammamet, 2012.

[NOY 13] NOYER J.-M., "La transformation numérique : quelques procès en cours", *Revue française des sciences de l'information et de la communication*, accessed February 2013, available at: http://rfsic.revues.org/377, 2013.

[NOY 17] NOYER J.-M., *Transformation of Collective Intelligences*, ISTE Ltd, London and John Wiley & Sons, New York, 2017.

[ORE 05] O'REILLY T., "What is Web 2.0?", available at: http://oreilly.com/web2/archive/what-is-web-20.html, 2005.

[ORL 00] ORLÉAN A., "L'individu, le marché et l'opinion : réflexions sur le capitalisme financier", *Esprit*, November 2000.

[ORR 08] ORRIGI G., Edge: The Reality Club, available at : http://www.edge.org/discourse/the_end_of_theory.html, 2008.

[ORW 49] ORWELL G., *Nineteen Eighty-Four*, Secker and Warburg, Paris, 1949.

[PAL 10] PALPACUER F., LEROY M., NARO G. (eds), *Management, mondialisation, écologie : regards critiques en sciences de gestion*, Hermès-Lavoisier, Paris, 2010.

[PEN 14] PENTLAND A., *Social Physics: How Good Ideas Spread The lessons from New Science*, Penguin Press, London, 2014.

[PER 01] PERRON B., "Le petit glossaire 'cinématographique' de la science cognitive", *Cinémas*, vol. 11, nos 2–3, pp. 275–290, 2001.

[PET 94] PETITOT J., "Topologie phénoménale : sur l'actualité scientifique de la phusis phénoménologique de Merleau Ponty", in MERLEAU-PONTY M., *Le philosophe et son langage*, Éditions Vrin, Paris, 1994.

[PEU 13] PEUGEOT V., "Les communs, une brèche politique à l'heure du numérique", in CARMÈS M., NOYER J.-M. (eds), *Les débats du numérique*, Presses des Mines, Paris, 2013.

[PRO 15] PROULX S., "La sociologie des usages, et après ?", *Revue française des sciences de l'information et de la communication*, vol. 6, accessed August 17, 2016, available at: http://rfsic.revues.org/1230, January 2015.

[ROD 10] RODHAIN F., FALLERY B., GIRARD A. *et al.*, "Une histoire de la recherche en Systèmes d'Information à travers trente ans de publications", *Entreprises et Histoire*, no. 60, 2010.

[ROG 13] ROGERS R., *Digital Methods*, MIT Press, Cambridge, 2013.

[ROG 15] ROGERS R., "Au-delà de la critique Big Data", in SEVERO M., ROMELE A. (eds), *Traces numériques et territoires*, Presses des Mines, Paris, 2015.

[ROS 10] ROSA H., *Accélération : Une critique sociale du temps*, La Découverte, Paris, 2010.

[ROU 07] ROULLEAUX-DUGAGE M., *Organisation 2.0 : The knowledge management new generation*, Éditions d'Organisation, Paris, 2007.

[RUP 13] RUPPERT E., "Doing the transparent state: open government data as performance indicators", in ROTTENBURG R., MERRY S.E., MUGLER J. *et al.* (eds), *A World of Indicators: The Production of Knowledge and Justice in an Interconnected World*, Cambridge University Press, Cambridge, 2013.

[SAS 03] SASSO R., VILLANI A. (eds), "Le vocabulaire de Gilles Deleuze", *Les Cahiers de Noesis*, no. 3, 2003.

[SAU 12] SAUVAGNARGUES A., "Machines, comment ça marche ?", *Chimères: Chaosmose, penser avec Félix Guattari*, no. 77, pp. 35–46, February 2012.

[SAU 03] SAUVAGNARGUES A., "Fulgurer", in SASSO R., VILLANI A. (eds), "Le vocabulaire de Gilles Deleuze", *Les Cahiers de Noesis*, no. 3, p. 164, 2003.

[SCH 60] SCHELLING T.C., *The Strategy of Conflict*, Harvard University Press, Cambridge, 1960.

[SCH 77] SCHANK R. C., ABELSON R. P., *Scripts, Plans, Goals and Understanding*, Lawrence Erlbaum Associates, Hillsdale, 1977.

[SCH 13] SCHOLZ T., *Digital Labor: The Internet as Playground and Factory*, Routledge, New York, 2013.

[SER 98] SERRES M., FAROUKI N. (eds), *Dictionnaire des sciences*, Flammarion, Paris, 1998.

[SER 00] SERIEYX H., "Préface" in PRAX J.-Y., *Le guide du knowledge management : concepts et pratiques du management de la connaissance*, Dunod, Paris, 2000.

[SFE 02] SFEZ L., *Technique et idéologie*, Le Seuil, Paris, 2002.

[SIM 58] SIMONDON G., *Du mode d'existence des objets techniques*, Aubier, Paris, 1958.

[SIM 89] SIMONDON G., *L'individuation psychique et collective*, Aubier, Paris, 1989.

[SLO 00] SLOTERDIJK P., *La domestication de l'être*, Éditions des Mille et une Nuits, Paris, 2000.

[SLO 02] SLOTERDIJK P., *Sphères I. Bulles. Microsphérologie*, translated by Olivier Mannoni, Pauvert, Paris, 2002.

[SLO 05] SLOTERDIJK P., *Sphères III. Écumes. Sphérologie plurielle*, translated by Olivier Mannoni, Marell Sell Éditeur, Paris, 2005.

[SLO 06] SLOTERDIJK P., *Le palais de cristal : À l'intérieur du capitalisme planétaire*, Maren Sell Éditeurs, Paris, 2006.

[SLO 10] SLOTERDIJK P., *Sphères II. Globes*, Olivier Mannoni, translated by Marell Sell Éditeur, Paris, 2010.

[SOU 09] SOURIAU E., *Les différents modes d'existence*, Presses universitaires de France, Paris, 2009.

[STA 10] STAR L.S., RUHLEDER K., "Vers une écologie de l'infrastructure : Conception et accès aux grands espaces d'information", *Revue d'anthropologie des connaissances*, vol. 4, no. 1, pp. 114–161, January 2010.

[STE 04] STENGERS I., "Résister à Simondon ?", *Multitudes*, no. 18, pp. 55–62, available at: http://www.cairn.info/revue-multitudes-2004-4-page-55.htm, April 2004.

[STE 10] STENGERS I., *Cosmopolitics*, University of Minnesota Press, Minneapolis, 2010.

[STI 94] STIEGLER B., *La technique et le temps*, vol. 1, Éditions Galilée, Paris, 1994.

[STI 08] STIEGLER B., *Le design de nos existences à l'époque de l'innovation ascendante*, Éditions des Mille et une Nuits, Paris, 2008.

[STI 10a] STIEGLER B., *Ce qui fait que la vie vaut la peine d'être vécue : De la pharmacologie*, Flammarion, Paris, 2010.

[STI 10b] STIEGLER B., "Le carnaval de la nouvelle toile : de l'hégémonie à l'isonomie", in NOYER J.-M., JUANALS B. (eds), *Technologies de l'information et transformation des intelligences collectives*, Hermès-Lavoisier, Paris, pp. 57–86, 2010.

[STI 12] STIEGLER B, "Le bien le plus précieux à l'époque des sociotechnologies", in STIEGLER B. (ed.), *Réseaux sociaux : Culture politique et ingénierie des réseaux sociaux*, FYP, Limoges, 2012.

[SUC 87] SUCHMAN L., *Plans and Situated Actions: The Problem of Human-machine Communication*, Cambridge University Press, Cambridge, 1987.

[SUS 14] SUSHA I., ZUIDERWIJK A., JANSSEN M. *et al.*, "Benchmarks for evaluating the progress of Open data adoption: Usage, limitations, and lessons learned", *Social Science Computer Review*, December 2014.

[TAR 99] TARDE G., *Monadologie et sociologie*, Les Empêcheurs de penser en rond, Paris, 1999.

[TAR 01] TARDE G., *Les lois de l'imitation*, Les Empêcheurs de penser en rond, Paris, 2001.

[TEI 91] TEIL G., Candide . Un outil de sociologie assistée par ordinateur pour l'analyse quali-quantitative de gros corpus de textes, PhD thesis, École des Mines de Paris, 1991.

[TEI 95] TEIL G., LATOUR B., "The Hume machine: Can association networks do more than formal rules?", *Stanford Humanities Review*, vol. 4, no. 2, pp. 47–65, 1995.

[THE 04] THEUREAU J., "L'hypothèse de la cognition (ou action) située et la tradition d'analyse du travail de l'ergonomie de langue française", available at: http://activites.revues.org/1219, 2004.

[THÉ 06] THÉVENOT L., *L'Action au pluriel : Sociologie des régimes d'engagement*, La Découverte, Paris, 2006.

[TIS 02] TISSERON S, *L'intimité surexposée*, Hachette Littérature, Paris, 2002.

[TOF 70] TOFFLER A., *Future Shock,* Random House, United States, 1970.

[TOF 83] TOFFLER A., *Previews and Premises*, William Morrow, New York, 1983.

[VAR 89] VARELA F.-J., *Autonomie et connaissance : Essai sur le vivant*, Le Seuil, Paris, 1989.

[VEL 00] VELTZ P., *Le nouveau monde industriel*, Gallimard, Paris, 2000.

[VEN 09] VENTURINI T., LATOUR B., "Le tissu social : traces numériques et méthodes quali-quantitatives", in CHARDRONNET E. (ed.), *Actes Futur en Seine*, Cap Digital, Paris, 2009.

[VIR 77] VIRILIO P., *Vitesse et politique : Essai de dromologie*, Galilée, Paris, 1977.

[VIR 91] VIRILIO P., "Dromologie : logique de la course", available at: http://multitudes.samizdat.net/Dromologie-logique-de-la-course, 1991.

[VIR 92] VIRNO P., "Quelques notes à propos du general intellect, available at: http://www.multitudes.net/Quelques-notes-a-propos-du-general/.", 1992.

[WAT 90] WATERMAN JR., ROBERT H., *Adhocracy: The Power to Change*, W.W. Norton & Company, New York, 1990.

[WEN 02] WENGER E., MAC DERMOTT R., SNYDER W.M., *Cultivating Communities of Practice*, Harvard Business School Press, Boston, 2002.

[WHI 95] WHITAKER R., "Self-organization, autopoiesis, and enterprises", *Association for Computing Machinery*, available at: http://www.johnpolly.co.uk/hnd/resources/lecture/self-organisation.pdf, 1995.

# Index

interface, 1, 9, 14, 18–20, 23, 25, 26,
29–31, 33, 34, 36, 39, 43, 47, 59,
61, 63, 65–70, 72–74, 76–78, 98,
102, 104, 108, 116, 118, 142, 146,
148, 149, 157, 166, 172–179, 182,
185, 188–194, 200–204, 206, 207,
209, 217, 219, 221, 222, 226, 228,
235, 237, 238, 264
intranet, 1, 28, 31, 41, 45, 47–51,
55–57, 62, 89, 95–97, 110, 111,
114, 121, 122, 124–126, 130–132,
137, 139, 141, 143–146, 148–151,
155, 178, 185, 187, 191, 192, 194,
195, 207–216, 222, 243, 251

**L, M**

Latour, 2, 3, 5–11, 13–18, 24–26, 73,
75, 76, 78–80, 91, 94, 96, 98, 101,
119, 142, 143, 169, 174, 186, 200,
205, 206, 245, 246, 248, 250, 263,
265–269
Lyotard, 83, 86–89, 91, 93, 98, 102,
109
machine, 8,  94, 97, 102, 105, 108,
112, 113,116, 126, 134, 135, 140,
153, 155, 156, 165, 174–180, 182,
185–187, 208, 212, 213, 246, 247,
250, 264, 266, 268, 271
management, 5, 13–15, 21–23, 25,
27–29, 31–39, 41, 43–45, 47, 49–51,
54–59, 62–65, 67, 68, 70, 71, 77,
88, 94, 95, 97, 98, 101, 102, 104,
109, 111, 113, 116–121, 123, 125,
126, 129, 131–134, 141, 143–157,
165, 169, 173, 180, 184, 185, 189,
190, 193–196, 205, 209–214, 217,
221, 222, 224, 227, 230, 233, 234,
236, 237, 240, 243, 246, 247
molar/molecular, 179, 180

**N, O, P**

narratique, 106, 107, 109, 113–120,
126, 127, 130, 132, 136, 137, 141,
142, 146, 152, 153, 156, 161, 173,
222, 264
Noyer, 3, 30, 84, 153, 178, 179, 182,
201, 202, 258
Open
Data, 141, 147, 157–169, 180
Gov, 141, 157, 160–164, 166
organization-network, 143, 146
organizational network analysis, 230
performation, 7, 12, 13, 17, 30–32,
34, 46, 51, 78, 81, 82, 85, 88,
97–106, 108, 110–113, 115–117,
127, 128, 130, 131, 134, 137, 140,
147, 157, 166, 171, 173, 179, 180,
187, 189, 203, 207, 209, 222, 230
desired, 105, 106
experiential, 51, 128, 209
technical, 32, 130, 131, 230
performativity, 46, 47, 51, 75, 81, 82,
92, 96–99, 104, 116, 117, 118, 132,
181
political economy of interfaces, 179
practices
socio-digital practices of
employees, 156
work, 1, 54, 63, 144
pragmatic sociology, 1, 2, 9, 79
public
actor, 204
data, 157, 160–163, 236

**R, S**

regime
of connectivity, 184, 193, 194,
204
of reflexivity, 184, 190

Other titles from

in

Information Systems, Web and Pervasive Computing

## 2018

ARDUIN Pierre-Emmanuel
*Insider Threats*
*(Advances in Information Systems Set – Volume 10)*

CHAMOUX Jean-Pierre
*The Digital Era 1: Big Data Stakes*

FABRE Renaud, BENSOUSSAN Alain
*The Digital Factory for Knowledge: Production and Validation of Scientific Results*

GAUDIN Thierry, LACROIX Dominique, MAUREL Marie-Christine, POMEROL Jean-Charles
*Life Sciences, Information Sciences*

GAYARD Laurent
*Darknet: Geopolitics and Uses*
*(Computing and Connected Society Set – Volume 2)*

IAFRATE Fernando
*Artificial Intelligence and Big Data: The Birth of a New Intelligence*
*(Advances in Information Systems Set – Volume 8)*

REYES-GARCIA Everardo, BOUHAÏ Nasreddine
*Designing Interactive Hypermedia Systems*
*(Digital Tools and Uses Set – Volume 2)*

SAÏD Karim, BAHRI KORBI Fadia
*Asymmetric Alliances and Information Systems:Issues and Prospects*
*(Advances in Information Systems Set – Volume 7)*

SZONIECKY Samuel, BOUHAÏ Nasreddine
*Collective Intelligence and Digital Archives: Towards Knowledge*
*Ecosystems*
*(Digital Tools and Uses Set – Volume 1)*

# 2016

BEN CHOUIKHA Mona
*Organizational Design for Knowledge Management*

BERTOLO David
*Interactions on Digital Tablets in the Context of 3D Geometry Learning*
*(Human-Machine Interaction Set – Volume 2)*

BOUVARD Patricia, SUZANNE Hervé
*Collective Intelligence Development in Business*

EL FALLAH SEGHROUCHNI Amal, ISHIKAWA Fuyuki, HÉRAULT Laurent,
TOKUDA Hideyuki
*Enablers for Smart Cities*

FABRE Renaud, in collaboration with MESSERSCHMIDT-MARIET Quentin,
HOLVOET Margot
*New Challenges for Knowledge*

GAUDIELLO Ilaria, ZIBETTI Elisabetta
*Learning Robotics, with Robotics, by Robotics*
*(Human-Machine Interaction Set – Volume 3)*

HENROTIN Joseph
*The Art of War in the Network Age*
*(Intellectual Technologies Set – Volume 1)*

KITAJIMA Munéo
*Memory and Action Selection in Human–Machine Interaction*
*(Human–Machine Interaction Set – Volume 1)*

LAGRAÑA Fernando
*E-mail and Behavioral Changes: Uses and Misuses of Electronic*
*Communications*

LEIGNEL Jean-Louis, UNGARO Thierry, STAAR Adrien
*Digital Transformation*
*(Advances in Information Systems Set – Volume 6)*

NOYER Jean-Max
*Transformation of Collective Intelligences*
*(Intellectual Technologies Set – Volume 2)*

VENTRE Daniel
*Information Warfare – 2$^{nd}$ edition*

VITALIS André
*The Uncertain Digital Revolution*
*(Computing and Connected Society Set – Volume 1)*

# 2015

ARDUIN Pierre-Emmanuel, GRUNDSTEIN Michel, ROSENTHAL-SABROUX
Camille
*Information and Knowledge System*
*(Advances in Information Systems Set – Volume 2)*

BÉRANGER Jérôme
*Medical Information Systems Ethics*

BRONNER Gérald
*Belief and Misbelief Asymmetry on the Internet*

IAFRATE Fernando
*From Big Data to Smart Data*
*(Advances in Information Systems Set – Volume 1)*

KRICHEN Saoussen, BEN JOUIDA Sihem
*Supply Chain Management and its Applications in Computer Science*

NEGRE Elsa
*Information and Recommender Systems*
*(Advances in Information Systems Set – Volume 4)*

POMEROL Jean-Charles, EPELBOIN Yves, THOURY Claire
*MOOCs*

SALLES Maryse
*Decision-Making and the Information System*
*(Advances in Information Systems Set – Volume 3)*

SAMARA Tarek
*ERP and Information Systems: Integration or Disintegration*
*(Advances in Information Systems Set – Volume 5)*

## 2014

DINET Jérôme
*Information Retrieval in Digital Environments*

HÉNO Raphaële, CHANDELIER Laure
*3D Modeling of Buildings: Outstanding Sites*

KEMBELLEC Gérald, CHARTRON Ghislaine, SALEH Imad
*Recommender Systems*

MATHIAN Hélène, SANDERS Lena
*Spatio-temporal Approaches: Geographic Objects and Change Process*

PLANTIN Jean-Christophe
*Participatory Mapping*

VENTRE Daniel
*Chinese Cybersecurity and Defense*

## 2013

BERNIK Igor
*Cybercrime and Cyberwarfare*

CAPET Philippe, DELAVALLADE Thomas
*Information Evaluation*

LEBRATY Jean-Fabrice, LOBRE-LEBRATY Katia
*Crowdsourcing: One Step Beyond*

SALLABERRY Christian
*Geographical Information Retrieval in Textual Corpora*

## 2012

BUCHER Bénédicte, LE BER Florence
*Innovative Software Development in GIS*

GAUSSIER Eric, YVON François
*Textual Information Access*

STOCKINGER Peter
*Audiovisual Archives: Digital Text and Discourse Analysis*

VENTRE Daniel
*Cyber Conflict*

## 2011

BANOS Arnaud, THÉVENIN Thomas
*Geographical Information and Urban Transport Systems*

DAUPHINÉ André
*Fractal Geography*

LEMBERGER Pirmin, MOREL Mederic
*Managing Complexity of Information Systems*

STOCKINGER Peter
*Introduction to Audiovisual Archives*

STOCKINGER Peter
*Digital Audiovisual Archives*

VENTRE Daniel
*Cyberwar and Information Warfare*

# 2010

BONNET Pierre
*Enterprise Data Governance*

BRUNET Roger
*Sustainable Geography*

CARREGA Pierre
*Geographical Information and Climatology*

CAUVIN Colette, ESCOBAR Francisco, SERRADJ Aziz
*Thematic Cartography – 3-volume series*
*Thematic Cartography and Transformations – Volume 1*
*Cartography and the Impact of the Quantitative Revolution – Volume 2*
*New Approaches in Thematic Cartography – Volume 3*

LANGLOIS Patrice
*Simulation of Complex Systems in GIS*

MATHIS Philippe
*Graphs and Networks – 2nd edition*

THERIAULT Marius, DES ROSIERS François
*Modeling Urban Dynamics*

# 2009

BONNET Pierre, DETAVERNIER Jean-Michel, VAUQUIER Dominique
*Sustainable IT Architecture: the Progressive Way of Overhauling*
*Information Systems with SOA*

PAPY Fabrice
*Information Science*

RIVARD François, ABOU HARB Georges, MERET Philippe
*The Transverse Information System*

ROCHE Stéphane, CARON Claude
*Organizational Facets of GIS*

## 2008

BRUGNOT Gérard
*Spatial Management of Risks*

FINKE Gerd
*Operations Research and Networks*

GUERMOND Yves
*Modeling Process in Geography*

KANEVSKI Michael
*Advanced Mapping of Environmental Data*

MANOUVRIER Bernard, LAURENT Ménard
*Application Integration: EAI, B2B, BPM and SOA*

PAPY Fabrice
*Digital Libraries*

## 2007

DOBESCH Hartwig, DUMOLARD Pierre, DYRAS Izabela
*Spatial Interpolation for Climate Data*

SANDERS Lena
*Models in Spatial Analysis*

## 2006

CLIQUET Gérard
*Geomarketing*

CORNIOU Jean-Pierre
*Looking Back and Going Forward in IT*

DEVILLERS Rodolphe, JEANSOULIN Robert
*Fundamentals of Spatial Data Quality*

Printed and bound by CPI Group (UK) Ltd, Croydon, CR0 4YY